The Oil of Gladness

Also edited by Martin Dudley and Geoffrey Rowell:

Confession and Absolution (London: SPCK; Collegeville: Liturgical Press, 1990)

The Oil of Gladness

Anointing in the Christian Tradition

Edited by Martin Dudley and Geoffrey Rowell

SPCK · London
Liturgical Press · Collegeville

First published in Great Britain 1993
Society for Promoting Christian Knowledge
Holy Trinity Church
Marylebone Road
London NW1 4DU

First published in the United States 1993
The Liturgical Press
St John's Abbey
Collegeville
MN 56321

ISBN 0–8146–2245–3

British Library Cataloguing-in-Publication Data
A catalogue record for this book is available from the British Library
ISBN 0–281–04645–X

Typeset by Deltatype Ltd, Ellesmere Port, Cheshire
Printed in Great Britain by
Biddles Ltd, Guildford and Kings Lynn

Contents

Contributors

Rebecca Abrams, author and journalist.

Norman Autton, formerly Chancellor, Llandaff Cathedral and Chaplain of the University Hospital of Wales, Cardiff.

Angus Bowie, Fellow and Tutor in Classics, The Queen's College, Oxford.

Sebastian Brock, Reader in Syriac Studies, University of Oxford, and Fellow of Wolfson College.

Stephanie Dalley, Senior Research Fellow, Somerville College, Oxford, and Shillito Fellow in Assyriology, Oriental Institute, University of Oxford.

Martin Dudley, Vicar of Owlsmoor, Berkshire, and Visiting Lecturer in Anglican Studies and Liturgy, Simon of Cyrene Theological Institute, London.

Roger Greenacre, Chancellor and Canon Residentiary, Chichester Cathedral.

W. Jardine Grisbrooke, formerly Lecturer of Liturgy, The Queen's College, Birmingham, and St Mary's College, Oscott, Birmingham.

Christine Hall, Vice-Principal, Chichester Theological College.

John Halliburton, Chancellor and Canon Residentiary, St Paul's Cathedral, London.

Brian Horne, Lecturer, King's College, London.

Jeffrey John, Vicar of Holy Trinity, Eltham.

Maureen Palmer, Chaplain and Succentor, Birmingham Cathedral.

J. Roy Porter, Emeritus Professor of Theology, Exeter University.

Geoffrey Rowell, Fellow, Chaplain and Tutor in Theology, Keble College, Oxford.

Hugo Slim, Senior Research Officer, Save the Children, London.

Preface

In our earlier collection of essays, *Confession and Absolution*, we sought to provide a comprehensive survey of the Christian tradition, pastoral practice, liturgical texts and theological assessment. The same model has been used for this new collection on oil and anointing in the Christian tradition. We are grateful to our colleagues on the Church Union Theological Committee who have both contributed to and encouraged us in putting together this book, and we are also grateful to those not on the committee who responded generously to our invitation when asked for contributions to ensure that this book would have a wide and appropriate coverage.

In his introduction Roger Greenacre considers the immediate Church of England context of these essays, but their significance, we believe, is much wider, for we know of no comparable study of anointing in the Christian tradition. We hope that this thorough exploration of the historical, theological and liturgical background, and of contemporary pastoral practice will not only be informative but a further encouragement to the renewed understanding and use of anointing in the church. A wise Mother Superior of a religious community which welcomes many for counsel and retreat said to one of us that in her opinion 'anointing was today's sacrament'. The growth of such things as aromatherapy outside the church may indicate part of the reason why this may be so. Although olive oil is in our culture no longer the main source of light, with a corresponding diminution of its symbolic power, nevertheless its sacramental use, with its rich background in Scripture and the Christian tradition, reminds us that incarnational religion is always sacramental, and that Christianity affirms our bodiliness as good in God's creation and in his new creation.

Martin Dudley
Geoffrey Rowell

Introduction

Roger Greenacre

In 1990 *Confession and Absolution*, also edited by Martin Dudley and
Geoffrey Rowell, was published by SPCK and Liturgical Press. It
arose out of the reading of papers and their discussion at meetings of
the Church Union Theological Committee, and a majority of the
ensuing contributions to the book were written by members of the
Committee and began life as papers read to the Committee. We were
encouraged by the welcome given to that book to continue our
exploration of sacramental theology and we decided that our next
book would be a study of the anointing of the sick; a decision
subsequently widened by common consent to embrace the whole field
of the sacramental and liturgical use of oil. In the present case there is
a higher proportion of contributors who are not members of the
Committee, and the Committee as a whole did not discuss the drafts of
particular chapters; we were happy to delegate overall responsibility
to our editors and I have been asked, on behalf of the Committee, to
write a commendatory preface to the resulting volume.

In the Preface to *Confession and Absolution* I referred to the
confusion and controversy within the Church of England on the
subject of priestly absolution which was reflected in the failure of a
proposed modern language rite for the Reconciliation of a Penitent to
acquire the necessary two-thirds majority in the House of Laity of the
General Synod in 1983. In fact at that period General Synod was being
asked to approve a threefold package, consisting of orders of service
for *Ministry to the Sick, The Reconciliation of a Penitent* and *The
Blessing of the Oils*. The only one of these three orders to survive was
the first, which has been authorized for use from 1983. Opposition to
the form for the Reconciliation of a Penitent was not unexpected; the
failure of the Form for the Blessing of the Oils to get the necessary
two-thirds majority at Final Approval stage in the House of Laity in
November 1982 by a very narrow margin was certainly far more of a
surprise.

As someone quite closely involved at the time, not only as a member
of General Synod but also as a member of the Joint Revision
Committee for all three rites, I hope it may not be inappropriate for
me to make a few observations on that *débâcle* and its consequences.

First, the need for all three rites clearly arose from the perceived
incompleteness of the provisions of the newly authorized ASB. If we
confine our attention to the use of oil, this incompleteness is
particularly striking. Note 23 of the notes prefixed to the Rite A Order
for the Eucharist suggests that 'when Holy Communion is ministered

to the sick, the Laying on of Hands or Anointing may follow the Absolution (section 28 . . .).' Yet no texts either for the Laying on of Hands or for Anointing are provided in the book – nor, for that matter, any form for Communion of the Sick. However the Canon Law of the Church of England already contained a canon (B37: of the Ministry to the Sick) which directed:

> If any such person so desires, the priest may lay hands upon him and may anoint him with oil on the forehead with the sign of the Cross using a form of service authorised by Canon B1 and using pure olive oil consecrated by the bishop of the diocese or otherwise by the priest himself in accordance with such form of service.

The Church of England now has a series of rites authorized by General Synod in 1982 under the title *Ministry to the Sick* and these include a form for *The Laying on of Hands with Prayer, and Anointing* (which removes the implication in the ASB notes that one has to choose between one or the other). The introductory rubrics refer back to Canon B37 and its requirement that the oil should be blessed by the bishop or by the priest himself, but a prayer of blessing is not provided since at the time it was expected that the parallel rite for the Blessing of the Oils would also receive synodical authorization. The more recent booklet, *Ministry at the Time of Death*, commended by the House of Bishops and published in 1991, provides in introductory Note 4 a form for blessing the oil which may be used by a priest. Those who make careful comparison of the notes in the 1982 and 1991 orders of service will observe that the question of the minister of anointing is not left unambiguously clear. Canon B37 restricts this ministry to bishops and priests; the 1982 order allows others to join with the priest in the laying on of hands and a deacon or 'authorized lay minister' to preside over the ministry of the laying on of hands in the absence of a priest. But anointing, described in note 9 as 'a sacramental ministry', is apparently reserved to priests, though note 7 allows the president of the eucharist to delegate the ministry of anointing to 'other lawful ministers', without specifying who they might be. The notes to the 1991 order go a step further and seem to allow the anointing of the sick to be performed by 'a deacon authorized for this ministry by the Bishop'.

When we turn to the use of oils in the Rites of Christian Initiation the *lacunae* are even more glaringly obvious. At no point do the actual texts of the rites of Baptism and Confirmation in the ASB ever mention the use of oil; that is left to the Introductory Notes. One note points out that the signing with the cross may take place either before the baptism in the section headed *The Decision* or immediately after the baptism. It goes on to provide that 'the sign of the cross may be made in oil blessed for this purpose'. Another note permits the bishop to anoint those he is confirming 'with oil he has previously blessed for this purpose'. The combined effect of these Notes is to raise almost as many questions as they solve (if they solve any!), but before we identify these questions we should turn to the only other parts of the ASB where the oils are mentioned – the Proper (Sentences, Collect and Readings) for *The Blessing of the Oils* (the plural must be assumed to be deliberate) and the Proper Preface referred to in that Proper but printed with the other Proper Prefaces of Rite A. It is indeed a classic case of 'the mint with the hole'; everything necessary is provided for the Blessing of the Oils – except the Blessing formulae themselves! It is also strange that the Proper is placed between the Proper for Maundy Thursday and that for Good Friday and the Proper Preface similarly follows the Maundy Thursday Preface, a curious inversion of the traditional order.

The priest without some knowledge of liturgical history – indeed, the bishop without some knowledge of liturgical history, if we may dare even to contemplate so awful a possibility – will face a number of perplexing questions once he begins to consider whether to use oil in the Rites of Christian Initiation. How many oils should there be? If there is more than one, how are they to be distinguished? Simply by designated use, by content (pure olive oil or oil mixed with balsam or other perfumes) or by the degree of solemnity of the prayer of blessing and a distinction between oil which may be blessed by a priest and oil which only a bishop may bless? And what formula – if any – accompanies the anointing? And in baptism (if one feels bound to accept that the ASB probably rules out two anointings) which position – before or after the baptism – is to be preferred? Even for those priests with some knowledge of liturgical history – or perhaps, rather, especially for such priests – there is a real problem with this last question.

The case for opting for the pre-baptismal anointing could be argued as follows. The signing of the cross was part of the rite for admitting a catechumen; the anointing with the oil of baptism (or oil of exorcism or oil of the catechumens) also belonged to the pre-baptismal ceremonies. So indeed did the giving of a name and, whereas the Prayer Book rite could give the impression that the conferring of a name and the signing were essential parts of the baptismal act itself, successive revisions have tried to separate the signing and naming from the act of baptizing. In the ASB rite it is claimed that the earlier position for signing and naming (and for the use of the name at the signing it is once more necessary to turn to the Notes) was the preferred option of the compilers of the ASB;[1] in that position it links clearly and in a coherent and logical sequence with the Decision which precedes it and the prayer for deliverance from evil which follows it.

In this context of renunciation of evil, of fighting under the banner of Christ and of deliverance 'from the powers of darkness' (a modern equivalent of exorcism) anointing with the oil of baptism at this point is clearly appropriate. In dioceses where all three oils are blessed this appropriateness is further underlined, and in the Diocese of Chichester where this is the case (and where the notes to the Diocesan Service for the Blessing of the Oils explain that the symbolism of this oil is 'that of an athlete or soldier using oil to make his limbs supple and strong for his contest') the Diocesan Order for Baptism and Confirmation within the Eucharist opts for the pre-baptismal signing 'which may be with the oil of baptism'.

The case for opting for a post-baptismal anointing with chrism is based partly on a negative and partly on a positive argument. The negative argument is based on the fact that – as Martin Dudley explains in Chapter 9 – the Roman Catholic Church now allows for the omission of the pre-baptismal anointing, since the symbolism of the oil of catechumens is not very obvious in most modern cultures. The positive argument is based on the more fundamental importance and richer symbolism of the oil of chrism and on the fact – also analysed by Martin Dudley – that the post-baptismal anointing with chrism is provided for by at least five other Provinces of the Anglican Communion, while the Church of England alone makes provision for pre-baptismal anointing. The principal difficulty is that the words in the ASB rite fit the pre-baptismal position perfectly and the post-baptismal position not at all. Using chrism therefore involves going beyond what the ASB provides, with a pre-baptismal signing (with or without oil) and a chrismation after the actual baptism with a formula 'borrowed' from Rome or from another Anglican rite.[2]

A similar though less complex choice faces a bishop who uses chrism at confirmation. Theoretically, he could try to anoint and lay on hands at the same moment (as in the former Roman Rite) while saying the formula, 'Confirm, O Lord . . .' In fact, the anointing with chrism nearly always follows the laying on of hands and in many diocesan orders a form of words is provided; in Chichester, for example, it is 'Receive the seal of the Spirit'.

Second, the failure of the Form for the Blessing of the Oils to acquire the requisite synodical majority in 1982 was a source of great disappointment to many of us at the time – especially to those of us who had expended much time and labour on the Joint Revision Committee. Ten years later it is possible to take a less tragic view of this defeat and to see the seeds of failure in the weaknesses and ambiguities inherent in the ASB initiation rites themselves. It is important even today to note carefully the arguments expressed in the General Synod debates at the time; if they are not satisfactorily answered we can expect no breakthrough. As C. S. Lewis wrote,

'There is always hope if we keep an unsolved problem fairly in view; there's none if we pretend it's not there.'[3]

On the positive side, it is vital to note that there was no opposition at all to the anointing of the sick. A Latimer House publication, which could well be expected to speak for the more conservative evangelicals in the Church of England, allowed that it was 'perfectly reasonable to maintain the custom'; it argued however that there is no suggestion in the Letter to James 'that the oil is to be prayed over, consecrated, blessed or in any way treated as other than every day (presumably olive) oil'.[4] In the synodical debate, one prominent evangelical priest testified to the fact that he did anoint the sick – but using 'just God's good oil as it came from the shop'. Another drew a parallel with evangelical difficulties over Communion from the Reserved Sacrament and argued that it was 'far more in keeping with the dynamic view of a sacramental action' if the blessing of the oil was always performed by the local minister and in the course of the actual ministration. Provision for a service for the Blessing of the Oils by the bishop was 'carrying the notion of extension too far'. Another speaker affirmed that there was no evidence in Scripture that inanimate objects can be blessed; he had previously described the Blessing of the Oils as 'rather like a form of white magic'.[5] Others feared that the use of chrism in some confirmations and not in others would cause confusion and result in 1st class and 2nd class confirmations, and doubted that it was necessary to provide for three separate oils. The most telling criticism came from Peter Dawes, now Bishop of Derby. After pointing out that provision in the ASB for the use of oil in the rite of Christian Initiation was something of an afterthought and that assurances were given at the time that the Church of England was attaching no particular meaning to it, he attacked the lack of theological seriousness in bringing forward a rite for the Blessing of the Oils on a side-wind. Another speaker took up this point and pleaded for serious theological consideration to be given beforehand to issues which are the subject of liturgical revision. From our point of view we must have every sympathy with this line of argument and make it clear that we are not interested in mere ritualism or mere antiquarianism but concerned for the expression in the Church's *lex orandi* of the Church's *lex credendi*. If this volume can be seen as a serious contribution to this vitally important process of theological reflection it will have justified its publication.

Third, it is clear that since synodical debates in 1981 and 1982 the subject has by no means gone dead in the Church of England. Christian Initiation is very much in the forefront of the Church's theological, pastoral and liturgical thinking in the 1990s and a whole cluster of questions – not all of which directly concern the next stage of liturgical revision – is engaging the attention of the Church of England

and its ecumenical partners.[6] Some of these questions involve the possible use of oil, including the relatively new one of the pastoral need for liturgical celebration of the renewal of baptismal faith for those who often demand 're-baptism' after an experience of conversion. The growth of interest in the subject and of liturgical experimentation is not confined to the rites of Christian Initiation. It is quite common for priests to be anointed with chrism at their ordination and on at least one recent and well-publicized occasion a bishop was anointed at his enthronement (not, as tradition and precedent would suggest, at his ordination or consecration).

As Christians, we take our name from Jesus, the Christ, the Messiah, the Anointed One. A concern for the place of anointing in the life of the Church is therefore far from peripheral; it relates to our doctrine of Christ, of the Holy Spirit, of the Holy Trinity. Much of this preface has been concerned with the recent history of the Church of England and with specifically Anglican problems, but these are rooted in a concern which should be shared by all Christians. We hope that what we have written will appeal to many outside the tradition which we represent; we do not necessarily ask for agreement with all we have to say, but we do ask for our concern to be shared and for our contribution to elicit serious and constructive response.

Notes

1. cf. R. C. D. Jasper and P. F. Bradshaw, *A Companion to the Alternative Service Book* (London 1986), p. 353.
2. If chrism is used both at baptism and at confirmation a theological question, not yet fully resolved, is posed by the relationship between them. Particular importance therefore attaches to the form of words used.
3. *Letters to Malcolm* (London 1964), p. 83.
4. D. S. Allister, *Sickness & Healing in the Church* (Latimer Studies 11, Oxford 1981).
5. The Church Union Theological Committee is already planning to publish a theological and liturgical study of Blessing; it will need to address this question, among others.
6. cf. *Christian Initiation* (GS Misc 365), a Discussion Paper by Canon Martin Reardon (London 1991).

1

The Sacramental Use of Material Things

Brian Horne

Ever since the creation of the world his invisible nature, namely, his eternal power and deity, has been clearly perceived in the things that have been made (Rom. 1. 20).

I

In the fourth book of the *Institutes of the Christian Religion* John Calvin adumbrated a theory of the sacramental universe. He asked his readers to consider the rainbow – given by God to Noah as a sign of the promise of his faithfulness (Gen. 9) – and trenchantly addressed the objections of sceptical materialists who could see in this physical phenomenon nothing more than an effect of colour produced as light was refracted by moisture left in the air after rain:

> Therefore, if any philosopher, to mock the simplicity of our faith, contends that such a variety of colours naturally arises from rays reflected upon a cloud opposite, let us indeed admit it, but laugh at his stupidity in failing to recognize God as lord of nature, who according to his will uses all the elements to serve his glory. If he had imprinted such reminders upon the sun,

stars, earth, stones, they would all be sacraments for us (Book IV, 8).

He took the idea no further; this was an adumbration and not a developed theology, for his main purpose in this section of the *Institutes* was, on the one hand, to correct the erroneous belief that sacraments could somehow, of their very nature, 'justify and confer grace' (Book IV, 7), and, on the other, to establish a principle that was to become a cornerstone of Protestant sacramental theology – namely, that the existence of a sacrament depended solely upon the divine word of promise. That concept of the primacy of the word came to dominate Protestant religion, not least in the sphere of sacramental theology. Nevertheless, Calvin could see no necessary contradiction between the promise that was made by God in his word and the means by which the promise was apprehended – in this instance, the rainbow. While no natural object could be regarded as inherently sacred or by its own power be the channel of supernatural grace, matter (sun, stars, earth, stones) was, none the less, capable of bearing the weight of divine glory. Behind this we may perceive what is not stated explicitly: a realization that sacramental theology (and sacramental worship) is grounded not only in the doctrine of salvation: 'I set my bow in the cloud, and it shall be a sign of the covenant' (Gen. 9.13), but also in the doctrine of creation: 'And God saw everything that he had made, and behold, it was very good' (Gen. 1.31). The conviction that the word of promise is truly given by God is, strictly speaking, rooted in the doctrine of salvation. But the complementary conviction that the promise is accompanied by physical signs and attached to material substances – bread and wine, oil and water – is, strictly speaking, rooted in the doctrine of creation. It is when one of these doctrines is emphasized at the expense of the other that a distorted theology of the sacraments emerges.

The complementarity of the doctrines of salvation and creation was not a principle that was to be pursued in Protestant theology or maintained in Protestant devotion (partly because of the influence of Calvin himself); and Protestantism never developed a theory of a sacramental universe. Indeed, it is a concept that became alien to its spirit. In its intellectual rejection of Natural Theology and its instinctive fear of idolatry, Protestantism came to stress the difference between God and the world; it was concerned to contrast the fallenness of the created order with the holiness of its creator; to emphasize the necessity of redemption rather than the possibility of transformation; to preach justification rather than sanctification; to command obedience to the word rather than participation in the sacrament. And so it assisted not only in the process of the desacralization of nature, but also contributed to the alienation of man from nature. Four hundred years after Calvin, D. H. Lawrence complained bitterly: 'The Christian religion lost, in Protestantism finally, the togetherness with the universe, the togetherness of the body, the sex, the emotions, the passions, with the earth and sun and stars.'[1]

But the picture is not, of course, monochrome: there have been remarkable attempts, from within Protestantism, to recover what had been lost: notably by P. T. Forsyth in his *The Church and the Sacraments* (1917). And no one spoke more prophetically of the tragedy of Protestantism than Paul Tillich when he pleaded with his fellow Protestants in *The Protestant Era* for 'a new understanding of the intrinsic powers of nature which constitute an essential part of the sacraments'. 'The very destiny of Protestantism,' he argued, 'depends upon the solution of the problem of "nature and sacrament".' He was not trying to introduce into Protestant Christianity a pantheistic strain, nor trying to replace the life of moral obligation with one of aesthetic appreciation, nor trying to turn the celebration of sacraments into quasi-magical rituals. He was perfectly aware of these dangers and specifically warned against any kind of disguised nature mysticism: 'there can be no sacramental object apart from the faith that grasps it.' But he did make a powerful plea for the recognition that

> nature is not the enemy of salvation; it does not have to be controlled in scientific, technical and moral terms or be deprived of any inherent power in order to serve the 'Kingdom of God', as Calvinistic thinking is inclined to believe; rather nature is a bearer and an object of salvation. This is the basis for a Protestant rediscovery of the sacramental sphere.[2]

It is also a basis for Christians, in our polluted world, to rediscover the true relationship of human beings to their environment. At the same time we shall recover the perception that the doctrine of creation is one of the foundations for building a true theology of the sacraments. The issue of the state of the world in which we live is not a separate issue from that of the sacramental life in the Church.

II

Whereas classical Protestantism never developed a theory of the sacramental universe or a sacramental principle, Anglicanism did; and the roots of the typically Anglican articulation of the theory are to be found in the writings of a man who stands at the very beginning of a specifically Anglican way of thinking and whose influence upon the subsequent tradition can hardly be overestimated: Richard Hooker. This great contemporary of Calvin, in his defence of an Anglican position against the arguments of the Puritans, provided the Church of England with an essay in systematic theology unsurpassed in its intellectual brilliance and majestic coherence. It may not have been his intention to create such a 'system' of doctrine or to give the Church in England a kind of confession of faith. His aim was, ostensibly, simpler: to construct a comprehensive theory of law; but undergirding this attempt was a set of convictions about the nature of revelation and divine action, and upholding his theory of law was a doctrine of creation. And it is largely because of Hooker that there has been greater attention paid to the doctrine of creation in the theology of the Church of England than in any other Church in the West. It was Hooker's belief about the doctrine of creation that determined his perspective on the sacraments of the Church. We shall not find phrases like 'a sacramental universe' or 'the sacramental principle' appearing in his prose, yet when he came to describing the place and purpose of the sacraments in his ecclesiastical polity he located them firmly in the nexus of both doctrines: salvation and creation. They were not to be understood merely as instruments the Church had at its disposal offered by a merciful deity to a sinful world for the spiritual sustenance of the faithful; instead, they were concrete manifestations of God's providential activity in the ordering of the universe. The kind of world that God had brought into being, and that his law controlled, was one in which the whole natural order praised and revealed him:

> All other things that are of God have God in them and he them in himself likewise . . . God hath his influence into the very essence of all things, without which influence of Deity supporting them their utter annihilation could not choose but follow. Of him all things have both received their first being and their continuance to be that which they are. All things therefore are partakers of God, they are his offspring, his influence is in them, and the personal wisdom of God is for that very cause said to excel in nimbleness or agility, to pierce into all intellectual pure, and subtle spirits, to go through all, and to reach unto everything that is. Otherwise, how should the same wisdom be that which supporteth, beareth up, and sustaineth all?[3]

C. S. Lewis rebuts the accusation that the tendency of Hooker's mind was to secularize with the contrary assertion that when one really scrutinizes the 'model' of the universe in Hooker's system one sees that 'few models of the universe are more filled – one might say drenched – with Deity than his'.[4] The biblical justification for such a model is to be found not only in the numerous passages from the Old Testament that speak of the creation hymning its creator, but also in the first chapter of St Paul's letter to the Romans and the fourth

chapter of the letter to Timothy in which the author sets his face
against a gnostic dualism: 'For everything created by God is good, and
nothing is to be rejected if it is received with thanksgiving; for then it
is consecrated by the word of God and prayer' (1 Tim. 4.4). In
constructing his theory of Natural Law, Hooker clearly depicted a
world in which the glory of its creator shone through it – what we
should call a 'sacramental universe'. This reading of the doctrine of
creation did not disappear from Anglican theology and devotion: it is
vividly present in the writings of Hooker's contemporaries, Lancelot
Andrewes and George Herbert;[5] it appears later in the seventeenth
century in Thomas Traherne's *Centuries of Meditation* and John
Pearson's *Exposition of the Creed*; and it rose strongly to the surface
again two centuries later in the theology and devotion of the Oxford
Movement. When John Keble came to edit Hooker's works in the
1830s, he believed that he had found the basis of a sacramental
theology that was not only part of the spiritual heritage of the Church
of England, but one that was firmly and truly grounded in the
traditions of the early Church: 'And thus did the whole scheme of
material things, and especially those objects in it which are consecrated by scriptural allusion, assume in their eyes a sacramental or
symbolical character.'[6] In Keble's own poetry the frequency of
allusions to nature and the manner in which these are turned into
images of divine revelation demonstrates as powerfully as his
theological essays the underlying assumption of the sacramental
principle in Keble's thought.

The most comprehensive exposition of the notion in Anglican
theology came fifty-eight years after Keble's death when William
Temple published, in 1934, his Gifford lectures, *Nature, Man and
God*.[7] It is also, in its way, an Anglican systematic theology, and at its
climax is the nineteenth chapter which Temple called 'The Sacramental Universe'. All the previous arguments about personality,
spirit, revelation and history have been leading to this: the perception
of the universe as sacramental, of the natural world (both human and
non-human) as the place in which and by which the personal God is
encountered and revealed: 'It is to such a view that our whole course of
enquiry has been leading us; and it is such a view which affords the
strongest hope for the continuance in reality and power of religious
faith and practice.' It is precisely this concept of the sacramental
universe that I should like to lay as part of the foundation of a theology
of creation. By means of this we may reach a better understanding of
the proper relationship between the human being and his environment; and also a clearer understanding of the relationship between the
natural and supernatural. And in such a context we may better
understand what it is we are doing when we take bread and wine,
water and oil, and celebrate the sacraments of the Church: 'In Nature

we find God; we do not only infer from Nature what God must be like, but when we see Nature truly, we see God self-manifested in and through it.'[8] Such a statement seems to press beyond what was contained in classical Catholic dogmatic formulations about the revelation of God in and through the material world. Thomas Aquinas had indeed taught that all knowledge of God was mediated, but the knowledge is acquired more by the process of rational inference than by that of direct apprehension – that is, the 'things' themselves reveal the glory of their creator. And it is a long way beyond the classical Protestant concept of the necessity of the word of promise accompanying the physical sign:

> We affirm then that unless all our existence is a medium of Revelation, no particular Revelation is possible. . . . Only if God is revealed in the rising of the sun in the sky can He be revealed in the rising of a son of man from the dead . . . only if nothing is profane can anything be sacred.[9]

What is being argued here is not only that the created order and human life have been 'graced' by the incarnation of the Son of God in Jesus Christ, but that creation was 'graced' from the beginning, and has, despite evil and corruption, remained 'graced': the incarnation becomes, in this theology, the perfection of the creation.[10] We do not have to embrace Temple's philosophical terminology – drawn, to some extent, from a combination of idealism and process philosophy – to accept his concept of the sacramental universe. His theology of creation is not dependent upon the thought of Samuel Alexander or A. N. Whitehead; what we are given is a picture of the world which, like Hooker's, is 'drenched with Deity'.[11] Where we might begin to feel uneasy with Temple's theology is his failure, at least in this work, to make a strong enough connection between the sacraments of the Church and the history of salvation. They seem, almost, to float free from that in which they should be grounded: the historical facts of the life, death and resurrection of Jesus of Nazareth. It was this failure that brought criticism from many thinkers who suspected an incipient nature-mysticism which would not only bypass the history of salvation, but also evade the question of sin and the problem of the disorder of the natural world. It need hardly be said that Temple was alive to these dangers – and the even greater danger of pantheism – and never advanced down this avenue: he tried to deal directly with the problem of evil, and central to his whole scheme was the uniqueness of the incarnation. Moreover, he can be defended on the grounds that his very use of the word 'sacramental' – suggesting events and objects that are both themselves and, at the same time, signs of something other than themselves – prevented him from lapsing into a kind of idolatry of nature. G. S. Hendry correctly interpreted Temple's position when he wrote:

On the sacramental view . . . all the elements of the world of nature continue to be what they are and to possess the properties ascertained by the natural sciences; but above and beyond (or 'in, with, and under') their natural properties the elements are elevated as bearers of higher properties, which, in turn, reflect back on their natural properties and colour the perception of those who use them. All natural objects continue to be what they are, and they are to be used according to their natural properties, but to those who perceive them in the light of the incarnation they become charged with the promise of something more than what they are, and they will be treated accordingly.[12]

It can be seen, however, that a kind of pantheism, or at least a belief that nature is inherently sacred, if not actually to be worshipped, pervades much of the apologetic literature of current writing on environmental issues. Those who are the most vociferous in their efforts at protecting the natural world from pollution and destruction are often those who are most reverential in their attitude to that world. It can also be seen that Christian apologists who, under the pressure of valid criticism of non-Christians, are having to develop and re-interpret the Christian doctrine of creation, have found the subversive pantheism of their attackers hard to resist; especially in an intellectual climate in which the uniqueness of the revelation of God in Jesus Christ is often doubted by Christians themselves.

Paul Tillich saw the problem clearly and warned against the dangers in 1951: 'Where nature is not related to the events of the history of salvation its status remains ambiguous.'[13] His condemnation of the incipient pantheism of those whose approach to nature is one of reverential awe is strong and needs to be heeded by all those, like myself, who are trying to locate their theology of the sacraments in a general theory of the sacramental universe: 'It is only through a relation to the history of salvation that it [nature] is liberated from its demonic elements and thus made eligible for a sacrament.'[14] When the creator ceases to be seen as the lord *over* nature and is collapsed into and identified *with* nature, nature takes on the character of the demonic; and human beings, no longer crucially related to and saved through specific historical events, become trapped in the natural process: 'In so far, however, as nature participates in the history of salvation, it is liberated from the demonic and made capable of becoming a sacrament.'[15] Behind this discussion lies the theology of St Paul in the eighth chapter of his letter to the Romans: 'For the creation waits with eager longing for the revealing of the sons of God . . . because the creation itself will be set free from its bondage to decay and obtain the glorious liberty of the children of God' (Rom. 8.19–21). Exactly how nature 'participates in the history of salvation' will be discussed later.

A still more critical attitude to the theory of the sacramental universe was brought from a quite different perspective two years later by E. L. Mascall in a book which did much to shape the ecclesiology of many Anglicans for a generation, *Corpus Christi*. Although he stands firmly on the principle that grace perfects nature without destroying it, he equally firmly places the sacraments of the Church in 'the order of grace'. They are to be found only in that body which comes into being as a consequence of the incarnation of the Son of God:

> They derive their existence and their efficacy not from the act by which God omnipotent perpetually preserves the world in existence, lovely and beautiful even in its fallen condition, but from the act by which God incarnate, entering into his world and, as it were, making himself part of it, died and rose again that it might be created afresh and more lovely and beautiful still.[16]

In view of this he goes on to define the purpose of the sacraments as being acts of Christ in his mystical body whose function is 'to establish, to maintain and to extend, to vivify and to unify, the mystical Body of the whole Christ, made up of Head and members in one organic and coherent pattern of life, to the glory of God the Father'.[17] I am no longer persuaded that this reinterpretation of classical Thomist teaching provides an adequate basis for a theology of the sacraments, although I still accept it is a valid criticism of a certain kind of naïve and simplistic version of the sacramental principle. Where Mascall is wrong is in maintaining that while matter may be seen to be capable of bearing the weight of divine glory and being the channel of divine grace, that fact has 'little or nothing to do with the doctrine of the sacraments'. Moreover, to confine the sacraments 'in the order of grace' and to limit their significance to the maintenance, extension, vivification and unity of the Church seems to contradict the very principle which he has established earlier, of the '*organic* relation between the order of nature and the order of grace' (my italics).[18] This is too narrow (and Western) a perspective on the purpose of the sacraments, and hence on the whole worship of the Church. There is lacking in this picture the sense that the worship of the Church is not merely the articulation of the adoration of rational creatures, but that of the whole of creation; that the sacraments are not merely for the sanctification of persons, but are related to the ultimate destiny of the whole of nature.

III

When Paul Tillich in *The Protestant Era* spoke of nature 'participating in the history of salvation' he, unfortunately, did not go on to indicate how this participation would and should happen. A more developed sacramental theology, one growing out of the closer integration of the doctrines of creation and incarnation, might show us how this participation comes about. Most Western theology, Catholic and Protestant alike, has tended to base its sacramental theology on the doctrine of the incarnation partly because the doctrine of creation has for so long been a kind of stepchild in the family of Christian doctrines, assumed but not much discussed. There was even debate, until recently, about the propriety of treating the doctrine as though it were a major theological issue.[19] Times have changed, but there is still an air of suspicion about the introduction of the doctrine into the central areas of Christian life and worship. An interesting example can be cited. In 1987 Michael Moreton wrote an expert and incisive essay on eucharistic sacrifice entitled 'The Language of the Christian Mystery of Redemption'. In the course of his mordant and, on the whole, thoroughly justified criticism of the 'language' of the Alternative Service Book of the Church of England, he condemns the fact that at the offertory there is no offering of the gifts 'with consecration in view':

> Instead, there is first the bizarre praising God for his gifts of bread and wine – bizarre because this makes of the offertory an agricultural sacrifice; and secondly, contrary to Prayer Book tradition, the offerings of the people, i.e. the collection, are presented, as though this were part of the eucharistic action.[20]

Presumably Moreton would have preferred the liturgical action at this point to be something similar to that of the modern Roman rite in which the gifts are offered with the specific intention that they will be consecrated to become the 'bread of life' and 'spiritual drink'. If this is an accurate interpretation of his position, I am only in partial agreement with him. The modern Roman prayers are, in themselves, inadequate. They begin with the blessing of God, the lord of creation, but he is being praised solely in order to ensure that the fruits of the earth may be transformed into something that will provide the worshipper with spiritual sustenance; the sacrifice is performed solely for the sake of the persons who will receive the sacrament. Moreton's antipathy towards the idea of an agricultural sacrifice seems to imply that his theology of the Eucharist is very much the same as that expressed in the offertory prayers of the Roman rite. By contrast, I would suggest that there *is* an element of agricultural sacrifice in eucharistic worship and that this is not at odds with the other parts of the sacrifice. To exclude this element would result in the danger of limiting the sacrifice of the Eucharist to being only a sacrifice for sin and solely for the purpose of saving mankind. I, on the other hand, see the presence of these pieces of matter as symbolic of the whole of the non-human, natural order brought into the eucharistic celebration and presented there by the priest of creation, mankind.

In the seventh century Leontios of Neapolis described the relationship of humanity to the rest of creation thus: 'The creation does not venerate the Creator through itself directly but it is through me that the heavens declare the glory of God, through me the moon offers him homage, through me the stars ascribe glory to him, through me the waters, rain and dew worship and glorify him.'[21] This perception is based upon the notion (already present in much patristic theology) that the human being is the microcosm of the universe. It is only when human beings begin to achieve sanctification that the whole natural order can begin to enter its own destiny in God. This has been a recurrent motif of the theology of creation in Eastern Orthodox theology and is beginning to be received in the West:

> Man no longer saves himself through the universe, but the universe is saved through man. For man is the hypostasis of the whole cosmos which participates in his nature. . . . To the universe, man is the hope of receiving grace and unity with God, and also the danger of failure and fallenness.[22]

The natural world is as much the explanation of Christ as he is the means of its redemption. Considered theologically, the incarnation is already implicit in creation: the creative process begun 'ex nihilo' only reveals its true purpose in the divinization of human nature by the act in which the divine word appears in history as a human being. And with this joining of the natural and the supernatural in Christ goes the possibility of the sanctification of the whole universe:

> . . . these closely linked themes of the revelation of God's glory in and through the created universe, and the place of the material creation in the prayer and praise we offer to God, are not peripheral or secondary to our concern for Christian worship. Rather, they are essential to the fullness of the tradition. The whole earth, not man alone, is the temple of God's glory. Man comes before God not in isolation from the rest of creation, not in mind and heart alone, but in the fullness of his being, bodily as well as spiritual, social as well as personal, bringing with him all this material universe of which he forms a part.[23]

And thus we have arrived at an extended and enriched understanding of the theory of the sacramental universe. We use elements of the natural order – bread, wine, water and oil – not merely because we are bodily creatures in a material creation that can manifest the divine splendour and convey the divine presence, but because if we do not use these elements in this way we shall not be performing our priestly task of sanctifying the universe that has been entrusted to us. As we are washed in water in baptism and are anointed with oil in chrism, as we offer and receive bread and wine in the Eucharist, we close the gap between nature and history; nature 'participates in the history of salvation'. No one has expressed this insight with greater intensity or more felicity than the man whom T. S. Eliot described as 'the first great preacher of the English Catholic Church' speaking 'with the old authority and the new culture': Lancelot Andrewes.[24] Preaching on Christmas Day in 1623 on the subject of the nativity, he said:

> . . . as there is a recapitulation of all in heaven and earth in Christ, so there is a recapitulation of all in Christ in the Holy Sacrament. You may see it clearly. There is in Christ the Word eternal, for things in heaven; there is also flesh, for things on earth. Semblably, the sacrament consisteth of a heavenly and of a terrene part (it is Irenaeus' own words); the heavenly – there the Word too, the abstract of the other; the earthly element. And in the elements, you may observe there is a fulness of the seasons of the natural year; of the corn-flour or harvest in the one, bread; of the wine-press or vintage in the other, wine. And in the heavenly, of the wheat-corn whereto he compareth himself – bread, even the Living Bread that came down from heaven; the true Manna, whereof we may gather each his gomer. And again, of him, the true Vine as he calls himself – the blood of the grapes of that vine. And both these issuing out of this day's recapitulation, both in *corpus autem aptasti mihi* of this day.[25]

Lancelot Andrewes's profound apprehension of the co-inherence of the creative and redemptive acts of God – the integration of the doctrines of creation and incarnation – issues in a sacramental theology that comes as close as anything ever written in the history of the Church to articulating the mystery of our religion.

Notes

1. 'A Propos of *Lady Chatterley's Lover*' (1929), in *Phoenix II*, uncollected, unpublished and other prose works by D. H. Lawrence, ed. W. Roberts and H. T. Moore (London 1968), p. 512.
2. P. Tillich, *The Protestant Era* (London 1951), pp. 114, 122 and 125.
3. R. Hooker, *Works*, arranged by John Keble, 3rd ed. (Oxford 1855), II (Book V, ch. lvi), p. 247.

4. C. S. Lewis, *English Literature in the Sixteenth Century* (Oxford 1954), p. 459.
5. See A. M. Allchin, *The Dynamic of Tradition* (London 1981), pp. 55ff.
6. Introduction to Hooker, *Works*, I, p. xci. Keble goes on to observe: 'Surely, on this point, as on many others, Hooker's sympathy with the fourth century rather than the sixteenth is perpetually breaking out, however chastened by his too reasonable dread of superstition' (p. xciv).
7. W. Temple, *Nature, Man and God* (London 1934), p. 486.
8. ibid., p. 266.
9. ibid., p. 306.
10. He refers to this possibility only obliquely: 'Yet the self-revelation so given is incomplete and inadequate. Personality can only reveal itself in persons. . . . If in the midst of the World-Process there should occur an instance of Human Nature free from all blemish or defect there might be found there the perfect self-expression of God to those who share that Human Nature' (p. 266).
11. It is primarily in his exposition of the incarnation that the determinative influence of process philosophy becomes evident. But it is worth noticing that Temple became critical of this influence later in life and acknowledged a growing interest in Thomism.
12. G. S. Hendry, *Theology of Nature* (Philadelphia 1980), pp. 217–18.
13. Tillich, *The Protestant Era*, p. 123.
14. ibid., p. 123.
15. ibid., p. 123.
16. E. L. Mascall, *Corpus Christi* (London 1965), p. 41.
17. ibid., p. 43.
18. ibid., p. 40.
19. See, for example, G. Von Rad's commentary on Genesis: *Genesis* (London 1979).
20. J. Greenhalgh and E. Russell, eds *Signs of Faith, Hope and Love* (London 1987), p. 55.
21. quoted by K. Ware, in 'The Value of the Material World', *Sobornost* 6:3 (1985), p. 85.
22. V. Lossky, *Orthodox Theology: An Introduction*, (Crestwood, NJ, 1978), p. 71.
23. Allchin, *The Dynamic of Tradition*, p. 128.
24. 'Lancelot Andrewes' (1926), in T. S. Eliot, *Selected Essays* (London 1934), p. 344.
25. *Ninety Six Sermons*, I (Oxford 1841), p. 281.

2

Anointing in Ancient Mesopotamia

Stephanie Dalley

'Pure oil, clean oil, shining oil, purifying oil of the gods, oil that relaxes the muscles of men, . . . oil of spells, . . . oil of pacification.' The functions that oil was perceived to have by the Babylonians themselves are described in an incantation to oil, given in the magical series *Maqlû*.

Anointing in ancient Mesopotamian sources consisted of either rubbing or pouring various types of oil on to a person, a divine statue, or an object representing or intimately connected with a person or a deity. Four categories can perhaps be distinguished from laconic and fragmentary cuneiform texts. First, in the context of washing and dressing, oil is rubbed into the flesh. Second, in the context of sacrificing, oil is rubbed upon divine statues and cult objects. Third, in the context of eating and drinking, oil is rubbed into the flesh when a legal contract is concluded, probably on the occasion of oath-taking, in which the oil together with the food and drink may contain a spell or potential curse on perjurers. Finally, in the context of marriage, oil is poured on to the head of the chosen person by the selector, perhaps to mark selection; this category can also be applied to the selection of vassal kings.

At a domestic level, unction follows washing in water as a preliminary to dressing. Although it follows cleaning, it is not a part of it, for whereas water is removed from the body taking dirt with it, thus purifying the flesh, oil sinks into the body, making it shine, smoothing roughened skin and (if the unguent is perfumed) adding

19

fragrance. Medicinal application of salves can also be added to this category. Washing and oiling are so different that it is extremely doubtful whether purification was considered to be a function of oiling the body; Akkadian texts do not seem to support the idea, although they clearly indicate that bathing with water purifies.

The soothing and beautifying effect of anointing can be illustrated from Babylonian mythology. In the story of the Flood as told in the *Epic of Gilgamesh* the hero supplied his workmen with 'hand oil' as they were building the Ark. In the *Epic of Creation* Marduk was oiled and dressed after killing the rebellious gods. When Assurnasirpal II entertained 69,574 guests at the inauguration of his palace at Calah, he said: 'I gave them food, I gave them drink, I had them bathed, I had them anointed.' The pleasing qualities of oil are implied by two curses on future oath-breakers: 'May naphtha be your ointment', and, 'May pitch be your ointment'.

Last rites carried out for a corpse before inhumation correspond to this regular, domestic toilette, a final ritual carried over from daily life, in which the 'oil of pacification' has the added effect of pleasing and pacifying the spirit of the dead man so that it will be disinclined to harm the living. Instructions for the body of Dumuzi (Tammuz) are given in *The Descent of Ishtar to the Underworld*: 'Wash him with clean water, anoint him with perfumed oil, dress him in a red cloth.' Once a body was buried, it was impossible to anoint it again; funerary unction with washing and dressing thus marks the end of an episode or a state and preparation for a new direction.

Important men often had a statue made of themselves, as Gilgamesh made for Enkidu, or a *narû*-stele inscribed with biographical details; or they might deposit a written record of their fame, sometimes in the foundation of a public building. Pious descendants had a duty to anoint such statues, steles and inscriptions, and texts express the urgent wish that this be done. 'Whoever among the kings my descendants renovates this temple, may he anoint my clay inscriptions and my steles with oil, make a sacrifice, and return them to their places,' wrote Shamshi-Adad I (King of Assyria *c*.1800BC). Nearly 1,000 years later, another Assyrian king reconstructed a palace in the capital city Assur and proclaimed: 'I deposited my steles. I anointed with oil the steles of earlier kings, my forefathers, made sacrifices and returned them to their places.' This phenomenon is not restricted to royal or divine objects. The stele of a governor of Suhu province on the Middle Euphrates in the eighth century BC, Shamash-resh-uṣur, calls upon future passers-by to respect his monument in this way, and since a porous stone was used, one can still see that its greasy top was indeed anointed.

The last indigenous king of Babylon, Nabonidus, writing shortly before the Achaemenid Persians overran his country, restored the temple of the moon god Sin in Harran. During the building work, inscriptions deposited by Assurbanipal a century earlier came to light. 'I saw inscriptions written with the name of Assurbanipal . . . and I did not alter them. I anointed them with oil, made sacrifices, put them with my inscriptions and returned them to their places.' This was done even though Nabonidus was not related to him and was king of Babylon, not of Assyria. In such inscriptions invocations to future rulers to do likewise indicate that the treatment would be rewarded by the gods: 'The gods will accept his prayers and bless him.'

In those examples the steles and inscriptions are not washed before anointing. The same appears to be true of divine statues: they are oiled and they are clothed, but never washed. When Marduk had defeated the rebel gods in the *Epic of Creation* the gods oiled and dressed him, but they did not wash him. The conclusion may tentatively be suggested, that whereas mortals were cleaned and purified by washing with water, divine beings were cleaned and purified by anointing with oil. This interpretation would fit the implied separation of functions in the incantation from the series *Maqlû* quoted above, which calls oil the purifier of gods but not the purifier of men.

A related situation seems to have come to light recently from texts found at two sites on the Middle Euphrates: at Mari in the Middle Bronze Age and at Emar in the Late Bronze Age. One aspect of the cult there was the erection of shaped stones, menhirs or baetyls (Akkadian *sik(k)an(n)u*, Ugaritic *skn*, Hittite *huwaši/^{na4}ZI.KIN* from which an Akkadian loanword *hamusum* appears to be derived) which were themselves divine and sometimes, perhaps always, belonged to or represented specific deities or deified ancestors. They were smeared with oil and with blood as part of the ritual of the *kukru*-festival, and the anointing was accompanied by sacrifice of a goat. In an Ugaritic legend a *skn* is set up by a man's heir and dedicated to Ilaba, a god who is thought by some to embody the principle of ancestor-worship. In these contexts anointing may come into the category of nourishment instead of (or in addition to) purification. Possibly this phenomenon should be compared with the act of anointing doorposts and thresholds, referred to in *Maqlû* IX 141, for the doorpost was regarded as a deity (Sumerian ^{d}Gandu, Akkadian ^{d}Hittu).

Unction, when it is performed with eating and drinking, and mentioned in legal record and treaty clauses, moves into the sphere of symbolic actions that have legal implications. Cuneiform records are written as laconic reminders of what took place before witnesses. Clauses need not describe each stage of contract-making, and references to symbolic actions are rare. However, enough examples are now published for us to be certain that, at least in the Middle Bronze Age, when one man bought real estate from another, both buyer and seller ate, drank and anointed their heads with oil together. The interpretation is still not certain, but it is likely that a ritual of oath-taking is involved, for the contracting parties are known from other texts to have sworn oaths by their king and city god that they would abide by the contract. From other kinds of texts we know that food, drink and oil were involved in rituals accompanying promises: by sympathetic magic a potential curse was laid upon the food, water and oil which entered the body of the oath-takers; if they broke their promises, they would activate the curses, as divine retribution. Loyalty oaths sworn by allies and vassal rulers to Esarhaddon, king of Assyria in the seventh century BC, make this clear: 'Just as bread and wine enter into the intestines, so may the gods make this oath enter into your intestines. . . . Just as oil enters your flesh, so may the gods cause this oath to enter into your flesh.'

In the *Epic of Creation* VI, the gods swore allegiance to Marduk 'in water and oil', and a clause in a neo-Assyrian slave sale record – 'by water, oil, snake and scorpion! – if she [the slave] dies or disappears, it is the responsibility of her father' – may refer to a promissory oath made by the guarantor. The ritual presumably included drinking water and anointing with oil which contained a potential curse; but it is ambiguous, since water may be for washing or for drinking. The same procedure was followed when Esarhaddon became king: his people swore oaths of loyalty to him, 'sworn on oil and water to guard my kingship'.

In real estate sales from Emar in the Late Bronze Age, clauses say: 'The money has been received, his heart is pleased, *hukku*-bread has been cut (for a *kispum*-offering to the dead), the table has been anointed with oil; one shekel has been given for the tomb on the property.' (Arnaud nos. 20,109 and 130.) In this instance a table is anointed as part of a ceremony performed when the owners of a property that included an ancestral tomb sold them to people outside their own family.

Eating, drinking and unction also come together in the exclusion clauses found in oracular queries to the Sungod, as three ways in which impurities may accidentally enter the body. The categorization as nourishment that may be contaminated is clear here.

Unconnected with the toilette or with nourishment, unction plays a part in marriage contracts, and in coronations of vassal kings, at least in some areas of the Near East. In these ceremonies oil is not generally rubbed on to the body, but is poured upon the head of one person. The evidence from Mesopotamian texts is deficient, for no complete account of a coronation ritual is known for any Babylonian or Assyrian king. However, Marduk's appointment as King of the Gods in the *Epic of Creation* is preserved in detail, and the text is silent on the rite of unction. For this reason it has sometimes been supposed that unction played no part in Mesopotamian enthronement, but is restricted largely to Israel and to the Hittites. Undoubtedly vassal kings were anointed by their overlords in the semitic world beyond Israel: an Amarna letter, written to the Pharaoh by Addu-nirari, king of Nuhašše, a kingdom south of Aleppo, implies that both Syrians and Egyptians knew of the practice: 'When your ancestor Manahpiya king of Egypt established my ancestor Taku as king of Nuhašše, he put oil on his head and spoke as follows: "Nobody shall [depose] anyone whom the king of Egypt has installed as king, and on whose head he has put [oil]." '

A similar usage is found in a ritual some two centuries later, from Emar, at the enthronement and marriage of the *entu*-priestess to the Weather God. The very first act to take place after the girl has been selected was that oil 'from the palace and from the temple of the goddess Bēlat-māti' was 'placed on her head'. In a Middle Assyrian marriage law of the same period 'a man poured oil on to [her] head', as one of the steps that makes the arrangement binding. In the case of a text from Ugarit, it is not certain whether the ritual marks manumission or marriage: the official in charge of the queen's house discharges a servant girl from the status of *harimtu*, pours oil on her head and declares her free or exempt (from her previous obligations?). She then immediately marries a man who pays money to the official. It is not clear in this text where the division between manumission and marriage arrangements occurs; manumission is normally accompanied by washing the forehead of the slave with water.

A treaty recently published from the seventh century BC shows that the evidence from Amarna and Emar for enthronement with anointing is not merely peripheral to Mesopotamia. 'Assurbanipal your lord put oil on you [plural, i.e. kings of Qedar in Arabia], put his friendly face towards you' refers to the coronation of successive vassal kings by the Assyrians. Both in this case and in the Amarna letter, it is the overlord (or his representative) who puts oil on the appointed ruler, as if to mark his choice. There is no trace of evidence to show that, in this case, the unction might be connected with oath-taking; indeed, the absence of water with oil suggests that no oaths are involved, and the act seems simply to mark selection. The ritual of the New Year festival in Babylon makes it clear that kingship there, although bestowed by the gods on man as part of his duty to serve heaven, could be revoked and had to be discarded symbolically each year by the king; moreover, he was reduced to tears by having his face slapped. It seems possible that the great kings of Babylonia and Assyria were not anointed at their coronation even though they anointed their own vassal kings. A neo-Assyrian letter has been interpreted as containing evidence for the anointing of the substitute king and queen, but this is extremely doubtful; the act follows drinking wine and washing with water, and the precise context is far from clear.

The Oil of Gladness

Thus several distinct uses of unction can be discerned: with washing and dressing as part of the toilette of mortals; to purify and nourish the statues of the gods and the stones that represent ancestors; rubbed into skin to convey a potential curse to bind oath-takers; and poured on the head of a girl chosen for marriage or the head of a man selected to be a vassal king.

Select Bibliography

Real Estate Sales

J-M. Durand, 'Sumérien et Akkadien en pays amorite', *Mari Annales de Recherches Interdisciplinaires* I (1982), pp. 80–82.

G. Boyer, *Textes Juridiques, Archives Royales de Mari VIII* (Paris 1958), text no. 13.

R. Harris, 'The archive of the Sin Temple in Khafajah (Tutub)', *Journal of Cuneiform Studies* 9 (1955), p. 92, text no. 59:10.

D. Arnaud, *Recherches au Pays d'Aštata Emar VI/3* (Paris 1986), texts nos. 109, 110, 111 and 130, with the interpretation offered by:

J-M. Durand, 'Tombes familiales et culte des ancêtres à Emar', *Nouvelles Assyriologiques brèves et utilitaires* (henceforth *NABU*) (1989), p. 86.

Statues and stones

J-M. Durand, 'Le culte des bétyles en Syrie', *Miscellanea Babylonica, hommage à M. Birot* (Paris 1985), pp. 79–83.

D. Arnaud, *Recherches au pays d'Aštata Emar VI/3* (Paris 1986), text nos. 369, 370 and 373.

D. Charpin, 'Le bétyle au pays de Sumer', *NABU* (1987), p. 41.

J-M. Durand, 'sikkannum = ᵈAbnum', *NABU* (1987), pp. 41–2.

J-M. Durand, 'Le nom des bétyles à Ebla et en Anatolie', *NABU* (1988), pp. 5–6.

J. C. L. Gibson, [legend of Aqhat in] *Canaanite Myths and Legends*, 2nd edn (Edinburgh 1978), p. 104.

A. K. Grayson, *Assyrian Royal Inscriptions*, vol. 1 (Harrassowitz 1972) and vol. 2 (1976), *passim*.

B. Lafont, 'La collection A des inscriptions de Šu-Sîn', *NABU* (1990), pp. 13–14.

S. Langdon, *Die neubabylonischen Königsinschriften, Vorderasiatische Bibliothek* 4 (Leipzig 1912), e.g. p. 223.

D. D. Luckenbill, *Ancient Records of Assyria and Babylon* 2 (Chicago 1926–7), *passim*.

Marriage Contracts and Coronation

R. Borger, *Die Inschriften Asarhaddons* (Osnabrück 1967), p. 43.

G. R. Driver and J. C. Miles, *Middle Assyrian Laws* (Oxford 1935) law no. 43.

F. Thureau-Dangin, 'Trois Contrats de Ras Shamra', *Syria* 18 (1937), pp. 248 and 253.

K. F. Müller, 'Das assyrische Ritual, Teil I. Texte zum assyrische Königsritual', *Mitteilungen der vorderasiatische-aegyptische Gesellschaft* 41/3 (1937), p. 8.

S. Parpola and K. Watanabe, *Neo-Assyrian Treaties and Loyalty Oaths, State Archives of Assyria* vol. 2 (Helsinki 1988), pp. 11, 49 and 68–9.

D. Arnaud, *Recherches du pays d'Aštata Emar* VI/3 (Paris 1986), text nos. 369, 370 and 373.

S. Parpola, *Letters from Assyrian Scholars, Alte Orient und altes Testament* 5/1 (Neukirchen-Vluyn) part I Texts, p. 21, 5/2; part II Commentary (1983), p. 36.

W. Moran, *Les Lettres d'El Amarna* (Paris 1987) text no. 51.

Other

K. R. Veenhof, [review of E. Kutsch, *Salbung als Rechtsakt im Alten Testament und im Alten Orient*, (Berlin 1963) in] *Bibliotheca Orientalis* 23, 5/6 (1966), pp. 308–13.

S. Dalley, *Myths from Mesopotamia* (Oxford 1989), pp. 111 and 258.

G. Meier, *Die assyrische Beschwörungssammlung Maqlû* (Osnabrück 1967), pp. 47–8.

I. Starr, *Queries to the Sungod, State Archives of Assyria* 4 (Helsinki 1990), especially pp. xxiv–xxv.

D. J. Wiseman, 'The Nimrud Tablets, 1953', *Iraq* 15 (1953), text ND 3441, pl. xii.

3

Oil in Ancient Greece and Rome

Angus Bowie

Asked how one might live a healthy life, the pre-Socratic philosopher Democritus replied, 'if one's body is moistened inside with honey and outside with oil'.[1] Oil was central to Greek and Roman life: Pliny said that it showed nature's forethought that she made it unnecessary to use up wine in haste, because it keeps and is anyway produced merely for intoxication, but caused oil not to keep, so that men could use it freely.[2] To the Greeks, the olive was an attribute of Athena, goddess of civilization and its technology.[3] Its frequency in everyday Greek and Roman life, especially after the bath or the gymnasium, as a protection against sun and cold, or as an internal or external medicine, stands however in contrast to its relatively specialized use in Greek cult practice, and, in Roman cult practice, its infrequency of use.[4]

Greece

There is ample archaeological evidence for the extensive use of olive oil and unguent in Mycenaean Greece, and its religious use is attested on the Linear B clay tablets.[5] From Pylos, there are a number of references to 'unguent-boilers', and it is most likely that the *aleiphar* used for making perfumed unguent was olive oil. The oil was flavoured with substances such as coriander seed, 'fruits', wine, honey, must; and we read of rose- and sage-scented oil or oil with two perfumes. Arrangements are made for the distribution of perfumed

26

oil and unguent to 'the gods' of a particular location, to specific gods such as Poseidon, Potnia, the Divine Mother, the Thrice-Hero, or to places, such as the precinct of Zeus, and perhaps festivals. Oil which is not specifically described as perfumed is a regular offering to gods: at Cnossus it is given to Dictaean Zeus, to the 'Daedaleion', to Erinys and to the Priestess of the Winds; other tablets refer to the gift of olive oil to human beings and trade groups. The religious use of oil is clear therefore, but exactly how it was used the tablets do not tell us: no doubt, as later, it was used for libations and unguent was smeared on cult-images; we have one specific reference to 'unguent for robes'.[6]

Our next evidence comes from Homer, where anointing with olive oil is generally practised before or after washing. It was also used for garments.[7] 'Ambrosia', which was clearly conceived of as an ointment of some kind, and oil infused with roses or 'aromatic' oil, are both restricted to the Olympians.[8]

If our evidence is too little for us to draw many conclusions about the nature of the uses of oil in the Mycenaean period, in the Classical period we can see that there is a tendency for oil to be used, either alone or alongside honey, milk, water[9] and neat wine, in rituals or stages of rituals that are marked in some way as unusual – perhaps in not involving the spilling of blood, or in rites connected with the uncanny or marginal.[10] These liquids stand in opposition to wine mixed with water, which was the regular liquid used in religious rites.[11] This opposition is also found in the belief that the earliest men did not offer blood-sacrifice, but instead other substances such as fruits, perfumes and unguent.[12]

Oil's use in an unusual ritual is clearly seen at Demeter's shrine at Phigaleia, where there was one altar on which they did not offer blood-sacrifice, but put on it the produce of cultivated trees, wine, honey, and wool that had not been treated, and then poured oil over it.[13] Not far away, at Lycosura, those who sacrificed to the Mistress, a goddess worshipped with many unusual rites, had to offer oil, myrrh, honey-comb etc.[14] At the annual sacrifice to those who died fighting the Persians at Plataea, a black bull, as befitted chthonic beings, was sacrificed on a pile of wood (not a regular altar); oil, unguent, milk and wine were offered and the chief magistrate, who at other times might not touch iron or wear any clothing except white, on this occasion bore a sword and was dressed in purple, and had the task of washing the grave-stele with water from a stream and anointing it with unguent.[15]

As for marginal situations, oil was regularly used in the burial and honouring of the dead. The body was washed and anointed with oil or unguent, and unguent could be poured into wounds.[16] Aphrodite anointed the body of Hector with oil infused with roses to protect it from Achilles' maltreatment.[17] More unguent could be placed next to the bier in bottles,[18] or poured into a trench as an offering to the dead.[19] Achilles was cremated with honey and unguents and to his ashes were added unmixed wine and more unguent.[20] These Homeric examples describe special burials, but his evidence coincides with that from archaeology.[21] In the Classical period, the most characteristic grave-offering is the oil-vessel (*lekuthos*); they were buried in the grave, hung on the grave-stone or placed next to it; some have small inner chambers and may have been used for libations of more precious oils.[22] Oil was also offered to the dead after burial, sometimes through tubes, and in summoning the ghost of her dead husband, Darius, Atossa offered him milk, honey, water, neat wine, oil and flowers.[23]

There is some evidence that mother and child might be purified by anointing after a birth.[24] Both bride and groom were anointed before marriage,[25] and those making the preparations might anoint their hands;[26] anointing with unguent could precede sexual congress.[27] Oil could be used in purifications. A murderer might rid himself of pollution by sitting on a fleece at the threshold of a shrine and anointing himself and leaving in silence.[28] In second-century AD Lindos, a man who had slept lawfully with a woman could make himself ritually pure the same day by anointing himself with oil and washing.[29]

Anointing was used as a prelude to magical rites. Demeter anointed a child with ambrosia and hid him in the fire in an attempt to make him immortal,[30] and Medea anointed Jason with chrisms that protected him from fire-breathing bulls.[31] Statues were anointed before magical rites, for which the celebrant would have to anoint himself too.[32] The whole body or just the hand might be anointed. Anointing, not with oil but with animal fat, was popularly believed to protect one against wild animals: the fat of the elephant was particularly effective.[33] Bear fat would make one hairy,[34] and that of the sea-lion beautiful.[35] Here belongs the story of Isidas the Spartan, who stripped naked, oiled himself, and with spear and sword sprang at the Thebans at a crucial moment in a battle; he was harmed by no one on the Theban side.[36] The medicinal use of oils is a corollary of this.[37]

It was also used before certain less dramatic rites. One would anoint oneself before religious processions,[38] or during washing as a prelude to the Mysteries at Andania, where there was a special room for the purpose,[39] or before a dance: 'after the sea-battle at Salamis, Sophocles danced naked with a lyre before the men singing the paean began the victory ode'.[40] Anointing was part of the elaborate rituals used before consulting the underground oracle of Trophonius,[41] or before the relatively unusual practice of lifting a bull to bring it to a god.[42] Finally, when Plato describes the proposed treatment of the most skilled poet if he tried to enter the new state without producing the kind of poetry required there, he says they would 'reverence' him as a 'holy and marvellous man, pour unguent over his head and send him on his way'.[43]

Anointing oneself at the symposium was a common practice performed before and after the meal, and before the 'second table' was brought in for the drinking. Although originally this was probably not simply a secular act designed to give pleasure, but, like the hymns and sacrifice, had a sacral character, in the Classical and hellenistic periods many felt that it was taken to excess:[44] an extraordinary range of different oils, unguents and perfumes was available,[45] which were rubbed or poured over the body, different unguents sometimes being used for different parts of the body.[46] In some of its earliest attestations, unguent was associated with luxury, sexuality and effete foreign races like the Lydians.[47] It was said that in Homer no hero was anointed except Paris;[48] this is a misinterpretation, but a significant one. In his play about the Judgement of Paris, Sophocles brought on Aphrodite, representing pleasure, smelling of unguent, but Athena, representing good sense, smelt of simple olive oil.[49]

It was not only humans who were anointed. Sacred stones and cult statues were similarly treated. The statue of Dionysus was anointed yearly on Delos,[50] and those of Zeus Ktesios (Guardian of the Household) were anointed when set up.[51] At Delphi, the stone that was given to Cronus to eat instead of his son Zeus was daily anointed,[52] and the *omphalos*, the centre of the earth, was also anointed.[53] The superstitious would pour a few drops of oil on to smooth stones at crossroads.[54] The polished stones outside his palace on which Nestor sat to perform his function as king were 'glistening with unguent'.[55] Presumably there is here an element of demarcation, of fixing a centre or point of orientation; the marking of objects by animals has been compared to this practice.[56] Altars might also have oil put on them.[57]

Oil was also poured over or around statues with the more practical purpose of protecting them, but here too there is a religious element involved: Phidias gave orders that oil should be poured round his chryselephantine statue of Zeus at Olympia 'to keep it as immortal as far as possible';[58] *perfumed* oil was poured into the many holes in the wooden image of Artemis at Ephesus,[59] and at Chaeronea, an unguent of roses was used to stop wooden images from rotting.[60]

Rome

Many Roman uses of oil and unguent were similar to those of the Greeks, not least, from around the middle of the second century BC, because of Greek influence,[61] especially on the more lavish everyday customs[62] and in medicine.[63] However, in the Roman Republic, we find frequent expressions of suspicion of their use as a Greek practice.[64] The archaic *Twelve Tables* law-code forbade giving the dead the *servilis unctio* and *murrata potio* ('myrrh-scented drink'),[65] and unguents were forbidden by the Censors in 189 BC.[66] Explaining why, among many other prohibitions, the Flamen Dialis (priest of Jupiter) could not anoint himself in public, Plutarch says it was because of Roman suspicions of rubbing down with oil and 'their belief that nothing has been so much to blame for the enslavement and effeminacy of the Greeks as their gymnasia and wrestling-schools'.[67] Later, Roman practice fell in with Greek.[68]

As in Greece, it was believed that early Roman sacrifice was bloodless and consisted of similar substances to those found in Greek belief.[69] There is an interesting reflection of this belief in the rites of the Arval Brethren, priests of the Goddess Dia. On the first day, at dawn the 'Master' made an offering of incense and wine, 'dry' and 'green' fruits, and bread crowned with laurel, before anointing a statue of the goddess; the others followed suit.[70] On the second day, blood sacrifice was made, but there is no mention of the anointing of the statue at that point.[71] Thus a 'primitive' sacrifice involving unction precedes a 'normal' one, in a pattern familiar from Greek and Roman rites.

Oil again figures in liminal rites. A bride anointed the door-posts of her new husband's house with oil or wolf's fat, before she was carried over the threshold.[72] The Latin word for 'wife', *uxor*, was explained as a form of *unxor* 'anointress', and the goddess Unxia presided over this rite.[73]

At funerals, after the closing of the eyes and the lamentation, the dead were washed and anointed with perfumes (*pollinctio*);[74] they might even be embalmed in perfumes, or the ashes sprinkled with unguent.[75] In Vergil's detailed description of the burial of Misenus, the body is anointed and bowls of oil are poured out, as offerings to the spirit of the dead man.[76] Oil-bottles were left as offerings in or by graves.[77] Oil was also offered, with eggs, milk, honey, etc., privately to the *Manes* (shades of ancestors).

When Aeneas sacrifices to the underworld powers, before his descent into the underworld, oil is poured over the burning innards.[78] When he becomes one of the Indigetes divinities, Venus anoints him with 'divine perfume and ambrosia mixed with nectar'.[79] In literature, magic chrisms might be applied before an ordeal,[80] or by deities involved in magic.[81]

Stones are again anointed,[82] including boundary-stones, which were anointed and garlanded after the rites used to set them up and once they were in place.[83] So were a few statues of gods, such as Diana by the women and young girls of Segesta,[84] and of mortals, such as ball-player Ursus, who asks in his epitaph that friends anoint his image.[85] Oil was again believed to preserve ivory from decay: 'at all events, the inside of the statue of Saturn at Rome has been filled with oil',[86] and a man might leave money for his statue to be cleaned and anointed.[87] The eagles and standards of the legions were anointed with unguent on holidays,[88] and the arms of Quirinus were smeared at the Portunalia in August.[89]

If Romans used oil in these various ways, the undercurrent of disapproval remained: Pliny felt that 'when Lucius Plotius having been proscribed by the Triumvirs was given away in his hiding place by the scent of the unguent he had been using, this disgrace acquitted the whole proscription of guilt, for who would not consider that such people deserved to die?'[90]

Notes

1. *Ap*. Athenaeus, *Deipnosophistae* 46F (abbreviated as *Deipn*. hereafter). Cf. Pliny, *Naturalis Historia* 22.114, 14.150 (abbreviated as *NH* hereafter).
2. Pliny, *NH* 15.7.
3. For instance, an olive grew by her temple (the Erechtheum) in Athens, and with this plant she won the competition with Poseidon to be patron of the city; when Epopeus of Sicyon asked if his temple to her was pleasing, olive oil flowed in front of it (Pausanias 2.6.3).
4. On oil in antiquity, see A. S. Pease, 'Oleum', in A. Pauly and G. Wissowa, *Realencyclopädie der klassischen Altertumswissenschaft* 17 colls. 2454–74; for anointing, see J. Hug, 'Salben', ibid., 11a/12a colls. 1851–66.
5. M. Ventris and J. Chadwick, *Documents in Mycenaean Greek*, ed. J. Chadwick (Cambridge 1973), Index *s.vv*. 'olive oil', 'unguent', and esp. pp. 476–83; E. L. Bennett, *The Olive Oil Tablets of Pylos*, *Minos* Suppl. 2 (Salamanca 1958).
6. Fr 1225.
7. Homer, *Iliad* 18.596, Homer, *Odyssey* 7.107; for later times, cf. the story in Plutarch, *Alexander* 36.
8. Homer, *Iliad* 14.172f., 16.680, cf. 670, 23.186f.; Homer, *Odyssey* 8.364f., 18.190ff.; *Homeric Hymn to Demeter* 237f., *Homeric Hymn to Aphrodite* 61ff. etc.
9. Sacrifices that did not involve wine were called *Nephalia*, 'sober sacrifices': cf. L. Ziehen, 'Nephalia', in Pauly and Wissowa (see note 4) 16 colls. 2481–9, esp. 2484–6 on oil.
10. For a general discussion of Greek uses of oil, cf. C. Mayer, *Das Öl im Kultus der Griechen*, (Würzburg 1917) (not always reliable).
11. Plutarch, *Moralia* 672B, 'honey has a nature opposed to that of wine'; Athenaeus, *Deipn*. 693E. In general, cf. F. Graf, 'Milch, Honig und Wein. Zum Verständnis der Libation im Griechischen Ritual', in G. Piccaluga, ed., *Perennitas. Studi in onore di A. Brelich* (Rome 1980), pp.

31

The Oil of Gladness

209–21; A. Henrichs, 'The "Sobriety" of Oedipus: Sophocles *OC* 100 misunderstood', *Harv. St. Cl. Philol.*, 87 (1983), pp. 87–100.

12. Empedocles fr. 128 Diels-Kranz; Theophrastus, *ap.* Porphyry, *de Abstinentia* 2.20.2ff.

13. Pausanias 8.42.11; also Sophocles fr. 398 Pearson (wool, wine, preserved grapes, barley-grains, honey and oil).

14. F. Sokolowski, *Lois sacrées des cités Grecques* (Paris 1969), no. 68.13ff.; cf. Pausanias 8.37.1ff.

15. Plutarch, *Aristeides* 21.

16. Homer, *Iliad* 16.679f.

17. ibid. 23.186f.

18. ibid.23.170f.

19. Cleidemus *ap.* Athenaeus, *Deipn.* 410A. Oil with honey appears at Patroclus' funeral (Homer, *Iliad* 23.170) and has a parallel in the Mycenaean honey-tablet found among the oil-tablets with their record of offerings to gods (cf. Ventris and Chadwick (see note 5), p. 309).

20. Homer, *Odyssey* 24.67f., 73.

21. D. Kurtz and J. Boardman, *Greek Burial Customs* (London 1971), pp. 102–5 and 209.

22. A libation of oil was a *khoa*, in which the vessel was emptied at one go, as opposed to the *sponde* of wine in which only a portion was poured out.

23. Aeschylus, *Persians* 607ff.

24. Callimachus, *Hymn* 1. 17; Apollonius Rhodius, *Argonautica* 4.1311 (both of gods).

25. e.g. Aristophanes, *Plutus* 529.

26. Theocritus, *Idyll* 17.134.

27. e.g. Aristophanes, *Lysistrata* 938ff.

28. F. Sokolowski, *Lois sacrées des cités Grecques: supplément* (Paris 1962), no. 115 B 52f. (Cyrene, end fourth cent. BC).

29. Sokolowski (see n. 14), no. 139.14ff.

30. *Homeric Hymn to Demeter* 237–40.

31. Pindar, *Pythian* 4.221f.

32. e.g. C. Wessely, *Denkschr. K. Akad. Wissenschaften*, Ph.-Hist. Kl. 42 (1893), p. 51, line 941f.; ibid. 36 (1888), p. 78, lines 1339f.

33. Dioscorides, *de Materia Medica* 2.76; Aelian, *de Natura Animalium* 1.37. In general, anointing with substances other than oils was seen either as conservative (a Spartan woman of conservative tastes used butter (Plutarch, *Moralia* 1109B)), or barbarian (the Paeones of Thrace used 'oil from milk' (Hecataeus *ap.* Athenaeus, *Deipn.* 447D)).

34. Dioscorides, *de Materia Medica* 2.76.18.

35. Aelian, *de Natura Animalium* 14.9.

36. Plutarch, *Agesilaus* 34.

37. Theophrastus, *de Odoribus*; Dioscorides, *de Materia Medica* 1.7–68; Pease (see n. 4), colls 2461f.

38. Proclus on Plato, *Republic* 398A (p. 42 Kroll).

39. Sokolowski, (see n. 14) 65.108f.

40. *Vita Sophoclis* 2; cf. Athenaeus, *Deipn.* 20F; Homer, *Odyssey* 18.194 (Aphrodite).

41. Pausanias 9.39.7.
42. ibid. 8.19.2; cf. Strabo 14.1.44 on rite at Charonion of Acharaca (Ionia).
43. *Republic* 398A.
44. Solon forbade Athenian citizens to sell unguents (Athenaeus, *Deipn.* 612A), Sparta expelled sellers of them (ibid., 686F) and Socrates said olive oil was all a man required (Xenophon, *Symposium* 2.3).
45. Pliny, *NH* 13.8ff.
46. e.g. Athenaeus, *Deipn.* 553A ff.
47. ibid., 690 BC.
48. ibid., 18F.
49. Fr. 361; cf. Callimachus, *Hymn* 5.23ff.
50. *Bull. Corresp. Hell*, 14 (1890), pp. 498ff.; 32 (1908), pp. 14 A.32ff.
51. Anticleides *ap.* Athenaeus, *Deipn.* 473C.
52. Pausanias 10.24.6.
53. W. H. Roscher, *Omphalos* (Leipzig 1913), pl. 7.4.
54. Theophrastus, *Characters* 16.5.
55. Homer, *Odyssey* 3.406ff.
56. W. Burkert, *Structure and History in Greek Mythology and Ritual* (Berkeley, Los Angeles and London 1979), pp. 41–3.
57. Sokolowski (see n. 14), 55.10f.
58. Photius, *Bibliotheca* p. 293 b 1ff. Bekker.
59. Pliny, *NH* 16.214.
60. Pausanias 9.41.7.
61. Livy 39.6.7–9 ascribes 'the source of Eastern luxuriousness in Rome' to the victories of Cn. Manlius Vulso in Asia in 187 BC.
62. We find the same extravagant use at banquets, and the same complaints from the moralists, such as Scipio (Aulus Gellius 6.12.5) and Seneca (*Epistles* 108.16). Decent Romans would not smell of unguent before the *cena* (Juvenal 4.108), and 'a woman who smelt of nothing smelt properly' (Plautus, *Mostellaria* 272f.). Cf. J. Colin, 'Luxe orientale et parfums masculins dans la Rome alexandrine', *Rev. Belg. de Philol.*, 33 (1955), pp. 5–19.
63. Pliny, *NH* 23.75ff. On oil and unguents in Rome, see ibid., 13.1ff. and 15.1ff.
64. Pliny (*NH* 15.24) suggests that the reason Cato the Censor (*d.* 149 BC) does not mention any 'artificial oil' (i.e. not from olives) is that they did not then exist. In Pliny's time there were myriad types (cf. Pease (see note 4) 2454f.).
65. *XII Tabulae* 10.5b–6 (Loeb edn); Cic. *Leges* 2.23.59; Varro *ap.* Festus pp. 150–2 Lindsay.
66. Pliny, *NH* 13.24.
67. Plutarch, *Quaestiones Romanae* 40; Horace, comparing Roman and Greek achievements in the Greek activities of painting, dancing and wrestling, refers rather scornfully to the '*Achivi . . . uncti*' (*Epistles* 2.1.32f.).
68. Nevertheless, bequeathing oil for athletics and bathing at a festival could be a religious act (*Corp. Inscr. Lat.* 5.5279 (Comum)).

The Oil of Gladness

69. Dionysius of Halicarnassus, *Antiquitates Romanae* 2.74.4; Ovid, *Fasti* 1.337ff.; Pliny, *NH* 18.7; Plutarch, *Romulus* 12, *Numa* 16.
70. Frr. 88, 99–101 Pasoli, cf. I. Paladino, *Fratres Arvales: storia di un collegio sacerdotale romano* (Rome 1988), pp. 117f.
71. Paladino (see note 70), pp. 119–21.
72. Servius on Vergil, *Aeneid* 4.458. The wolf is an animal much associated with crossing of life's boundaries.
73. Arnobius, 3.25.
74. e.g. Ennius, fr. 147 Skutch; Persius, 3.104; Juvenal, 4.108f.; Apuleius, *Florida* 19.4 etc.; for the *pollinctor*, cf. Plautus, *Poenulus* 63.
75. Ovid, *Fasti* 3.561; Petronius, *Satyricon* 77.
76. Vergil, *Aeneid* 6.212–35, esp. 219, 224f. The passage is important for our knowledge of burial customs, though there are Greek elements taken from Homer's description of the burial of Patroclus (*Iliad* 23.161ff.). The offering of oil in *Eclogue* 5.67ff. is a quotation from Theocritus, *Idyll* 5.53f.
77. Petronius, *Satyricon* 71.
78. Vergil, *Aeneid* 6.254; the line is a quotation from Homer, but Vergil substitutes oil for Homer's wine.
79. Ovid, *Metamorphoses* 14.602ff.
80. Vergil, *Georgics* 4.415–18, with Servius' commentary; Ovid, *Metamorphoses* 2.122f.
81. Ovid, *Ibis* 227 (snake venom).
82. Lucian, *Alexander* 30; Apuleius, *Florida* 1.4; Minucius Felix, *Octavian* 3.1.
83. Siculus Flaccus, *de condicionibus agrorum*, p. 105 Thulin: in some cases the vegetable offerings included blood sacrifice (here and Ovid, *Fasti* 2.681f.), in others not (Plutarch, *Quaestiones Romanae* 15).
84. Cicero, *In Verrem* 2.4.77 (though Segesta was a Greek city).
85. *Corp. Inscr. Lat.* 6.9797.6ff.
86. Pliny, *NH* 15.32; cf. 33.122 and Vitruvius, *de architectura* 7.9.3 for preserving statues with oil mixed with wax.
87. *Corp. Inscr. Lat.* 8.9052 13f. (Mauretania Caesariensis).
88. Pliny, *NH* 13.23.
89. Festus, p. 238 Lindsay.
90. Pliny, *NH* 13.25.

4

Oil in the Old Testament

J. Roy Porter

Three kinds of oil can be distinguished in the Old Testament, although there is some degree of overlap in the terms used to designate them. The first is called *yiṣhār* and denotes the fresh oil produced by treading out the newly picked olives and thus the denominative verb means 'to press oil' (Job 24.11). This was the most highly valued of the products of the olive: it can be described as 'the choicest of the oil' (Num. 18.12). As the product of the land, in an untreated state, it regularly occurs, together with corn and new wine, in a stock expression symbolizing the richness of the land of Canaan and the divine bounty to Israel (Deut. 7.13; Jer. 31.12; Hos. 2.8; Joel 2.19). Thus the *yiṣhār* was one of the first fruits which were given to the priesthood (Deut. 18.4), and from it was taken the sacred tithe, to be consumed by the worshippers at the sanctuary before the Lord (Deut. 12.17). In accordance with its character and its method of production, the oil in question is also described as 'pure' and 'pounded'. As such, it was ritually used for the sacred lampstand or *meʿnorâh* which stood in the Jerusalem temple (Exod. 27.20; Lev. 24.2).[1] This accounts for the particular expression *beʿnē ha-yiṣhār*, 'sons of oil', for the two figures in Zech. 4.14, since they are there identified with the openings on the *meʿnorâh* through which the oil was discharged. Such highly valued oil often formed one of the gifts exchanged between monarchs in the lands surrounding Israel and a large quantity of it was part of the annual tribute paid by Solomon to the king of Tyre (1 Kings 5.11; Heb. 25). Again, this 'pure' or 'pounded' oil was used for the grain-offering that accompanied the twice daily corporate whole-offering in the Temple, which, after the exile, became the principal sacrificial celebration, viewed as a gift in homage to God (Exod. 29.40; Num. 28.5).

The second word for oil in the Old Testament is *šemen*. Properly speaking, this was oil of inferior quality, produced in larger quantities by repeated pressing of the olive pulp, but the word comes to be a general term for oil in the Bible. Thirdly, one particularly significant kind of *šemen* may be distinguished, described as 'the anointing oil' (Lev. 8.2), or 'the holy anointing oil' (Exod. 30.25). This was actually a compound of aromatic spices, with oil as the base (Exod. 30.23–24), and hence it can also be described as a 'perfume', *rōqaḥ* (Exod. 30.25). Its use was strictly confined to certain ritual purposes: a layperson was forbidden to make it or to apply it to the human body on pain of death (Exod. 30.32–33).

This elaborately prepared oil was applied to the sanctuary and the cultic apparatus (Exod. 30.26–28) in order to 'anoint' them (cf. Dan. 9.24). The word 'anoint', *māšaḥ*, properly means 'to rub or stroke with the hand' (Lev. 2.4), but here it has become a kind of technical term, whose meaning must be considered subsequently, for the objects of worship were anointed by sprinkling, *nzh* (Lev. 8.11). More significantly, the post-exilic high-priest was anointed, as part of his installation ceremony, by pouring, *yāṣaq*, the holy oil, on his head (Lev. 8.12), apparently in considerable quantity, if the picture in Ps. 133.2 is to be relied upon. Certain passages in the Old Testament appear to suggest that the ordinary priests were also anointed, at least at some stage (Exod. 30.30; Exod. 40.15; Lev. 7.35–36; Lev. 10.7; Num. 3.3). However, it seems unlikely that there was ever a rite of anointing for the priesthood in general analogous to that for the high-priest and perhaps these passages have in mind the ceremony referred to in Exod. 29.21 and Lev. 8.30, according to which blood and anointing oil was sprinkled – not poured – on the bodies and vestments of both the high-priest and the other priests; the effect of this was to make them holy, which, as will be seen, was the purpose of ritual anointing. In this connection, it is perhaps worth noting that the Mishnah distinguishes between the high-priest who is anointed with the holy oil and the one who is dedicated, *rhb*, by assuming the high-priestly vestments (Horayoth 3.4; Makkoth 2.6; Megillah 1.9): this probably reflects the abandonment of the specific high-priestly anointing in the Herodian and Roman periods, so that all priests were installed by putting on the vestments appropriate to their particular status.

As in ancient Mesopotamia, such anointing was not associated with purification which also in Israel was brought about by washing (Lev. 8.6). Rather, the purpose of anointing was to 'make holy' or to 'consecrate', in the case of the cultic impedimenta (Lev. 8.10), and the high-priest (Lev. 8.12). Consecration would appear to have comprised two aspects. On the one hand, it confers on the recipient, whether inanimate or human, a particular character, the quality of 'being holy', a quasi-physical capacity that can be transmitted, through contact, to other objects or persons (Exod. 30.29).[2] On the other hand, consecration sets the recipient apart from the circumstances of ordinary human life by creating a specially intimate relationship between him and God, and hence the anointing oil, in the case of the high-priest, is described as the oil 'of his God' (Lev. 21.12).

It is, however, the anointing of the king which holds the most characteristic and significant place among the various Old Testament anointings: we only hear of the anointed high-priest after the exile and the reason for this, as is now generally recognized, is that, with the disappearance of the monarchy, the chief priest of the Jerusalem Temple assumed many of the characteristics of the old Israelite king, including anointing. In the case of the first king (1 Sam. 10.1), and elsewhere in certain exceptional circumstances (1 Sam. 16.1, 13; 2 Kings 9.1–3), the designated ruler was anointed by the pouring on of his head of ordinary oil, but the fact that the royal anointing oil is called 'holy' in Ps. 89.20 (Heb. 21), and that it was kept in a sacred place (1 Kings 1.39), suggests that in the regular practice of the Judaean monarchy the oil was constituted in the same way as that employed for the later high-priest.

The royal unction conferred a special character on the king also: as 'Yahweh's Anointed', his person was inviolate (1 Sam. 24.6; 1 Sam. 26.11; 2 Sam. 1.14). Anointing also brought about an intimate union between the king and the deity which found expression in various ways. To curse Yahweh's Anointed merited death (2 Sam. 19.21; Heb. 22), just as cursing God did (Lev. 24.15, where the same verb is used), and Yahweh and his Anointed together could be invoked as witnesses to a person's solemn declaration of innocence (1 Sam. 12.3,5). By his anointing, the king received the endowment of the spirit of Yahweh to enable him to fulfil the duties of his office (1 Sam. 16.13; 1 Sam. 10.1,6; and compare 2 Sam. 23.1–2). Further, the designation 'Yahweh's Anointed' denoted a special kind of relationship between God and the king, which is to be understood in the light of the situation with respect to royal anointings in the ancient Near East generally. There the great kings, such as the Pharaoh or the rulers of Babylonia and Assyria, who were probably not anointed themselves, appointed vassal kings or high state officials by the rite of anointing, either personally or through a representative. But the true king of Israel was considered to be Yahweh himself (1 Sam. 12.12), a belief above all given liturgical expression in the worship of the

The Oil of Gladness

Jerusalem Temple, where Yahweh was venerated as 'a great king', enjoying universal dominion (Ps. 47.2; Heb. 3). The actual anointing of the earthly king was performed by a priest or a prophet, but this human agent was only Yahweh's representative and hence Yahweh can be spoken of as himself anointing the king (1 Sam. 10.1; 1 Sam. 15.17; 2 Sam. 12.7): indeed, the repeated expression in 2 Kings 9.3,6,12 (compare 1 Sam. 10.1) may represent the regular royal anointing formula. Thus anointing designated the king as Yahweh's vassal, whose relationship with the deity was governed by a covenant or treaty (Ps. 89.3; Heb. 4), corresponding to the treaties that the great kings of the ancient Near East imposed on their vassals.

It is thus obvious that there are different emphases in the Old Testament understanding of the sacerdotal and royal anointings respectively and this has led to claims that in fact they constitute two quite different rites. According to Giovanni Garbini, royal anointing 'materially sanctions a designation already made or a quality already possessed', whereas priestly anointing 'itself confers a particular quality', and he further states that 'the king is anointed (designated "messiah") because he is king; the priest becomes priest by virtue of being anointed (made "messiah")'.[3] Garbini does not explain what he understands by 'materially sanction' nor why such a sanction would be necessary for someone already 'designated' to a particular office. It is true that a man could be designated as king before being anointed, either by a divine oracle (1 Sam. 9.15–16; 1 Sam. 16.1,12), or by popular recognition and acclamation (1 Sam. 10.24; 2 Sam. 15.10; 1 Kings 1.25), or by a ruler appointing his successor from the royal family (1 Kings 1.30; 2 Chron. 11.22); but this does not mean that he thereby acquired that sacrosanct and inviolable quality so characteristic of Israelite kingship which, as already argued, the Old Testament associates with anointing. Nor is the situation altogether different in the case of the priesthood, for normally[4] the future high-priest was designated as such by being the son of the existing holder of the office (Neh. 12.10–11), and was in a sense a priest by virtue of descent, since it was held that the first priestly anointings had inaugurated a hereditary priesthood in perpetuity (Exod. 40.15). Garbini believes that royal anointing in Israel had the same significance as the anointing of high Egyptian officials, simply indicating 'a designation without any sacral character',[5] but it has been argued that in this case 'the oil coming from the Horus-king transmitted to the anointed one the power which he was called by the king to exercise in his name and as his representative',[6] where it is not difficult to see an analogy with what is implied by the endowment with Yahweh's spirit in Israelite royal anointing. Thus we may conclude that, in spite of the differences, there is a basic similarity in the Old Testament concept of both priestly and royal anointing.[7]

The ideas connected with anointing, especially that of kings, are developed in various ways. We may consider first what is usually described as the metaphorical or figurative use of the term. In Ps. 105.15, the patriarchs are described as 'anointed ones', although there is no indication that they were ever actually anointed. The whole tenor of the verse suggests that the word is primarily used here as denoting the sacrosanct inviolability which, as has been seen, anointing conferred on the king: we may also have to reckon with a tendency to view the patriarchs as royal figures, of which there are indications elsewhere in the Old Testament (e.g. Gen. 23.6; Gen. 35.11; with the latter compare 1 Kings 8.19). The verse in question also has 'prophets' in parallelism with 'anointed ones'[8] and some slender Old Testament evidence raises the question as to whether prophets were actually anointed with oil. At 1 Kings 19.15–16, Elijah is instructed by God to anoint two men as kings, but also Elisha as his successor-prophet. However, this is the only case in which anointing is envisaged as conferring prophetic authority and, in the sequel, neither Elisha nor the king of Aram are actually anointed, but only the king of Israel. Perhaps the easiest solution is that the word 'anoint' here has the sense of its synonym 'to make holy' or 'consecrate', that is, 'to set apart' for a new function, and does not necessarily involve the application of oil. What may also be significant here is the concept of *succession* (Ecclus. 48.8), the idea of the transference of a prophetic office from one person to another, so that again there is the possibility that the account has been influenced by a motif belonging to the royal sphere,[9] where succession to the kingdom is always emphasized. The anointing of a prophet in Isa. 61.1 is also probably figurative, but here it is the endowment with Yahweh's spirit that is determinative: the gift of the spirit, which anointing confers, is the sign that the prophet truly possesses the status that anointing brings.[10] By contrast, it is because 'Yahweh's Anointed' was the vassal of Yahweh that the title is applied, again figuratively, to Cyrus in Isa. 45.1, where the succeeding verses are to be understood as the terms of a vassal covenant or treaty.

Secondly, as has already been discussed, one effect of anointing is to create an intimate relationship with God and to bring the recipient into the divine sphere of holiness: thus in Lam. 4.20, Yahweh's Anointed is closely approximated to God – as all life derives from the divine breath (Gen. 2.7; Ps. 104.29–30), so the king is the breath of life to his people. This aspect is developed in some of the late Jewish pseudepigraphical literature into the concept of a superterrestrial anointing, which transforms a human person into a heavenly being and confers immortality. In 2 Enoch 22.8–10, in the seventh heaven, the archangel Michael is bidden by God to remove Enoch's earthly garments, to anoint him with 'delightful oil' and clothe him in garments of glory: this is done and then Enoch sees that he has become 'like one of the glorious ones', that is, the angels, 'without any observable difference'. That it was the anointing that played the leading part in Enoch's transformation is shown by the rhapsodical description of the oil: 'the appearance of that oil is greater than the greatest light, its ointment is like sweet dew, and its fragrance like myrrh, and its shining is like the sun'.[11] The 'dew' may well contain a reference to Ps. 133.3, the 'myrrh' to Exod. 30.23, while the description of the oil as 'shining' probably indicates the *yiṣhār*, since this is a possible meaning for the word, as many scholars have proposed. A similar concept seems to underlie the Greek 3 Baruch 15.1,[12] where the righteous receive baskets of oil as their heavenly reward: Enoch is also said to be 'anointed with the ointment of the Lord's glory' (2 Enoch 56.2), and the oil given to the righteous probably signifies their endowment with the divine glory.[13] The oil itself has a supernatural origin, for in Paradise, which 2 Enoch locates in the third heaven, there is an olive tree, 'flowing with oil continually' (2 Enoch 8.5),[14] from which Eve and her son Seth seek for oil to cure Adam (Apocalypse of Moses 9.3; 13.1).[15] Another heavenly anointing is found in the Testament of Levi 8.4–5[16] where the patriarch Levi is invested, according to the ritual for the installation of the high-priest, by seven angels, one of whom anoints him with holy oil. This reflects the well-known idea of the correspondence and the simultaneity of the earthly and heavenly ritual and it raises the question as to whether the actual high-priest[17] may have been considered in Israel to be raised by his anointing to the heavenly sphere and to have become an angelic being thereby.[18]

As a third consideration, some attention must now be given to the use of oil, *šemen*, more generally in Israel. It formed one of 'the chief necessities of human life, (Ecclus.39.26) – that is, it was a basic food. Part of the staple diet of Palestine consisted of cakes of flour baked in oil (Num. 11.8; 1 Kings 17.12–13), hence such cakes formed part of the grain-offering (Lev. 2.4–10), where the ritual preparations represent what was done at an ordinary meal.[19] At one place, the application of oil to a person's head is said to make it 'fat', *dāšēn* (Ps. 23.5), and there are a number of passages where *šemen* and its related words refer generally to a rich diet, which brings physical vigour and well-being and is a sign of prosperity (e.g. Gen. 49.20; Deut. 32.15; Ezek. 34.16; Neh. 8.10; Neh.9.25).[20] Here we probably find the explanation of Jacob's pouring oil on the top of the pillar that he had erected at Bethel (Gen. 28.18): this is intended not as a sacrifice or a consecratory act, but rather as a supply of strength to the sacred object, perhaps originally of conveying nourishment to the indwelling deity. So, in Jotham's fable (Judg. 9.9–13), the 'fatness' of oil exalts both gods and men, just as both are enlivened by wine (cf. Gen.

35.14). In the same way, the oil that makes the face of the one anointed to glow is a sign of vitality that is similarly bestowed by wine and food (Ps. 104.15; cf. Eccles. 9.7–8 and Dan. 10.3). Again, in Ezek. 16.13 and 16.19, the inhabitants of Jerusalem, who have grown beautiful by the consumption of flour, honey and oil, set the same things before their idols 'as an offering of soothing odour', while Mic. 6.7 suggests that lavish libations of oil could be offered to Yahweh also.

Oil was also employed as a medicament for the soothing of wounds (Isa. 1.6). No doubt this has to do primarily with the natural properties of oil, but, in the Apocalypse of Moses, to which reference has already been made, anointing with the paradisal 'oil of mercy' is a cure for every kind of illness (Apocalypse of Moses 8.2);[21] in the Testament of Adam 2.10 the priest mixes consecrated oil with the cosmic waters, anoints all who are afflicted and they are healed,[22] and in Joseph and Asenath 8.5, 15.5, 16.16, the two characters are anointed with the 'unction of incorruptibility'.[23] In these pseudepi-graphical works, then, oil is the vehicle of vigour, health and life; so, when Asenath has been anointed and has eaten bread of life and drunk a cup of immortality, she is told that 'from today your flesh will flourish like flowers of life from the ground of the Most High, and your bones will grow strong like the cedars of the paradise of delight of God, and untiring powers will embrace you, and your youth will not see old age, and your beauty will not fail for ever'. The idea that oil confers health and well-being is the significance of a rite in the cleansing of the 'leper' (Lev. 14.15–18), where the priest first consecrates oil by sprinkling some of it 'before Yahweh' and then applies it to the right ear, thumb and big toe and finally the head of the one to be cleansed.[24] This is not purification but the conveying of life,[25] as is suggested by the anointing of the head, which is mentioned separately; since to have oil on one's head was the right and normal thing in Israel and the sign of a good life, as such a passage as Eccles. 9.8 shows (cf. Mic. 6.15), this act indicates that the formerly ostracized person is accepted once more into the life of society.[26] It is understandable, then, that anointing with oil was left off during periods of mourning (2 Sam. 12.20; 2 Sam. 14.2), when, so to speak, the mourner removed himself from the conditions of ordinary life and associated himself with the realm of death.

The end of the period of mourning and the reintegration into daily life, marked by the resumption of anointing, was an occasion of happiness (Isa. 61.3). Anointing is associated with joyful events, especially with banquets (Amos 6.6; Ps. 23.5) or the celebration of a wedding (Ps. 45.7–8; Heb. 8–9). Perfumed oil, to which the 'finest of oils' in Amos 6.6 probably refers, was employed as a cosmetic, especially after bathing (Susanna 17). In particular, such anointing was viewed as a preparation for marriage or sexual intercourse, both for men and women (Song of Sol. 3.6; Song of Sol. 4.14; Ezek. 16.9; we may note also Ruth 3.3; Esth. 2.12; Judith 10.13; Judith 16.8–9, all passages which probably have sexual connotations).

Several of the ideas that have been reviewed in connection with anointing with oil in the Old Testament are brought together in the verse from which this volume takes its title (Ps. 45.7; Heb. 8). The anointing here may refer back to the coronation rite (cf. Ps. 2.2), or be re-enacting it, in which case one would see the king as Yahweh's vassal. More likely, perhaps, in view of the epithet 'gladness', the image is of Yahweh as the host who honours his guest on the occasion of a festal banquet. In any case, the anointing creates a bond between anointer and anointed, as is probably indicated by the obscure verse Ps. 141.5 where the psalmist appears to be saying that if he allowed wicked men to anoint his head he would thereby become a party to their crimes. The anointing endues the king with splendour and might which exalts him above his 'fellows' – perhaps, in view of verse 5 (Heb. 6), enemy monarchs whom he is enabled to subdue. But in verse 8 (Heb. 9) anointing is related to the wedding festivities: the subject of the two verses is anointed 'both as king and as lover'.[27]

In Ps. 92.10 (Heb. 11), the psalmist says 'I am doused' or 'freshened',[28] *bālal*, with new or 'green'[29], *ra^{ca}nān*, 'oil'[30] and, in the opinion of some scholars, it is again the king who is speaking here. However this may be, what is noteworthy is that it is closely linked with the statement that Yahweh has lifted up the speaker's 'horn' like that of a wild ox – in other words, has endued him with strength, of which 'horn' is a symbol. The pouring of oil confers power and might which revive the recipient to overcome his threatening enemies, verse 11 (Heb. 12). A similar picture is found in Ps. 23.5, where once more the king may be in view.[31] Here anointing is again associated with food and drink in a great banquet which Yahweh provides and which takes place 'in the sight of my enemies'. The foes are thus to realize that Yahweh extends his favour and protection over his servant or vassal, but this takes concrete form, in that the servant receives strength to confront his enemies from food and drink and the oil that means vitality.

A number of other miscellaneous references to oil in the Old Testament and the Pseudepigrapha are perhaps worth a brief mention. In the Assumption (or Testament) of Moses 1.17, Moses orders Joshua to set in order the books of the Pentateuch, then anoint them with cedar-oil and store them in jars.[32] Probably the oil is viewed here primarily as a preservative, but it may be noted that, in 2 Enoch 22.12, heavenly books, where the idea of preservation seems unlikely, are described in one manuscript as 'bright with myrrh' or 'smyrnium'.[33] It is thus possible that we have here something analogous to the Mesopotamian custom of anointing inscriptions. In

Hos. 12.1 (Heb. 2), Ephraim is said to 'carry oil to Egypt' and, in view of the parallel line 'he makes a treaty with Assyria', it has been suggested that the expression is a synonym for 'to conclude a treaty':[34] the oil would create a bond or covenant, in the same way that salt could do (Lev. 2.13; Num. 18.19; 2 Chron. 13.5; Ezra 4.14).[35] The difficult verse 18 in Ps. 109 may also point to a ritual use of oil: it perhaps refers to a rite of self-execration, as part of which there was an anointing with oil which, as suggested by Ps. 23.5 and Ps. 92.10 (Heb. 11), conferred inviolability from the recipient's enemies.[36] In Deut. 33.24, a blessing for Asher is that 'he may dip his feet in oil'. This is generally taken as an image of the richness of the tribe's territory, comparable to the formula denoting prosperity in Deut. 32.13 and Job 29.6. However, as the verse goes on to mention what are perhaps fortifications of fortresses and ends with the words 'your strength shall last as long as you live', the idea may be that the oil gives the vigour and fleetness of foot that a warrior needs.[37]

It may be said, then, that oil in the Old Testament appears fundamentally as a source of strength, vitality and life, and that its various significations all derive from this idea. As such, it is a basic food, a healing agent and even a revivifying force for the departed. Its cosmetic use means beauty and desirability, and when poured on a person's head it indicates individual vigour and radiance. Possession of oil is evidence of wealth and thus a rich harvest of oil becomes a stock symbol of a nation's prosperity. To anoint someone with oil is to pay him honour. Not surprisingly, then, anointing brings joy and gladness and is particularly appropriate on festal occasions. But also, oil creates a bond between contracting parties or between suzerain and vassal, where the anointer shows his authority but also assures support and protection. Most importantly, in sacral contexts, as in the case of the king, the high-priest or cultic objects, anointing 'acquires the weight and worth of a theological concept'.[38] Its effect is to consecrate, conveying a sacral character that finds expression in various ways – holiness, setting apart for a special relationship with the deity, inviolability, the gift of the spirit of Yahweh, and transformation into a heavenly being.

Notes

1. The Temple Scroll from Qumran has a special *yiṣhār* festival in the sixth month, in which the fresh oil was offered on the altar as first-fruits and burned in the sanctuary lamps. Cf. J. Maier, *The Temple Scroll* (1985), pp. 28 and 81.
2. The high-priest is to take care not to profane the sanctuary, which his own holiness preserves, because 'the consecration of the anointing oil

of his God is upon him' (Lev. 21.12). At Qumran, where apparently the whole priesthood is assumed to be anointed, the priests are forbidden to come into contact with the bodies of those slain in battle, because the priests 'are holy; they shall not desecrate the oil of their priestly anointment'. Cf. Y. Yadin, *The Scroll of the War of the Sons of Light against the Sons of Darkness* (1962), p. 300.

3. G. Garbini, 'From the Anointer to the Anointed: The "Messiah" ', in *History and Ideology in Ancient Israel* (1988), p. 67.
4. cf. W. Rudolph, *Esra und Nehemia* (1949), p. 193, note 1.
5. Garbini, 'From the Anointer to the Anointed', p. 69.
6. H. Bonnet, *Reallexikon der Ägyptischen Religionsgeschichte* (1952), p. 649.
7. See E. Kutsch, *Salbung als Rechtsakt im Alten Testament und im Alten Orient* (1963), pp. 52–63. Kutsch argues for two different kinds of royal anointing in Israel, one by the people (2 Sam. 2.4; 2 Sam. 5.3; 2 Kings 11.12; 2 Kings 23.30), the other by Yahweh or his representative. The first represents historical reality, the second is an interpretative theologoumenon. Garbini asks (p. 69), 'How could an assembly of citizens anoint, i.e. confer a supposedly sacred character on, a king?' But such an assembly would require a single consecrator to act for them and there is nothing to preclude the view that this would be a religious personage: for example, at 2 Kings 11.12 it is difficult to imagine that it was not Jehoiada the priest who performed the anointing, and so the singular verb in the Septuagint, though textually secondary, would reflect what really happened. It is noteworthy that the intervention of the people occurs only at the inauguration of a new monarchy (David) or on the occasion of a dynastic crisis (Joash, Jehoahaz) and we may therefore understand such texts as meaning simply that the people took the initiative in arranging for a particular king to be anointed. Nor is it easy to imagine the Chronicler, in 1 Chron. 29.22, envisaging the anointing of a chief priest by a lay assembly.
8. A Qumran text describes the prophets as 'Thine anointed ones.' See Yadin, *The Scroll of the War*, p. 310.
9. cf. G. Widengren, 'The Ascension of the Apostle and the Heavenly Book', *Uppsala Universitet Årsskrift* (1950), p. 33, note 3; J. R. Porter, 'The Succession of Joshua', in *Proclamation and Presence*, eds. J. I. Durham and J. R. Porter (1970), pp. 120f.
10. Once again, it is possible that a particular type of royal hymn lies behind the language of Isa. 61.1–3; cf. G. Widengren, *Sakrales Königtum im Alten Testament und Judentum* (1955), pp. 56f.
11. J. H. Charlesworth, ed., *The Old Testament Pseudepigrapha*, I (1983), pp. 138f.
12. ibid., p. 677.
13. ibid., p. 658.
14. ibid., p. 117. Cf. 2 Esd. 2.12, where the paradisal tree of life conveys 'an ointment of sweet savour'.
15. J. H. Charlesworth, *The Old Testament Pseudepigrapha*, II (1985), pp. 273 and 275. On this oil, cf. E. Quinn, *The Quest of Seth for the Oil of Life* (1962).

16. Charlesworth, *The Old Testament Pseudepigrapha*, I, pp. 790f.
17. And the king also, cf. Widengren, *Sakrales Königtum*, pp. 49–53.
18. This has been powerfully argued by M. Barker in *The Older Testament* (1987) and *The Gate of Heaven* (1991).
19. cf. J. R. Porter, *Leviticus* (1976) p. 25.
20. At Mic. 6.7, the true Septuagintal reading is *cheimarrōn pionōn*, 'rivers of fat things'.
21. Charlesworth, *The Old Testament Pseudepigrapha*, II, p. 273.
22. Charlesworth, *The Old Testament Pseudepigrapha*, I, p. 993.
23. Charlesworth, *The Old Testament Pseudepigrapha*, II, pp. 212, 226 and 229. Probably this is the significance of the anointing by angels of the bodies of Adam (Charlesworth, II, p. 291) and Abraham (Charlesworth, I, p. 895).
24. In 'The Life of Adam and Eve', the plagues from which Adam hopes to be cured by anointing afflict him 'from the top of the head and the eyes and the ears down to the nails of the feet' (Charlesworth, II, p. 272).
25. Anointing of shields (2 Sam. 1.21; Isa. 21.5) is perhaps best understood as burnishing metal shields (cf. the NEB rendering of Isa. 21.5) or preserving those made of leather. However, it is possible that this was viewed as a consecration (cf. J. Pedesen, *Israel III–IV* (1940), p. 12) or as conveying strength to the object. For further evidence of the association of oil and strength, cf. E. Cothenet, 'Onction', in *Supplément au Dictionnaire de la Bible* eds. L. Pirot, A. Robert and H. Cazelles (1960), VI, col. 717.
26. cf. Porter, *Leviticus*, pp. 112f.
27. J. H. Eaton, *Kingship and the Psalms* (1976), p. 119.
28. cf. Gesenius-Buhl, *Handwörterbuch über das alte Testament*, 17th edn (1949), p. 101.
29. cf. Eaton, *Kingship and the Psalms*, pp. 58f.
30. Hence the *yiṣ hār* is indicated here.
31. cf. Eaton, *Kingship and the Psalms*, pp. 36f.
32. Charlesworth, *The Old Testament Pseudepigrapha*, I, p. 927.
33. cf. H. F. D. Sparks, ed., *The Apocryphal Old Testament* (1984), p. 338.
34. cf. D. J. McCarthy, *Vetus Testamentum* 14 (1964), pp. 215–21. Following the Septuagint and parallel to Hos. 12.1 (Heb. 2), 1 Kings 5.15 (Eng. 1) is probably to be understood as sending oil for a diplomatic anointing, as a sign of homage or of covenant-making (cf. T. N. D. Mettinger, *King and Messiah* (1976), pp. 225ff.).
35. cf. A. H. J. Gunneweg, *Esra* (1985), p. 91.
36. cf. H.-J. Kraus, *Psalmen* (1959), pp. 749f.
37. If there is anything in this suggestion, consideration might be given to the Authorized Version's 'shoes' for *minᶜāl*, a meaning the word certainly has in post-biblical Hebrew, which would continue the reference to feet: Asher as a warrior would be shod with metal footgear. (f. Mic. 4.13.)
38. K. Seybold, 'māšaḥ I, māšiaḥ', in *Theologisches Wörterbuch zum Alten Testament* eds. G. J. Botterweck, H. Ringgren and H. J. Fabry, (1984), V, col 51.

5

Anointing in the New Testament

Jeffrey John

There are only two passages in the New Testament that have obvious bearing on the Church's practice of sacramental anointing. Both of these concern the use of oil in the healing of the sick. There is no such clear reference to the use of oil in Christian initiation (chrismation), but there are numerous passages that illuminate later custom – and a few that at least suggest that such a ritual was already known to their authors. Given the very close connection in the thought-world of the New Testament between spiritual and physical sickness, and given that it was the same Spirit of God, symbolized in oil, and the same Anointed One (Messiah) who supplied salvation to the soul and health to the body, it would be a mistake to make too hard and fast a distinction between the two kinds of anointing. Nevertheless, we will examine the more definite evidence first.

The anointing of the sick

Mark 6.13 and the Jewish background

The early Christians (and, we must assume, Jesus himself) inherited from their Jewish faith the conviction that sickness was the product of a fundamental disorder in creation, a symptom of man's, and indeed

46

the whole world's subjection to sin and demonic power. This was true not only of psychological illness, which might more readily be interpreted as demonic possession requiring supernatural treatment by exorcism, but ultimately of every kind of sickness, mental and physical. The Jewish mentality was in any case inclined to view the whole person as a psychosomatic unity, rather than, like the Greeks, to separate the condition of body and soul. Thus Luke's Gospel, for example, tells of Jesus casting out 'a demon which was dumb', and healing a crippled woman 'whom Satan bound for eighteen years'.[1] As Chapter 4 has shown, the idea that the devil and his minions were responsible for all moral and physical evil penetrated deeply into Jewish thought in the period following the Babylonian exile, but it became particularly prominent in orthodox as well as sectarian literature of the intertestamental period, along with a heightened interest in angelology, demonology and other esoteric lore. Ben Sira, writing around the start of the second century BC, is exceptional in giving a rationalistic appreciation of the physician's skill – though even here healing is said to depend primarily on the right disposition of both patient and healer before God.[2] Throughout the tradition the assumption that healing is a divine monopoly predominates, along with the corollary that if an individual showed a particular skill in healing this was strong evidence of special supernatural power, knowledge and authority.

The rabbis laid down certain medical procedures and forms of prayer to be used in various cases of disease, but charismatic healers abounded outside the institutional methods of dealing with sickness. Reviewing the evidence that bears on this period, Vermes[3] makes an interesting distinction between two kinds of spiritual healer. The first kind is the practitioner of specifically esoteric medicine, often bordering on the magical, who was usually dependent on the literal and precise observance of rules and procedures: 'the correct substances were to be employed possessing the right supernatural properties and the right conjurations uttered'. These 'rules' were generally claimed to be handed down in a secret tradition, often from Raphael or other angelic messengers, or from Noah or Solomon, who were proverbial for their secret wisdom. Such an exorcist or healer would regularly command the evil spirit to depart 'in the name of' his particular source, appropriating the authority of the named figure to his own action. The magical and manipulative dangers of this kind of healing and exorcism are obvious, and sometimes made it a source of suspicion to the rabbis, but it was never outlawed by mainstream Judaism. Among the sects the most prominent and organized practitioners of esoteric medicine were the Essenes (whose name may well mean 'The Healers'). They are reported by Josephus to have been avid guardians of secret traditions handed down in the books of past generations, among which 'they single out those which make for the welfare of soul and body; with the help of these they make investigations into medicinal roots and the properties of stones'.[4]

The second kind of supernatural healer Vermes compares with Jesus himself, who appealed to no external tradition or authority, and who, except for anointing with saliva on one or two occasions (saliva, like oil, was thought to have medicinal properties), seems to have used no particular props or rituals or secret incantations, but only unscripted speech and touch. The canonical stories about Elijah and Elisha are prototypes of this more dignified and authoritative form of healing, and apocryphal stories of miraculous healing attributed to heroes of the faith – such as Abraham, Moses, David and Daniel are of the same kind. In addition to historical figures, however, there were also one or two contemporary holy men, Hasidim, who can be distinguished in this way from the more vulgar category of wonder-workers. The most remarkable of these is Hanina ben Dosa, a Galilean Hasid whose ministry can be dated to the first century – some time before the destruction of the second temple in AD 70. There are numerous points of comparison between Hanina and Jesus. They include Hanina's teaching about poverty and detachment from possessions and his total reliance on God; his subordination of legal and ritual rules to the moral purpose of the heart, and his consequent disputes with the Pharisees; his miraculous power over natural phenomena; and his ability to heal, exorcize and even raise the dead by the power of prayer and simple command. Perhaps the most striking point of resemblance is the famous story of Hanina ben Dosa healing Gamaliel's son. When messengers beg him to come and heal the boy, Hanina retires to an upper room and prays, then returns to them with the words 'Go home, for the fever has departed from him'. On their return, Gamaliel confirms that 'that was the very hour the fever left him'.[5]

Intertestamental Judaism's pessimistic view of the world as a place enthralled to demonic powers is the essential backdrop to the Gospel's presentation of Jesus as the ultimate Healer. It is particularly important to the understanding of Mark's Gospel. Through a progressive series of dramatic disclosures, Mark reveals Jesus to be the Messiah, the Anointed One on whom the Spirit rests, the One in whom the powers of God's Kingdom have finally broken into the darkened world, and in whom the last battle between the powers of good and evil is joined. For Mark, Jesus' physical healings, his exorcisms, his declaration of the forgiveness of sins, his calming of the sea (understood as *chaos*, a place of demons), are all equivalent testimonies to the unique and ultimate authority of Jesus as the victor in this supernatural battle. Indeed, in this 'drama of secret epiphanies' it is the demons themselves who first let out the secret of his identity.[6]

It is the great sin – the unpardonable sin – of the Pharisees, that, seeing the power at work in Jesus, they ironically ascribe it not to God but to Beelzebub himself, the Prince of Demons. In Matthew's and Luke's versions, the Pharisees, noticing that Jesus (unlike other healers) invoked no external authority for his powers, ask him in whose authority he was acting. Jesus characteristically turns the tables: 'If I cast out demons by Beelzebub, by whom do your sons (meaning the exorcists in their own tradition) cast them out?'[7] The implication, soon to become explicit, is that they themselves are the agents of the devil.

In the sixth chapter of Mark's Gospel the battleground begins to extend outward. Jesus commissions his disciples and sends them out two by two, specifically 'giving them authority over unclean spirits'.[8] He tells them to take with them no other resource. They could take only a staff and the clothes and sandals they were wearing. Wherever they were made welcome, they were to stay; if they were rejected, they were to 'shake off the dust against' those who rejected them. The theological meaning of this commissioning in chapter 6 is clear. As apostles they go out not merely as representatives of Jesus, but as empowered representatives: as agents bearing the full authority of their sender. (The word 'apostle' itself, used by Mark at 6.30 and meaning 'one who is sent', is the Greek equivalent of the Hebrew word *shalich*, the term that was used in legal and religious spheres of Judaism for just such an empowered and accredited messenger – an understanding summed up in the dictum, 'the *shalich* of a man is as the one who sent him'.)[9] Despite their all-too-evident failings, Jesus imparts to the apostles the powers of the Kingdom that we have seen at work in him; and of these the most distinctive – because it shows most clearly the true nature of the fight – is their authority over evil spirits. Through the apostles, the Kingdom is to be extended outwards from Jesus himself, pushing back the frontiers of the darkness. They are to do what Jesus himself does: to heal and exorcize; to preach repentance and forgiveness. As Mark 6.10f. makes clear, they bring in their own persons the presence and challenge of the Kingdom of God. The command to shake the dust from their feet against those who reject them recalls the custom of pious Jews who, on re-entering the Holy Land, shook from their feet the dust of Gentile territory.[10] So acceptance or rejection of their message is in effect equivalent to acceptance or rejection of Christ and of God: 'He who receives you receives me, and he who receives me receives him who sent me' (Matt. 10.40); 'He who hears you hears me, and he who rejects you rejects me, and he who rejects me rejects the one who sent me' (Luke 10.16). The response of each individual places him either inside or outside the borders of the Kingdom.

Having related the terms of this commissioning, Mark tells us:

> So they went out and preached that men should repent. And
> they cast out many demons, *and anointed with oil many that were
> sick and healed them* (Mark 6.13).

> καὶ δαιμόνια πολλὰ εξέβαλλον, καὶ ἤλειφον ἐλαίῳ πολλοὺς
> ἀρρώστους καὶ ἐθεράπευον.

This is the first of our two most important texts. In contrast to Jesus,
who is never reported to have used oil in the process of healing or
exorcism, the apostles (according to Mark) anointed the sick in the
process of healing them. Such a procedure is entirely plausible
historically. Simply because we know that the later Church used oil in
healing, there is no need to be as sceptical as some commentators and
assume that the practice has been 'read back' into Mark's Gospel.[11] As
the preceding chapters have shown, anointing with oil as part of
ordinary medical treatment was widespread in the ancient world
among Jews and Gentiles alike. This everyday use is mentioned in the
Gospels in the story of the Good Samaritan, who bound up the
wounds of the man who fell among robbers 'pouring on oil and
wine'.[12] Rabbinic sources, following Old Testament usage, prescribe
the use of oil in an everyday context for the treatment of sciatic pains,
skin afflictions, headaches and wounds. In these cases the context is
not specifically supernatural, although the user might well have been
expected to accompany such treatment with prayer.[13] At the same
time, since parts of the Old Testament itself associated oil directly
with the supernatural healing activity of the Spirit, it is not surprising
to find that oil was used in the more explicitly supernatural and
exorcistic kind of medicine too. Several examples in Jewish intertestamental literature prescribe ritual anointing at the conjuration of
demons, and as part of the process for the healing and release of the
bewitched.[14] For example, in the Testament of Solomon (generally
agreed to reflect first-century Palestinian Judaism), a demon speaks:
'I am called Rhyx Physikoreth. I bring on long-term illnesses. If
anyone puts salt into [olive] oil and massages his sickly [body with it],
saying "Cherubim, Seraphim, help", I retreat immediately.'[15]

It is clear from the sense and context of the Marcan verse that the
practice of the apostles has more to do with the charismatic kind of
healing and anointing than with the everyday kind. Although the
aorist is used, ἤλειφον, the anointing is evidently regarded as an
action simultaneous with the miraculous healing rather than as a
separate action preceding it; Cole calls it an 'acted parable' of the
spiritual cure.[16] It is notable too that in this verse Mark distinguishes
'casting out demons' and 'healing the sick' as separate activities. We
have seen that the two activities are very closely related in the Gospels

and sometimes indistinguishable, but the distinction here is presumably between a case where demonic possession is the manifest, explicit cause of disorder, and healing, where demonic influence is only implicit but may still be presupposed. Despite the form of the verse, which seems to link anointing only with healing and not with exorcism, it is unlikely that Mark meant to exclude it from exorcism; he would probably have envisaged its application, as in the Jewish sources, to both circumstances.

Only Mark includes this reference to anointing. Matthew and Luke, although they knew Mark's Gospel and used it as the basis of their own, seem deliberately to have left it out. Swete argued that Mark kept it in because he wanted to make some distinction between the healing of Jesus himself, done on his own authority, and the healing of the disciples, done on their Master's authority.[17] We have already observed the fact that one or two of the most revered Hasidim were distinguished from the vulgar thaumaturges in that they too appeared to act on their own authority – or rather, by direct invocation of God – and eschewed the use of 'props'. So possibly the inclusion of oil, as the most innocuous of 'props' and in any case an orthodox symbol of the Spirit, is intended by Mark as a reminder that the disciples were using a power that was not their own. This explanation is given additional weight when one remembers a peculiar feature of Mark. Although he presents the Twelve as empowered representatives of Jesus and bearers of the Kingdom, he also goes out of his way to show that in their own persons they were utterly unworthy of their office. Matthew and Luke, by contrast, have a much more reverential attitude to the apostles and frequently omit or soften Mark's harsh portrayals of their stupidity, selfishness and cowardice. They may have wished to omit the oil precisely because it suggested that their manner of healing was in some way inferior to that of Jesus. We can also reasonably guess that whereas some form of anointing of the sick was practised in the ministry of Mark's own church, it was not practised in Matthew's or Luke's.

It is obvious in Mark 6.13 that when the apostles anoint, they expect and achieve physical healing. There is no possibility here, as there is in our other major text, Jas. 5.14, that this anointing can be understood in a merely spiritual sense, or that it would make sense to administer it prior to death. This is the main reason why, although this verse gives clear apostolic authority for the practice of anointing the sick, the Council of Trent could not take it as a proof-text for the sacrament of Extreme Unction, as it was then named and understood. It was therefore argued that the sacrament is merely 'hinted at' here (literally 'insinuated', *insinuatum*, rather than 'commended and promulgated', *commendatum ac promulgatum*, as it was held to be in the verse of James).[18] The Tridentine downgrading of the importance of this text was justified by the further arguments that in Mark 6.13: (i) the apostles were not yet 'ordained' in the fullest sense, since they had not yet received redemption by the cross and resurrection and had not received the Holy Spirit; (ii) those whom they healed were unbaptized persons outside the realm of salvation; (iii) there could therefore have been no sacramental imparting of grace, as a sacrament was defined as being operative on the soul – if it was operative on the body at all, then it was only 'accidentally and secondarily'.[19] Surprisingly, these arguments against linking Mark 6.13 with the sacrament are still reproduced in modern Roman Catholic writings on the sacrament, despite the Second Vatican Council's ruling that it should be renamed, and that it should no longer be regarded solely as a source of spiritual strengthening which normally precedes death, but as a source of healing for body and soul alike.[20] It is surprising because once this understanding of the sacrament has been restored, the secondary objections to the authority of Mark 6.13 are hardly compelling (points (ii) and (iii), for example, would rule out seeing the Last Supper as the institution of the Eucharist!); they derive from an outmoded and narrow definition of sacramental grace and a dualistic separation of soul and body which are both thoroughly unscriptural. As we noted above, Mark himself in mentioning anointing probably had in mind the custom of his own church, and by attributing it to the apostles was perhaps not only supplying it with apostolic credentials, but deliberately 'commending and promulgating' it. Those who wish to do the same in the modern Church – that is, to promote the restored use and understanding of the sacrament as a source of physical as well as spiritual healing – are entirely justified in appealing to the authority of this text.

Jas. 5.14–15

This is the *locus classicus* of the sacrament in Scripture; the text in which, according to Trent, it truly is *commendatum ac promulgatum*. It is worth giving it in its full context:

[13] Is any one among you suffering? Let him pray. Is any cheerful? Let him sing praise. [14] Is any among you sick? Let him call for the elders (presbyters) of the church, and let them pray over him, anointing him with oil in the name of the Lord; [15] and the prayer of faith will save the sick man, and the Lord will raise him up; and if he has committed sins, he will be forgiven. [16] Therefore confess your sins to one another, and pray for one another, that you may be healed.

[13] Κακοπθβεῖ τις ἐν ὑμῖν; προσευχέσθω, εὐθυμεῖ τις; ψαλλέτω. [14] Ἀσθενεῖ τις ἐν ὑμῖν; προσκαλεσάσθω τοὺς

πρεσβυτέρους τῆς ἐλκκλησίας, καὶ προσευξάσθωσαν
ἐπ'αὐτὸν ἀλείψαντες αὐτὸν ἐλαίῳ ἐν τῷ ὀνόματι τοῦ κυρίου. ¹⁵
Καὶ ἡ εὐχὴ τῆς πίστεως σώσειτὸν κάμνοντα, καί ἐγερεῖ
ἀυτὸν ὁ κύριος. κκἀν ἁμαρτίας ἢ πεποιηκώς, ἀφεθήσεται
αὐτῷ. ¹⁶ Ἐξομολογεῖσθε οὖν ἀλλήλοις τὰς ἁμαρτίας, καὶ
εὔχεσθε ὑπὲρ ἀλλήλων, ὅπως ἰαθῆτε.

This epistle purports to be written by James the 'brother of the Lord'
who became leader of the Jerusalem church after the resurrection, and
it is directed to 'the Twelve Tribes in the Dispersion', meaning not the
Jewish people, but the Christian congregations outside Jerusalem.
Probably the ascription to James is false, but the letter is strongly
Jewish in character; some commentators take the view that it is an
originally Jewish document that has been minimally christianized.
However, the author's apparent knowledge of and argument with
Pauline teaching make this view unlikely, and suggest a date after
James's martyrdom in AD 62, probably towards the end of the first
century.[21]

Who are the presbyters whom James makes responsible for this
ministry to the sick? The word πρεσβυτερος can mean simply 'older
man', and there are one or two Protestant commentators who take the
writer to be saying that the sick man should summon older and more
experienced Christians to perform the action of prayer and anointing.
It is much more likely, however, especially given the Jewish–
Christian character of this epistle, and the fact that it refers to 'the
elders of the church', that 'James' is referring to the presbyters or
'elders' as formal office holders. The Jewish synagogue organized
itself under a council of πρεσβυτέροι, of whom one was elected to
honorary presidency as the 'synagogue ruler' (ἀοχισυνάγωγος),
sometimes with a small board of other 'rulers' (ἄρχοντες).[22]
The institution of the presbyterate was ascribed to Moses who,
according to Num. 11.16ff., chose seventy elders and imparted to
them some of the Spirit he had received from God; that the laying on
of hands was his method of doing this was deduced from Joshua's
ordination in Deut. 34.9ff. [23] Presbyters and rabbis were ordained to
their office by the laying on of hands by others who had themselves
been ordained; however, in Jerusalem, at least after the Council of
Jamnia, the participation of the president in any ordination to the
sanhedrin was considered essential.[24]

The early Christian communities that stood nearest to the Jewish
tradition naturally organized themselves on similar lines, with similar
councils of πρεσβυτέροι. Presbyters appear in several of the church
settlements mentioned in the Acts of the Apostles, and in the
pseudonymous, Jewish–Christian epistles to Timothy and Titus, but
never in the genuine epistles of Paul. In Jerusalem itself, as it appears

from the account of the 'Council' in Acts 15, the Church was modelled on the Great Sanhedrin, where the high-priest presided over seventy-one presbyters; James himself, the putative author of our epistle, was regarded, at least by later Jewish–Christian tradition, as 'a Christian high-priest, presiding over a sanhedrin of Christian presbyters, exercising a real jurisdiction over the Christians of Palestine, and an undefined influence (through travelling delegates) over those elsewhere, especially converts from Judaism'.[25] In the second century, as is well known, the Church systematized its hierarchy into a formal structure with the presbyters grouped around, and under the authority of, a single 'monarchical' bishop. The situation in the New Testament is still much more complex and fluid; in particular, there is as yet no clear distinction between the functions of bishops and presbyters in the pastoral epistles, so that the two terms seem sometimes to be interchangeable (although it is notable that whereas the bishop is always referred to in the singular, the presbyters are always mentioned collectively).[26] The laying on of hands for ordination is variously practised.[27]

The Jewish presbyterate, although it might include rabbis and persons descended from the priestly line, and although it involved a form of ordination, had no special liturgical function and no particular charisms attached to the office. Any male adult Israelite could perform any function of synagogue worship. What is most striking in our passage is that the gift of healing, which was not connected with the Jewish office of presbyter, but regarded as an individual charism both in Judaism and in Paul's churches, has here been institutionalized and attached to the presbyterate: it is quite clear that they are to be summoned in virtue of their office – not because of some personal gift of healing that they may happen to possess. This development probably represents more than a general tendency to tame and systematize individual charisms in the settled Church; it is part of the process whereby the Christian presbyterate eventually inherited from the disappearing apostolate an inherent spiritual and liturgical authority that was foreign to the essentially lay character of the Jewish presbyterate. As we have seen in Mark 6, the gift of healing was in any case already partly 'institutionalized' in the Church by its association with the apostles. Not only the Gospel traditions, but the traditions underlying the Book of Acts and Paul himself regarded healing as one of 'the signs of an apostle', a power that attaches to the apostolic office itself. It seems entirely likely, though unfortunately the evidence does not allow us to trace the process precisely, that as the apostles disappeared and authority was delegated to local leadership in the settled churches, the apostolic power to heal was also considered part of the authority handed down, and became the property of the bishops and presbyters whom the apostles left behind.[28]

54

The presbyters are summoned in the plural; as always, they are felt to constitute a collective, a 'college'. This is not to say that all the members of the presbyterate had to be present at a healing, or even that one presbyter might not pray and anoint alone; but evidently to have several presbyters at an anointing was the norm. (This continued to be the custom in the early Latin Church, and it still continues in Eastern churches.) They are to 'pray over him, anointing him with oil'. The Greek in fact says 'let them pray over him, *having anointed him*'; but no doubt the actions are understood to be simultaneous, like the anointing and healing in Mark 6.13. In all probability the phrase 'pray over him' (ἐπ'αὐτὸν) implies not merely that the presbyters stood over the patient, but also that they laid their hands on him (ἐπ'αὐτὸν). The laying on of hands is a well-attested feature in Jewish healing as well as in ordination, and it appears as a very frequent element in the healing practice of Jesus and the apostles, so it is entirely to be expected here.[29] In the earliest patristic quotation of the verse, Origen in fact reads it in to James's instructions: *vocet presbyteros ecclesiae et imponant ei manus unguentes eum oleo . . .*[30]

They are to do this 'in the name of the Lord'. Bede, in his commentary on James, thought this phrase should be taken with ἐλαίῳ to mean oil that was previously blessed in the name of the Lord for the purpose of anointing.[31] However, there is no evidence that oil itself was blessed in this way before the early third century, and in any case Bede's meaning cannot be extracted from the construction of the Greek. Rather, the whole action – prayer and anointing together – is to be done 'in the name of the Lord'. Which Lord? Is this a reference to God or to the Lord Jesus? One important manuscript (B) omits the words τοῦ κυρίου, leaving only 'in the name'. Daube, along with others who see this epistle as a fundamentally Jewish text with later additions to bring it into Christian use, notes that to speak of 'healing in the Name' would be an obvious Jewish way of referring to healing in the name of God.[32] However, the testimony of a single manuscript is not very compelling, and in the received text as it stands there is little doubt that we are meant to understand the name of the Lord to be the name of Jesus. There is abundant evidence in the New Testament that the name of Jesus was widely invoked in the course of healing and exorcism. According to Mark 9.38 and Acts 19.13, this feature of the apostles' healing became so well known that even the Jewish thaumaturges began to add it to their repertoire of incantations. It is highly probable then that the healing activity intended here would also explicitly have invoked the name and power of Jesus (though there is no sign as yet of any particular form of words).

On the strength of the fact that several of the New Testament miracles involving the use of the name of Jesus are explicitly exorcisms, and because he believed the use of oil to be especially associated with exorcism in Jewish practice, Dibelius argued that the scene envisaged in James is also to be understood as an exorcism of the demon responsible for the disease.[33] This is an unnecessary confusion. We have already noted the underlying supposition in Judaism and Christianity that all sickness is ultimately caused by demonic forces, but that one might reasonably apply the category 'exorcism' to those cases where the distinctive vocabulary and motifs of demon-possession occur, and the category 'healing' where they do not. Mark, as we saw, distinguished the activities of exorcizing and healing in 6.13, even though both were regarded as victories over the demonic powers. If anything, Mark seemed to associate the anointing with healing rather than exorcizing, but we observed that in Judaism anointing was in fact deployed in both circumstances, and the double application no doubt continued in the Church. The author of this epistle is certainly aware of the demonic powers (2.19, 4.7), but he does not bring them *explicitly* into the picture here, so the category 'exorcism' seems inappropriate.

James does, however, associate sickness and sin. This connection is strong throughout Jewish tradition, though frequently challenged in its naïve form (as in the Book of Job, or the prophets who wrestled with the problem of innocent suffering). As a result, forgiveness and healing are strongly associated too; according to the Talmud, 'no sick person is cured of his disease until all his sins are forgiven him', and this appears to have been the common view.[34] It emerges frequently in the New Testament, along with some of the theological problems it raises. In some of Jesus' own miracles – the healing of the paralytic, for example – physical healing and forgiveness are treated as practically synonymous. In the Gospel of John, Jesus appears at one point to endorse a causal connection between personal sickness and sin (in his words, to the blind man healed at 5.14, 'Sin no more, that nothing worse befall you'), and at another point to deny it (in his answer to the question about another blind man, 'Rabbi, who sinned, this man or his parents, that he was born blind?' – 9.2f.).

Perhaps aware of the difficulties involved, James makes the connection a tentative one: '*if* he has committed sins, he will be forgiven'. The causation is admitted as possible, but not inevitable. The construction of the conditional clause is noteworthy too: κἂν ἁμαρτίας ᾖ πεποιηκώς. The perfect participle implies a past act of which the effect remains; thus one might paraphrase, 'If he is in the state of having committed sins, the effect of which remains, he will be forgiven.' Probably only serious sins are meant, of the kind that might be expected to entail disease (compare the distinction in the first epistle of John between 'mortal' and other sins). James himself says at 3.2, 'in many things we all stumble'; so when he writes '*if* he has committed sins' he presumably has a graver kind of sin in mind. A number of commentators, noting these points, argue that the author must be assuming that the patient, if he has sinned in this way, will have made a prior confession of it to the presbyters:

> Those to whom the Apostle (i.e. 'James') wrote would under-stand that the sick man is assumed to have manifested contrition, and to have confessed those weightier sins, which were endangering his soul, to the Presbyters, and to then have received from them the Absolution.[35]

That a confession to the presbyters is presupposed by the author does seem to be confirmed by the following verse, '*Therefore* confess your sins to one another . . .' It is hard to see what other causal connection 'Therefore' could imply. In verse 16 James recommends that Christians confess their sins to one another and to pray for one another in the ordinary course of things in order to receive healing (ὅπως ἰαθῆτε – a neutral word for healing that is regularly applied to the forgiveness of sins and need not imply sickness at all). If mutual confession is the way to deal with everyday 'stumbling', then *a fortiori*, James would have expected a confession to be made in the case of a graver sin with life-threatening consequences. However, the suggestion that the penitent would have received a form of 'Absolution' from the presbyters, apart from prayer for healing and forgiveness and the anointing itself, is much more doubtful and probably anachronistic. The act of healing and the act of forgiving are indistinguishable in James's thinking here; and presumably the 'prayer of faith' would have included a request for both. It is true to observe, however, that along with the healing, the forgiveness of sins is clearly felt to be guaranteed by the office of presbyter. Bound up in the action of healing is evidently the same kind of effective authority to forgive or retain sins that the rabbis called 'the power of the keys', that Paul exercised in the discipline of his churches, and that Jesus is portrayed as passing on to the apostles in Matt. 18.18 and John 20.23. Implied in their power to heal, but perhaps not yet formally distinguished from it, it is possible that the power to remit sins was already perceived as part of the presbyters' apostolic inheritance.[36]

How sick is the sick man in this passage? Pre-Vatican II Roman Catholic theologians, again with Trent and Extreme Unction in mind, used to argue that a case of mortal sickness is implied here, and that James was in effect recommending the use of this particular ministry prior to death. This view was always contested, and has now been widely discarded, on the apparently obvious and commonsense ground that the author is not speaking of a preparation for death in these verses, but plainly expects the object of the prayer and anointing to be restored to healthy life. As early as 1904 an Anglo-Catholic writer on the anointing of the sick lamented the error of the Tridentine view, and insisted that 'Unction with its accompanying prayers has for its object the restoration of the sick man to health; and . . . is in fact identical with the Unction administered by the Apostles during their first Galilean preaching-tour' (i.e. Mark 6.13).[37] A modern Roman Catholic exegete expresses a similar view:

> It is more in keeping with the context [of Jas. 5.14] to adhere to the simple idea of salvation from death and restoration to health. It is true that the sacrament will then be a sacrament of healing, not a sacrament of preparation for death. . . . The true sacrament of the dying is the *viaticum*: the first end of the sacrament of anointing is to *heal* – both physically and spiritually.[38]

Such an interpretation is certainly the most natural one, yet a close examination of the Greek vocabulary of the passage shows that the Tridentine view was not without evidence in the text. Evidently the sick person envisaged by James is at least quite seriously ill and unable to go to the presbyters, since they must be summoned to him. The word used for 'sick' in verse 14 (ἀσθενέω) is neutral; it is sometimes used in the New Testament to refer to mortal sickness, but it may also have the quite general sense of 'being ill'. More compellingly, the word 'save' (σώζω) in verse 15 does imply healing from serious (but not necessarily mortal) illness (it frequently occurs in Gospel healing miracles), or rescue in a life or death situation; and it is also the regular word meaning 'save' in a purely spiritual sense. Most strikingly of all, the word used for 'sick man' in verse 15 (κάμνων) is very much stronger than the usual ἀσθενέω. Its fundamental sense is that of physical exhaustion or debility, but it was also widely used to mean 'sick beyond hope, withering away', and it may even mean 'dead'. The word ἐγερεῖ, 'will raise up' in verse 15, is also ambivalent. It may simply mean 'raise up from the sick-bed'; but it is also the word regularly used in the New Testament for resurrection from the dead.[39]

There is therefore a quite remarkable and thoroughgoing ambiguity in the promise, ἡ εὐχὴ τῆς πίστεως σώσει τὸν κάμνοντα, κὰι ἐγερεῖ ἀυτὸν ὁ κύριος. It could mean, as most naturally fits the context, 'The prayer of faith will *heal* the *sick* man and the Lord will *cure* him.' But it *could* also mean, 'The prayer of faith will *save* the *mortally ill / dead* man and the Lord will *resurrect* him.' The most obvious interpretation is certainly the former, and so almost all recent commentators conclude that the form of prayer and anointing envisaged here was intended to be applied in the case of quite serious but not necessarily mortal illness, and with the expectation of recovery. This must be right, but it does not seem to be the whole truth. The vocabulary is so strikingly and systematically ambiguous that one is forced to wonder whether the author himself made it deliberately so. The basic expectation, as at Mark 6.13, is no doubt that following the presbyters' ministrations the sick man would recover; but it is highly likely that James, writing with practical pastoral concerns for a settled Church, was aware that in some cases it would not, and the patient would die. So, like the modern Roman Catholic rite of anointing, he appears to hedge his bets accordingly. In a case where prayer and anointing were duly performed by the presbyters according to the instructions of the epistle, but the sick man died, their ministry need not seem to have failed. On the contrary, it could then be understood according to James' own words as an effectual guarantee of post mortem forgiveness of sins, salvation and resurrection – in other words, precisely as a sacrament of Extreme Unction. This verse can therefore quite legitimately be seen as authorizing the administration of prayer and anointing to the sick under *both* circumstances.

Chrismation

Vocabulary

The New Testament uses two different Greek verbs for the two types of anointing.[40] As we have seen, in the contexts that concern the anointing of the sick it uses the word ἀλείφω. This is the more general word meaning to 'anoint' or 'pour [oil] over'. It is the word used in the Gospel accounts of the anointing of Jesus' body for burial; in the accounts of Jesus' head or feet being anointed by a woman in anticipation of burial; and in the reference in the Sermon on the Mount to anointing the head and washing the face when fasting. The other verb χρίω, with its related noun χρίσμα from which we derive the English word 'chrismation', is the one used in contexts where, following the Old Testament symbolism, the spiritual connotation of anointing is to the fore – in particular, the concept of anointing with the Spirit or the pouring out of the Spirit. χρίω is therefore the word that is almost always used to translate the Hebrew verb *mashach*, from which is derived the Hebrew word 'Messiah', the Anointed One. It is from the past participle of χρίω that we get Χριστός, Christ, the Greek equivalent of 'Messiah'.

The fact that the word 'anoint' has such a widespread figurative use in connection with the Spirit's anointing means that in many New Testament passages we cannot be sure whether an actual oil-anointing is being referred to, or whether the word is simply being used as a metaphor for the action of the Spirit. Throughout this discussion we shall have to try to distinguish in the texts between anointing as a *concept* and anointing as a *rite* that symbolizes the concept. The English word 'chrismation' is used here strictly to mean the latter.

The baptism of Christ and the anointing of the Spirit

The early Church understood the baptism of Jesus in the Jordan as the prototype of all Christian baptism.[41] It is a new kind of baptism, differing from the baptism of John or Jewish proselyte-baptism in that it is a baptism not only with water as a sign of repentance and cleansing, but a baptism with the Spirit, an effective imparting of the Spirit to the believer. The baptism of Jesus is reported with variations in all four Gospels, but in each case we are told that after Jesus emerged from the water the Holy Spirit descended upon him like a dove. This moment, immediately following the water-baptism, is understood to be the moment 'when God anointed Jesus of Nazareth with the Holy Spirit and with power', as Peter explains it in Acts 10.38. It is this moment of spiritual anointing that makes Jesus, or declares him to be, 'the Christ', the Anointed One, the Messiah. And because the purpose of his baptism was to transmit the same baptism to his followers, the meaning of his own anointing as the Christ determines the meaning of our own spiritual anointing as Christians, whether that anointing is expressed in an act of chrismation, or whether it was not – as in the case of Christ himself. Lampe quotes Athanasius: 'The descent of the Spirit upon Jesus at his baptism was a descent upon us, because of his bearing our body; and it happened for our sanctification, that we might share his anointing.'[42]

The story of Jesus' baptism gathers up many strands of Old Testament tradition about anointing; these were examined in Chapter 4 and it will be useful to summarize the points here:

The Spirit anoints Jesus as Messianic King. According to 1 Sam. 10.1, when Samuel poured the anointing oil over Saul, the first king of the Jews, 'the Spirit of God came mightily upon him and he prophesied'. Similarly, in the case of David, 'the Spirit of the Lord came mightily upon David from that day forward'.[43] The anointing with oil symbolizes the anointing with the Spirit that is simultaneous with it. 'The Anointed One' (i.e. the Messiah) became the regular Old Testament designation of the king, and so by extension came to be used of the hoped-for, eschatological king. The New Testament of course presents Jesus as the fulfilment of this hope. In the Synoptic Gospels' account of Jesus' baptism, the words spoken from heaven when Jesus emerges from the water, 'Thou art (in Matthew: "This is") my beloved Son', recall the words of Ps. 2. This is a coronation psalm, in which God ratifies the coronation and adopts the king as his son, with the formula: 'Thou art my son, today I have begotten thee' (verse 7). Therefore the baptism of Jesus – or more precisely his endowment with the Spirit immediately following the baptism – is understood as his anointing with the Spirit as messianic king, and also as his adoption (in Mark perhaps) or declaration (Matthew and Luke) as God's Son. It is the Spirit-anointing of the long-awaited Messiah. In the famous description of the Messiah and his Kingdom in Isa. 11.1– 9, it had been prophesied that 'the Spirit of the Lord will *rest* upon him'. Permanent possession of the Spirit (as opposed to periodic inspiration), and hence the power to bestow it on others, had come to be seen as one of the Messiah's defining characteristics.[44] So it is that in John's Gospel the Baptist identifies Jesus as the one of whom God had said, 'He on whom you see the Spirit descend *and remain*, this is he who baptizes with the Holy Spirit.'[45]

The Spirit anoints Jesus as high-priest. Except in the epistle to the Hebrews, the concept of Jesus as high-priest is not a leading one in the New Testament, but it is present – for example, in John's reference to Jesus' seamless robe, the high-priest's distinctive garment, and in the description of Christ in the Book of Revelation.[46] The idea that the Church corporately inherits this 'royal priesthood' is also important, as we shall see.[47] In the account of the ordination in Exodus and Leviticus the Lord instructs Moses first to wash Aaron and his sons with water, then to take the anointing oil and pour it on Aaron's head and to anoint him;[48] the washing with water prior to the anointing is a striking analogy with baptism. The recipe for the 'anointing oil' (χρίσμα ἅγιον in the Greek Bible) is given in the following chapter of Exodus: it is a blend of olive oil and precious fragrant spices and perfumes. Ps. 133 speaks of the anointing of Aaron, and 'the precious oil upon the head, running down upon the beard, upon the beard of Aaron, running down on the collar of his robes'.[49] At times when Israel was without a king, the term 'anointed one', messiah, came to be associated with the high-priest rather than the king. In the period immediately after the exile we find both kinds of messiah together: the prophet Zechariah presents a vision of two 'anointed ones', 'sons of oil', who are identifiable as the contemporary king and high-priest, Zerubbabel and Joshua.[50] This double messianic idea eventually became 'eschatologized' into a future hope and reappears in later literature, most notably in the 'priestly messiah' and the 'kingly messiah' of the Qumran texts.[51] Both strands of expectation are realized in the baptism of Jesus.

The Spirit anoints Jesus as a prophet. 1 Kings 19.16 tells of God commanding Elijah to anoint Elishah to be prophet in his place; and we have seen that the power to prophesy is mentioned as a side-effect of kingly anointing in the case of Saul and David. There is no evidence, however, that anointing with oil was a ritual regularly attached to initiation into the prophetic office, as in the case of kings and priests. Here perhaps the idea is already largely figurative, the power of prophecy being seen as a natural symptom of the spirit-filled state; this would explain why Elijah never literally anoints Elisha with oil, but sends down a double portion of his spirit upon him at the Jordan.[52] The text that most clearly associates Jesus with a specifically prophetic spirit of anointing is Luke 4.16. Here, following his baptism at the very beginning of his ministry, Jesus takes on his lips the words of the prophet himself from Isa. 61.1, 'The Spirit of the Lord is upon me, because he has anointed me to bring good news to the poor . . .'

The Spirit anoints Jesus as the Servant. The original identity of the Servant in the mind of second Isaiah is a vexed question (as it was for the Ethiopian eunuch in Acts 8.34). Is he a corporate symbol for righteous and suffering Israel; is he himself a king – Cyrus or Zerubbabel; or is he a prophet himself, or yet some other? For the New Testament writers the enigma was solved: the servant who will establish justice, who will bring light to the Gentiles, who was despised and rejected and wounded for our transgressions, is of course Christ. Elements of Isaiah's description of the Servant enter strongly into the New Testament's presentation of Jesus. In the first verse of the first Servant passage (Isa. 42.1–4) Isaiah had said of him, 'Behold my servant [παῖς] whom I uphold, my chosen in whom my soul is pleased [εὐδόκησεν]. I have put my spirit upon him . . .' So the Servant too is understood to be anointed with the Spirit. Further-more, the Greek word παῖς can mean 'servant' or 'son'; and the phraseology of this verse in Greek leaves little doubt that the evangelists saw this text as well as the coronation psalm echoed in the words at the baptism, 'This is [Thou art] my son, in whom I am well pleased' (εὐδόκησα). Later in his Gospel Matthew makes the identification explicit: quoting Isa. 42.1–4 in full, he uses the text to explain Jesus' reticence about the healing miracles, identifying him with the humble Servant who bears the Spirit, of whom Isaiah had said, 'He will not wrangle or cry aloud'.[53]

As we would expect, the tradition about Jesus' own baptism was reflected in the baptismal practice of the early Church. In particular, the two main stages in Jesus' baptism, the descent into the water and the anointing with the Spirit, set the pattern for the Church's rite of initiation, at least in the mainstream of the tradition. The clearest examples of a twofold initiation process in the New Testament are in the Book of Acts. In chapter 8 the apostles in Jerusalem hear that there are converts in Samaria and send to them Peter and John, 'who came down and prayed for them that they might receive the Holy Spirit; for it had not yet fallen upon any of them, but they had only been baptized in the name of the Lord Jesus'. The apostles lay hands on them and they receive the Spirit.[54] Similarly, in chapter 19, Paul encounters a group of disciples at Ephesus who had been baptized with John's baptism. Paul explains that John's baptism was only an act of repentance in preparation for faith in the One who was to come after him, Jesus. He therefore baptizes them in the name of Jesus, then lays his hands upon them and they receive the Holy Spirit.[55] In the first case of course the delay between the water-baptism and the giving of the Spirit is exceptional; the normal pattern appears in the second, where the baptism and the giving of the Spirit are inseparable, but nevertheless distinct and successive, as in the case of Jesus' baptism.

The sequence of events within this pattern (going down into the deep; rising up again; receiving the Spirit) is also of fundamental importance because it relates theologically to the sequence of Jesus' death, resurrection and (in Luke–Acts) Pentecost. The baptism of Jesus himself anticipates the saving events; Christian baptism recapitulates them. Jesus himself calls his forthcoming death and resurrection a 'baptism' in the Synoptic Gospels and tells his disciples they will share in it;[56] and baptism 'into' Jesus means, as Paul explains it, incorporation into his body: dying and rising with him. The giving of the Spirit, then, is consequent upon baptism as Pentecost is consequent upon the death and resurrection of Jesus. Only Luke–Acts describes Pentecost, but a similar theological pattern can be assumed in Matthew and Mark, since they too portray Jesus as the one who will baptize with the Spirit. It is certainly the same in John, where Jesus explains to the disciples that his death is necessary in order that the Spirit may come; the Spirit cannot be given until Jesus is glorified. The only difference is that in John's sequence of events the giving of the Spirit to the remaining apostles happens on the evening of the day of the resurrection rather than fifty days later.[57]

There is, however, another strand of tradition within the New Testament, in which the gift of the Spirit seems to *precede* baptism. As Lampe emphasizes, not all the initiations in Acts occur on the pattern of events in chapters 8 and 19.[58] In Acts 10.44–48, for example, St Peter baptizes Cornelius and his household *after* it is said that the Spirit has fallen upon them. This may well reflect an earlier understanding, since the evidence in Paul's letters, our earliest texts, also tends in this direction.[59] Paul's teaching, unlike the evidence of the Gospel tradition, does not easily admit a formal distinction between the work of the Spirit and the function of baptism as the means whereby we are made members of Christ's Body and united in his death. 'By one Spirit we were all baptized into one body'; 'You were washed, you were sanctified, you were justified in the name of the Lord Jesus Christ and in the Spirit of our God'.[60] If there is any idea of precedence, it is the Spirit who prompts us to baptism in the first place. In Gal. 3.2f. we are said to 'start with the Spirit', which we receive not by baptism, but 'by hearing with faith'. 'No one can say "Jesus is Lord" except by the Holy Spirit', says Paul in 1 Cor. 12.3. Since 'Jesus is Lord' is very likely to have been the earliest confessional declaration at baptism, preceding the trinitarian formula, the statement that no one can make it except by the Spirit is highly significant. This also appears to be the order of Paul's own conversion as it is described in Acts 9.17f.: Ananias commands, 'Be filled with the Holy Spirit'; Paul regains his sight, and *then* he is baptized. It is possible, then, that whereas the later initiation practice of the churches in East and West overwhelmingly followed the pattern of Jesus' own baptism in the gospels and of Acts 8 and 19, in which the Holy Spirit is imparted by apostolic hands after baptism, the Syriac custom of pre-baptismal chrismation follows this earlier Pauline tradition.[61]

The origin of ritual chrismation

So far we have seen no hint in the texts of the literal use of oil in baptism. It does not figure in the accounts of Jesus' baptism, nor in any of the accounts of apostolic initiation in Acts; the only external expression of the giving of the Spirit that we have seen is the laying on of hands. Other evidence in the New Testament texts, as we shall shortly see, is ambiguous; and the same is true of Catholic sources throughout the second century. Where anointing is mentioned by Justin, Irenaeus, Theophilus of Antioch, Clement, Barnabas and Hermas, there is no certainty that it refers to any distinct rite.[62] Our earliest safe testimony to the practice in the mainstream Church comes from Tertullian at the beginning of the third century.[63]

We do know, however, that at least by the second half of the second century chrismation was practised by Gnostic groups. Probably the earliest unambiguous reference to a baptismal rite of chrismation is in *The Gospel of Philip*, a second-century Valentinian text. Like the Orthodox, the author traces a connection via the apostles between the anointing of Christ and our anointing as Christians; but he is unorthodox in divorcing chrismation from baptism, and seeing the former as not only distinct from, but superior to, the latter:

> The chrism is superior to baptism, for it is from the word 'chrism' that we have been called 'Christians', certainly not because of the word 'baptism'. And it is because of the chrism that 'the Christ' had his name. For the Father anointed the Son,

and the Son anointed his apostles, and the apostles anointed us.
He who has been anointed possesses everything. He possesses
the resurrection, the light, the cross, the Holy Spirit.[64]

There is also evidence that chrismation was practised in the second
century by the Marcionites (like the Valentinians, a very numerous
and widespread group) and also by the Syrian Naassenes; and the rite
is very frequently referred to in later Gnosticism.[65] Its popularity with
the Gnostics, whose favourite self-designation was οἱ πνευματικοί,
the 'spirituals', to distinguish them from the ordinary, unspiritual
Catholics, was no doubt a result of their claim that the Spirit was their
exclusive possession. If, as Lampe believes,[66] they were the first
Christians to introduce it, the motive of the rite may well have been to
express and emphasize their spiritual superiority over ordinary
Christians who as yet practised only water-baptism. Dix, agreeing
that the earliest unambiguous evidence for chrismation is Gnostic,
argues that it is unthinkable that the Church should have taken over
any practice from its doctrinal enemies.[67] This may be a naïve
assumption, however, since we know that the Valentinians in
particular remained as long as possible inside the Catholic Church,
worked hard to disseminate their ideas within it, and were highly
flexible in accommodating their doctrine to different viewpoints.[68]

We are not bound, however, to assume Gnostic influence, and it
may be pure accident that it is a Gnostic text that gives the earliest
definite attestation of the rite. From both a Gnostic and a Catholic
point of view, the concept of chrismation is so central to the
understanding of Christ and the Christian (including of course the
very words 'Christ' and 'Christian'), and is so well grounded in
Scripture, with Old Testament texts that directly enjoin the practice
and New Testament ones that could be taken as doing so, that on both
sides the step towards crystallizing the concept into a rite must have
been easily taken. It should be remembered too that the use of oil as
soap during bathing and as a cosmetic afterwards was normal in the
ancient world, and certainly figured, without any special symbolic
significance, in Jewish ritual washing and proselyte baptism.[69] So it is
entirely possible that this everyday use of oil entered into Christian
baptismal washing from the first as a matter of course, but only gained
mention in the sources when it had begun to be given a ritual
theological significance as a sign of spiritual anointing.

Turning to Tertullian, our earliest certain witness to chrismation in
the Catholic Church, we find that he derives the practice not from the
New Testament, and of course not from the Gnostics, but from the
anointing of the levitical priests in the Old Testament:

> When we have come out of the font we are thoroughly anointed
> with a blessed unction, in accordance with the ancient discipline

65

whereby, since the time when Aaron was anointed with Moses, men were anointed to the priesthood with oil from a horn; from which they are called 'anointed ones' (*christi dicti a chrismate*) from the chrism, that is the anointing, which also lent its name to the Lord.[70]

Its force may not be immediately apparent, but here Tertullian has in fact chosen the most logically relevant scriptural reference available to him. At 1 Pet. 2.5, the Church collectively is termed 'a holy priesthood to offer spiritual sacrifices . . . a royal priesthood'. The author of Revelation similarly calls the Church 'a kingdom and priests to our God'.[71] In both texts the double messiahship of Jesus as King and high-priest is understood to have been conferred on his people, and the natural inference is that it is conferred through their own baptismal anointing. Tertullian, evidently following these scriptural precedents, sees the baptismal chrismation as a sort of ordination to the royal priesthood of all believers, 'a consecration to the universal priesthood which all Christians possess in virtue of their membership of Christ, the true Priest'.[72] The historical value of his statement that it derives from levitical ordination is hard to assess, but it is certainly possible that the introduction of the rite into Christianity, whether by Gnostics or Catholics, was consciously influenced by the scriptural account of the chrismation of the Aaronic priesthood. In this connection, it may even be significant that the rite of anointing by pouring oil and signing with the sign of the cross, reported in the third-century *Apostolic Tradition*[73] conforms closely to evidence in the Talmud about the mode of anointing the levitical priests: 'Our rabbis taught: How were the kings anointed? – In the shape of a wreath. And the priests? – In the shape of a *chi* (X).'[74]

The detail of the signing with the cross will be discussed later. As Mitchell notes, 'the similarity of Jewish and Christian practice is astounding',[75] and in view of Tertullian's testimony it is hard to disbelieve that, however indirectly, this Old Testament tradition bore some influence.

Ritual chrismation in the New Testament?

The besetting problem remains that of knowing whether the New Testament references to anointing are literal or figurative. Are spiritual anointing and 'royal priesthood' no more than metaphorical concepts in the New Testament, only later to be expressed in a rite modelled on compatible elements in Jewish tradition? Or are we justified in supposing that a Christian rite was already undergirding the metaphor? There are a few New Testament texts that we need to examine, where the vocabulary of anointing is arguably more than figurative.

In 1 John 2.20 the author contrasts the faithful with certain
secessionists whom he calls 'antichrists', who have left the fold and
fallen away into false doctrine: 'But you have been anointed [χρίσμα
ἔχετε] by the Holy One, and you all know [or: 'you know
everything']. At 2.27f. he adds:

> I write this to you about those who would deceive you; but the
> anointing [χρίσμα] which you received from him abides in you,
> and you have no need that anyone should teach you; as his
> anointing [χρίσμα] teaches you about everything, and is
> true, and is no lie, just as it has taught you, abide
> in him.

As we would expect, the most obvious meaning of the anointing
possessed by John's addressees is the Holy Spirit. The statement that
the anointing 'abides' recalls the teaching of John's Gospel that Jesus
himself is called the one on whom the Spirit abides; and it is his gift
and promise that the Spirit/Paraclete will abide with the disciples also.
They will 'receive' the Spirit that 'the world cannot receive'. In John's
Gospel too the Spirit is called 'the Spirit of truth'; and the disciples are
promised, 'he will teach you everything'.[76] The equation: anointing =
Holy Spirit, then, is not to be denied. However, three arguments have
been adduced for believing that the author also has in mind a literal
anointing with oil: (i) The word χρίσμα occurs in the New Testament
only in these verses; and Greek neuters ending in -α are usually
things, not actions. Bultmann, Schnackenburg and others therefore
translate χρίσμα as 'oil' or 'chrism', rather than anointing.[77] (ii)
Although this anointing or chrism is thought of as a present
possession, it is said to have been 'received' at a particular point in the
past, presumably upon entry to the community in baptism. (iii) The
main point of these verses is that the anointing preserves the true
believers from the error of the antichrists. Yet the author never says
that the secessionists, the 'antichrists', were not themselves anointed
before they split away, although if it had been possible to say this it
would have made an excellent polemical point.[78] Might it therefore be
(as R. E. Brown has argued) that the author has in mind two kinds of
anointing: the physical, which all received at baptism; and the
spiritual, for which the only evidence can be the adherence of the
believer to doctrine he originally professed?

All three of these arguments can be contested. (i) There *are* one or
two nouns in -μα which denotes action rather than things; and in any
case even if one translates 'chrism' this does not of itself prove that the
word refers back to an actual anointing with oil. (ii) Although the
anointing was received at a point in the past, probably baptism, the
same could be said of receiving the Spirit, without presupposing any

accompanying rite of chrismation. Argument (iii) is perhaps the strongest, but it is an argument from silence, and if there is a distinction in the author's mind between an actual and a figurative anointing one might have expected him to make it plainer. All in all, the case remains unproved.

A second case is that of the healing of the blind man in John 9.1–9. Several features make it virtually certain that this miracle was intended by the author as a symbol of baptism. The blind man is healed only when washed in the pool of Siloam. We are told that the name Siloam means 'one who has been sent' – and in John's Gospel Jesus is constantly presented to us as 'the one who has been sent' by the Father. Washing in this pool therefore naturally implies a baptismal washing 'in Christ'. Furthermore, it was water from Siloam which was used in the temple ceremony at the Feast of Tabernacles; and the Gospel has already shown us that Jesus is the fulfilment of this ceremony, when he proclaims at the Feast, 'He who believes in me . . . "Out of his heart shall flow rivers of living water" '.[79]

Secondly, it is stressed that the blind man is *born* blind. 'Enlightenment' is a term explicitly applied to baptism elsewhere in the New Testament,[80] and since there is such play in the story and its aftermath between physical and spiritual blindness, with the Pharisees later accusing the man of having been 'born in sin', the underlying idea is evidently that sin and spiritual blindness can only be healed by washing in the new waters that Jesus promises will flow from him. Finally, and most significantly for our enquiry, before sending the man to wash in Siloam Jesus makes an ointment of clay and spittle and *anoints* his eyes. The word ἐπέχρισεν, although it may simply mean 'rub' or 'smear', because of its connection with χριω is more likely to be a liturgical reference than if John had used a more obvious alternative such as ἀλείφω or ἐπιτίθημι. Again, however, even if there is a deliberate reference to anointing in the use of this word, we cannot be sure that an external rite is in mind rather than the general connection between Spirit-anointing and baptism. There is circumstantial evidence in the fact that this story, including the detail of the anointing, appears several times in early catacomb art as an illustration of baptism;[81] and the two gestures of Jesus – anointing and the use of spittle – were both widely adopted into later baptismal ceremonies. But whether such things figured in the practice of the author's own church still remains a guess.[82]

In 2 Cor. 1.21 Paul writes: 'It is God who establishes [βεβαιῶν] us with you in [ἐις] Christ, and has anointed [χρίσας] us; he has put his seal [σφραγισάμενος] upon us and given [δοὺς] us his Spirit in our hearts as a guarantee [ἀρραβῶν].' Thornton finds here an 'unmistakeable reference to confirmation',[83] by which he means confirmation in the sense of the second part of the baptismal rite, including chrismation and signing and the laying on of hands. The verse certainly contains the technical vocabulary of the later rite, and was quoted by patristic commentators to elucidate it,[84] but we must beware of interpreting it anachronistically. The context is certainly liturgical: Paul has just said that Christ is the final affirmation of all God's promises: 'All God's promises find their Yes in him; that is why we utter the Amen through him to the glory of God' (verse 20). Paul now explains that it is God who 'establishes' or 'confirms' us in these promises (βεβαιῶν) 'in Christ'. The Greek means literally *'into'* Christ (εἰς), which naturally suggests 'baptism into Christ', the standard Pauline phrase expressing the act of incorporation into his Body. In the Greek there is a word-play between χριστὸς and χρίσας, similar to that in the passage of *The Gospel of Philip* discussed above, also implying the Christian's baptismal participation in Christ's own spiritual anointing.[85] The overall action of 'confirming' us in Christ that is expressed in the present participle βεβαιῶν is unpacked in the three aorist participles that follow: he has confirmed us in that he has anointed us; he has set his seal on us; he has given us the Spirit as a guarantee. As Lampe points out, these three aorists clearly refer to a single moment in the spiritual history of Paul's readers, and that the moment is baptism is equally clear.[86] In fact, few commentators deny that baptism is in Paul's mind here (or at least at the back of it); what is in doubt is the significance of the vocabulary with which he refers to it. Are all three actions that constitute the 'confirmation into Christ' simply equivalent metaphors for the baptismal reception of the Spirit (anointing, sealing, guaranteeing); or are anointing and sealing and even confirming already technical terms reflecting a rite of chrismation and 'signing' in conjunction with baptism?

Argenti, believing that such a rite can be assumed in 2 Cor. 1.21f., finds his view confirmed in the following chapter, 2 Cor. 2.14–16, where Paul writes:

> But thanks be to God, who in Christ always leads us in triumph, and through us spreads the knowledge of him everywhere. For we are the aroma [εὐωδία] of Christ to God among those who are being saved and among those who are perishing, to one a fragrance [ὀσμή] from death to death, to the other a fragrance [ὀσμή] from life to life.

Argenti notes that 'this metaphor would be very strained and artificial unless it recalled a rite familiar to Christian readers; it is by chrismation that we are the aroma of Christ'.[87] Here he evidently assumes that the oil of chrism would have been a fragrant mixture of olive oil and perfumed essences, as laid down in Exodus for the anointing of the levitical priests, and as adopted by the Church. Most commentators, however, do not understand the 'fragrance' in this sense at all. Barrett, noting Paul's reference to a triumphal procession in verse 14, interprets εὐωδία in terms of processional incense as a symbol of the knowledge of God spreading among men, and ὀσμή as the 'sweet-smelling savour' of sacrifice as in Eph. 5.2 and Phil. 4.18 and many Old Testament texts.[88] Alternatively and rather more simply, one can interpret 'fragrance' throughout as a metaphor for the true wisdom or knowledge which is the living gospel itself. The reference to knowledge in verse 14 makes this the obvious interpretation of εὐωδία, and ὀσμή is a word applied to Wisdom elsewhere in biblical literature.[89] The apparently strange idea in verse 16 that this 'fragrance' brings life or death is then seen to be the relatively commonplace one that knowledge of the gospel is a 'two-edged sword', bringing judgement with it. The statement is in fact very close in form and virtually identical in meaning to 1 Cor. 1.18, 'the word of the cross is folly to those who are perishing, but to us who are being saved it is the power of God'. The argument cannot be closed, but an interpretation along these lines seems much more probable than Argenti's. It also removes his supporting evidence for a liturgical understanding of the reference to anointing in 1.21f., which must remain equally in doubt.

Postscript on the seal in 2 Corinthians, Ephesians and Revelation

In view of the importance of sealing (i.e. signing a cross, usually with the chrism itself) as a subsidiary rite alongside chrismation in later baptismal practice, Paul's reference to sealing in 2 Cor. 1.21f. needs further examination. The basic idea of the seal, σφραγίς, is clear: it is a mark denoting possession or belonging, the claim of the owner over the thing owned. In the ancient world slaves as well as animals, objects and commercial documents might bear such a mark, or their owner's name, and this too was termed a seal. In Judaism circumcision was frequently called a seal, denoting membership of God's people, and Paul himself calls it this in Rom. 4.11.[90] Possibly it was his meditation on the work of the Spirit as the new circumcision, the circumcision of the heart (e.g. Rom. 1.29, Phil. 3.3, Col. 2.11–13), which led him to apply the term σφραγίς to the Spirit, since there is no evidence for such a description of the Spirit prior to Paul. In 2. Cor. 21.21f. Paul is saying that it is the Spirit who marks out the Christian as belonging to God. The metaphor is primarily commercial; the sealing is part of the whole transaction which 'confirmed us into Christ'. Extending the metaphor, he also called the Spirit an ἀρραβών, a pledge of salvation or 'first instalment' in the present of the blessings of the life to come.

In Eph. 1.13 the same vocabulary reappears, in a passage that the probably pseudonymous author seems to have based on 2 Cor. itself: 'In him . . . you were sealed [ἐσφραγίσθητε] with the promised Holy Spirit, which is the guarantee [ἀρραβών] of our inheritance until we acquire possession of it . . .' And in Eph. 4.30 he writes: 'Do not grieve the Holy Spirit of God, in whom you were sealed [ἐσφραγίσθητε] for the day of redemption.'

The fact that Ephesians, like 2 Cor., refers to the 'sealing' as an action accomplished in the past, again suggests that baptism is in mind as the actual moment of sealing. In both passages the application of the word 'seal' to the Spirit makes perfect sense without presupposing a separate rite of signing with oil or water such as appeared in the later Church. Until the end of the second century, just as there is no unambiguous evidence for a literal rite of chrismation, there is no unambiguous evidence that the 'seal' refers to a rite of signing. Where it does not refer directly to the Spirit, it refers to the reception of the Spirit through the rite of initiation seen as a whole. In *2 Clement*, baptism itself is called the seal. *Hermas* says more specifically that the seal is the *water* of baptism: ἡ σφραγίς τὸ ὕδωρ ἐστιν. The seal means baptism in the *Epistle of Barnabas*, which also states the Pauline view that baptism is the replacement in the New Covenant of what was called the 'seal of circumcision' under the Old.[91] This evidence makes it all the more hazardous to read a rite of chrismation into the Pauline passages, or to assume that the Pauline 'seal' has yet been associated with an act of signing.

There is, however, another Old Testament tradition of sealing, connected not with the idea of circumcision as a mark of belonging to God's people, but with a sign on the forehead as a mark of redemption and salvation from the eschatological wrath of God. In Ezekiel's vision (9.4) the righteous in Jerusalem receive such a mark on their foreheads; this will save them from the slaughter that is about to befall the city. The Greek text mentions merely a mark or sign, but the original Hebrew specifies the letter Tau, which would be written thus: X or +.[92] This episode of Ezekiel's vision was borrowed by the author of the Book of Revelation and incorporated into his own picture of the Last Judgement, where an angel seals the servants of God with the seal of God upon their foreheads, so that they escape the plagues of wrath.[93] Since the author is so close to his source in Ezekiel he must also have had the Tau in mind, perhaps reinterpreted as the sign of the cross, or as the initial letter of Christ's name, Χριστός.[94] This is how Tertullian interprets the Ezekiel passage:

> He [Christ] has signed us with that very seal of which Ezekiel spoke, 'The Lord said to me, Go through the gate, through the midst of Jerusalem, and set the mark Tau upon the foreheads of

the men'. Now the letter Tau and our own letter T is the very form of the Cross, which he predicted would be the sign on our foreheads in the true and catholic Jerusalem.

Tertullian, in saying that Christ has signed us with a literal sign of the cross, must be referring to a signing ceremony in baptism, although there is no means of knowing how or at what stage of the ceremony it was done in his church. But does a baptismal understanding also underlie the passage in Revelation? Shepherd and others have argued that the whole context of Rev. 7 is baptismal, since it seems to allude to certain features of later baptismal ceremony: renunciation of Satan, profession of faith, washing, sealing, and investment with white garments.[95] Yet again the most one can say is that this is a possibility; the majority of commentators interpret all these elements without reference to baptism, and find it more likely that the rituals arose later, perhaps partly under the influence of this text.[96] The mention of the saints 'who have come out of the great tribulation and washed their robes and made them white in the blood of the Lamb' more naturally suggests their status as martyrs under persecution than their baptism.[97] And a particular difficulty in the matter of the sealing is that it is presented as a future hope, not as a present possession. The saints are sealed for redemption immediately before the battle; there is no indication that they have been already sealed in any sense on earth.

Recalling the talmudic tradition that the levitical priests were anointed with oil in the form of the cross, one wonders whether this custom itself arose from Jewish meditation on the cross-shaped mark in Ezekiel, but it is difficult to imagine that the mark of eschatological redemption would have been seen as the exclusive property of priests. The more probable explanation is that the mark X was used generally as the conventional owner's mark, so that it seemed appropriate to sign priests in this way as men possessed and set apart by God. If Tertullian is right in deriving the Church's custom of baptismal anointing ultimately from the ordination of the levitical priests, the rite of signing the cross in oil may well have come in with it. But whatever its proximate source was, it gave objective expression to a remarkable complex of scriptural ideas: the signing of priestly ordination; Paul's concept of the 'seal of the Spirit', understood as fulfilling the seal of circumcision and already associated with baptism; the cross-shaped seal of eschatological redemption as it appears in Ezekiel and Revelation; the Greek initial letter of Christ's name as 'owner'; and the sign of his cross.

Notes

1. Luke 11.14 and 13.16.
2. Ecclus. 38.1–15.
3. G. Vermes, *Jesus the Jew* (London 1973), esp. pp. 58–80.
4. Josephus, *The Jewish War* 2.136, quoted in Vermes, *Jesus the Jew*, p. 63.
5. Compare Matt. 8.5–13/Luke 7.1–10 and John 4.46–53. On Hanina ben Dosa, see Vermes, *Jesus the Jew*, pp. 72–8 and notes ad. loc.
6. Mark 3.11.
7. Mark 3.22–30; Matt. 12.24–32; Luke 11.14–23.
8. Mark 6.7, repeating 3.15.
9. See M. Dudley and G. Rowell, *Confession and Absolution* (London 1990), pp. 16–18 and notes.
10. See D. E. Nineham, *Saint Mark* (London 1963), p. 170.
11. ibid., p. 171.
12. Luke 10.34.
13. See F. J. Dolger, *Der Exorzismus im altchristlichen Taufritual* (Paderborn 1909), pp. 137–57; H. Schlier, article on 'Ἀλειφω', in G. Kittel, *Theological Dictionary of the New Testament* (Grand Rapids, 1964) vol 1, p. 230. Texts in H. L. Strack and P. Billerbeck, *Kommentar zum Neuen Testament aus Talmud und Midrasch* (1922), 1:428f., II:11f.
14. Evidence in Schlier, article on 'Ἀλειφω', p. 230.
15. *The Testament of Solomon* 18.34.
16. R. A. Cole, *The Gospel According to St Mark* (Grand Rapids 1961), p. 109.
17. H. B. Swete, *The Gospel According to St Mark* (London 1902), p. 119.
18. Conc. Trident. Sess. xiv, *De Sacramento Extremae Unctionis* cap. 1.
19. cf. Cardinal Bellarmine, *De Extr. Unct.* Lib. 1 cap. 2; C. Pickar, 'Is Anyone Sick Among You?', *Catholic Biblical Quarterly*, 7 (1945), pp. 165–74, esp. pp. 165f.; C. Ruch, 'L'Extrême Onction dans l'Ecriture', in *Dictionnaire de Théologie Catholique* (Paris 1913), cols 1897–1927, esp. 1926f.; B. Poschmann, *Penance and the Anointing of the Sick* (London 1964), esp. p. 233.
20. A. Flannery, ed., *Vatican Council II vol. 2* (New York 1975), pp. 13f.: 'The Apostolic Constitution on the Sacrament of the Anointing of the Sick'. See, for example, J. Ziegler, *Let them Anoint the Sick* (Collegeville, MN, 1987), p. 28, and I. Scicolone, 'Unzione degli Infermi', in *Anamnesis, vol 3: I Sacramenti* (Genoa 1986), pp. 213f.
21. See P. H. Davids, *The Epistle of James* (Exeter 1982), pp. 1–22; S. Laws, *A Commentary on the Epistle of James* (London 1979), pp. 1–42; M. Dibelius, *James* (ET Philadelphia 1976), Introduction.
22. See G. Bornkamm, article πρέσβυς κ. τ. λ. in *Theological Dictionary of the New Testament*, 6, pp. 651–83, esp. p. 660; G. Dix, 'The Ministry in the Early Church', K. Kirk, ed., *The Apostolic Ministry* (London 1946), pp. 183–303, esp. pp. 232–42; E. Schweizer, *Church Order in the New Testament* (London 1961), esp. chs 24–26.
23. Bornkamm, πρέσβυς κ. τ. λ., pp. 655f.; E. Lohse, article on χειρ, Kittel, *TDNT*, pp. 424–37, esp. pp. 429, 431–4; Dix 'The Ministry in

the Early Church', pp. 233f. Texts in Strack and Billerbeck, *Kommentar zum Neuen Testament aus Talmud und Midrasch*, II, pp. 647–61, esp. *Sifre Numbers* 140 and *Sifre Deuteronomy* 357.

24. Dix, 'The Ministry in the Early Church', pp. 235f. Evidence in *Mishnah Sanhedrin* 1.19a, 43.

25. Dix, 'The Ministry in the Early Church', p. 233; Bornkamm, πρέσβυς κ. τ. λ., pp. 658f., 663.

26. Bornkamm, πρέσβυς κ. τ. λ., p. 667.

27. Paul and the presbyters are said both to have laid hands on Timothy, perhaps simultaneously, on the Jewish model of president and presbyterate acting together. Paul himself and Barnabas in Acts 13 are apparently commissioned by the whole Church in Antioch; and the apostles collectively lay hands on the 'Hellenists' in Acts 6 (thereby arguably making them an order of presbyters rather than deacons, since the episode is undoubtedly modelled on the ordination of the presbyters in Num. 11). See Lohse, χειρ, pp. 33f.

28. Schweizer represents the most sceptical view (*Church Order in the New Testament*, esp. pp. 211–19), but none of his points gainsay this possibility. Bultmann assumes such a development: *Theology of the New Testament* (London 1955), 2, pp. 103–11.

29. Laws, *A Commentary on the Epistle of James*, p. 230; Lohse, χειρ, pp. 431ff.

30. Origen, *Homily on Leviticus* (Latin) 2.4.

31. Bede, *Expositio super Divi Jacobi Epistolam*, in Migne, *Patrologia Latina* xciii, col. 39.

32. D. Daube, *The New Testament and Rabbinic Judaism* (ET London 1973), p. 236.

33. Dibelius, *James*, p. 252.

34. Babylonian Talmud, *Nedarim* 41a. See Laws, *A Commentary on the Epistle of James* p. 229, and Vermes, *Jesus the Jew*, pp. 66–8, who argues that Jesus' claim to forgive sins 'was not outstandingly novel or unique' among Jewish healers.

35. See F. W. Puller, *The Anointing of the Sick in Scripture and Tradition* (London 1904), pp. 30f.; similarly Poschmann, Pickar, Ruch, etc. K. Condon disagrees ('The Sacrament of Healing', in T. Worden, ed., *Sacraments in Scripture* (London 1966), pp. 172–86; see p. 185).

36. Dudley and Rowell, *Confession and Absolution*, pp. 35f.

37. Puller, *The Anointing of the Sick*, pp. 40f.

38. Condon, 'The Sacrament of Healing', pp. 183, 186.

39. Older Roman Catholic commentaries interpreted ἐγερεῖ to mean 'will comfort, strengthen' (so as to help patients through death). This evidently arose from a mistake in the Vulgate which translated ἐγερεῖ as *alleviabit* ('will alleviate') instead of *allevabit* ('will raise up').

40. Discounting μυρίζω at Mark 14.8.

41. On the significance of the story of Jesus' baptism as the prototype of Christian baptismal practice, cf. O. Cullmann, *Baptism in the New Testament* (ET London 1950), ch. 1, esp. pp. 21f.; G. W. Lampe, *The Seal of the Spirit* (London 1951), p. 6; C. Argenti, 'Chrismation', in M. Thurian, ed., *Ecumenical Perspectives on Baptism, Eucharist and*

Ministry (Geneva 1983), pp. 46ff.; L. L. Mitchell, *Baptismal Anointing* (London 1966), p. 17. G. R. Beasley-Murray takes a differing view: *Baptism in the New Testament* (London 1962), ch. 1.

42. Athanasius, *Against the Arians* 1.47 (Lampe, *The Seal of the spirit*, p. 6).
43. 1 Sam. 16.13.
44. Evidence in Lampe, *The Seal of the Spirit*, p. 30.
45. John 1.33.
46. Heb. 2.17, 4.14–5.10, 7.1–10.22; John 19.23, Rev. 1.13.
47. cf. 1 Pet. 2.5,9; Rev. 1.6, 5.10, 20.6.
48. Exod. 29.4,7; Lev. 8.1–13.
49. Ps. 133.2.
50. Zech. 4.
51. 4 Q Florilegium 1.11 cp. Damasc. 7.18–20 (9.8–10); 1 Q Sa 1.1, 2.11–14.
52. 2 Kings 2.1–14.
53. Matt. 12.17–21.
54. Acts 8.14–17.
55. Acts 19.1–7.
56. Mark 10.38, Luke 12.50 (Matt. 20.22f. in certain MSS); Rom. 6.3–11, etc.
57. John 7.39, 16.7, 20.19–23.
58. Lampe, *The Seal of the Spirit*, ch. 5.
59. See T. W. Manson, 'Entry into the Early Church', *Journal of Theological Studies*, 48 (1947), pp. 25–33.
60. 1 Cor. 12.13, 6.11.
61. Manson 'Entry into the Early Church', p. 26.
62. Lampe, *The Seal of the Spirit*, ch. 6.
63. Discussed below.
64. *The Gospel of Philip* (NHL II.3) 74. 13–22.
65. Tertullian *Adv Marc* I.14; Hippolytus on the Naassenes, *Adv Haer* v.7; further evidence in Lampe, *The Seal of the Spirit*, pp. 120–8.
66. Lampe, *The Seal of the Spirit*, p. 127: 'It is in all probability to such curious sects that we must go to find the separation of water-baptism and spirit-baptism which we meet in the third century, and to these circles we must look for the introduction of subsidiary ceremonies such as postbaptismal unction.'
67. G. Dix, *The Apostolic Tradition of Hippolytus* (London 1937), p. xxxiv.
68. See for example, G. Quispel, 'La Sympathie pour le Catholicisme', in *L'Epître de Ptolémée à Flora* (Paris 1949), pp. 14–17.
69. See J. Jeremias, 'Der Ursprung der Johannes-Taufe', *Zeitschrift für die neutestamentliche Wissenschaft und die Kunde des Urchristentums* 28 (Giessen 1929), pp. 312–20; G. Dix, *Confirmation or Laying on of Hands?* (London 1935), p. 10.
70. Tertullian, *De Baptismo* 7.
71. 1 Pet. 2.5,9; Rev. 1.6, 5.10, 20.
72. Lampe, *The Seal of the Spirit*, p. 158.
73. *Ap. Trad.* 22.1–4.
74. *The Babylonian Talmud*, ed. I. Epstein (2nd edn London 1961): *Kerithoth* p. 36; *Horayoth* p. 85.

75. Mitchell, *Baptismal Anointing*, p. 23.
76. John 1.33, 14.6, 14.17, 15.26, 14.26.
77. R. Bultmann, *The Johannine Epistles* (ET Philadelphia 1973), p. 37, thinks the χρίσμα 'was connected in all likelihood with baptism and the laying on of hands in the primitive church'. R. Schnackenburg translates χρίσμα as the oil of anointing, but takes it to be symbolic of sound doctrine: *Die Johannesbriefe* (Freiburg 1970), p. 152.
78. See R. E. Brown, *The Epistles of John* (London 1982), pp. 341–7 and 368–71.
79. John 7.38. See R. E. Brown, *The Gospel According to John* (Republished London 1984), 1, pp. 369–82.
80. Heb. 6.4, 10.32. Note the start of Tertullian's *De Baptismo*: 'The present work will treat of our sacrament of water which washes away the sins of our original blindness . . .'
81. cf. F.-M. Braun, *Jean le Théologien et son Evangile dans l'Eglise Ancienne* (Paris 1959), pp. 149ff.
82. cf. E. Hoskyns's note on the use of John 9 in the lectionaries and liturgies of the early Church: *The Fourth Gospel* (London 1947), pp. 363–5.
83. L. Thornton, *Confirmation, its Place in the Baptismal Mystery* (London 1954), p. 7.
84. e.g. Didymus, *Trinity* 2.6.
85. The most thorough investigation of the text has been made by E. Dinkler, who while accepting its baptismal reference doubts the possibility – without excluding it – that actual rites of chrismation and sealing are referred to: 'Die Taufterminologie in 2 Kor 1.21f' in *Signum Crucis* (Tübingen 1967) pp. 99–133.
86. Lampe, *The Seal of the Spirit*, pp. 5f.
87. Argenti, 'Chrismation', p. 51.
88. C. K. Barrett, *A Commentary on the Second Epistle to the Corinthians* (London 1973), pp. 97–102.
89. Eccles. 24.15 and 39.14; cf. 2 Baruch 67.6.
90. See G. Fitzer, σφραγίς, Kittel, *TDNT*, 7, pp. 939–53, esp. pp. 947f.; Dinkler, 'Die Taufterminologie in 2 Kor 1.2f', pp. 109ff.
91. *2 Clement* 6.9, 7.6, 8.6; *Hermas* 9.16, 3–4; *Barnabas* 9.6.
92. cf. W. Eichrodt, *Ezekiel* (ET London 1970), pp. 130ff.; Lampe, *The Seal of the Spirit*, p. 14.
93. Rev. 7.1–4. A Qumran document also quotes Ezek. 9.4 (explicitly) in its description of the final judgement, but without further explanation of the mark: *CDC* 19.12.
94. See J. Massyngberde Ford, *Revelation* (New York 1975), pp. 116f. and 121–4.
95. M. H. Shepherd, *The Paschal Liturgy and the Apocalypse* (London 1960), esp. pp. 83, 90ff. cf. Mitchell, *Baptismal Anointing*, pp. 19f.
96. e.g. Massyngberde Ford, *Revelation*, p. 116; G. R. Beasley-Murray, *Revelation* (London 1974), pp. 142f.
97. Rev. 7.13f.

6

Anointing in the Early Church

John Halliburton

Any threat to monopolize or frustrate the production of oil in the early years of the Roman Empire and during its ascent to world dominance would have (compared with our own day) caused scarcely a ripple in the political arena, but enormous upsets on the domestic front. Oil as a mineral was certainly not unknown.[1] But it was oil as a household necessity, oil crushed from the olive, palm, coconut and nutmeg – vegetable oil, as we would call it, closely related to the liquefied fat of animals – which was considered essential to a civilized way of life.[2] Oil in cooking was as integral as today's margarine or butter. You could technically survive without it (ascetics in the Church 'gave it up' for Lent),[3] but it was a poor table that served up a dry meal, and an inadequate kitchen that did not have its flask of amber liquid in the larder. Besides which, oil had other uses. It fuelled the lamps of the late dinner parties.[4] It was the secret of the smooth and fragrant complexions of the young (and not so young) who listened and intrigued with their husbands about their social and political prospects. It was a universal salve – for sore feet, sore eyes, rough skin, broken skin. It could also be taken internally, based on the belief that internal pain was like external pain: an abrasion in need of soothing. What better than oil?[5] Thus its production was at a premium.

In Numidia, for example, it was the foundation of the farming economy. Harvesting the olive crop required seasonal casual labour; every tree had to be beaten until the last fruit had fallen. Hence a rustic labour force, which by all accounts swallowed the last forkful of

77

their harvest supper and then went on hire to the Donatists in order generally to disrupt Catholic farmers and Catholic townships.[6] All this is on Augustine's doorstep. He knows the oil business well. He knows the farmers; he has stood by their oil presses. He has watched the black olive poured by the thousand into the wooden press, piled in and then crushed, the disgusting mess of the skins, stones and surviving pulp having to be filtered off, the golden luxurious liquid disappearing secretly into the vats. An image of the Church, perhaps? An image of the good and bad coexisting to the end of the age (rather like the wheat and the tares growing together until the harvest).[7] But throughout the oil is the image of goodness, of salvation, of fragrance, of beauty – as it is in Christian rite and symbol throughout the years of a developing theology of regeneration and healing.

Anointing and baptism

The use of oil in Christian liturgy begins not, as might be supposed, with services for healing (after the example offered by St James) but instead with baptism. It is significant that the rite described by St James cannot be traced in the ante-Nicene Church. Theologians like Origen (and after him John Chrysostom) use Jas. 5 to illustrate their theology of the forgiveness of sins and not as a warrant for the practice of anointing the sick.[8] So for many years, oil, liturgically, belongs to the font and not the bedside. Its use in initiation may have been very early. Cyril of Jerusalem,[9] for example, believes (and he may well here be inheriting a very ancient tradition) that the final anointing at baptism relates directly to 'the anointing from the Holy One' mentioned in 1 John which preserves Christians in the truth. Christ, after all, is the Messiah, the Anointed One, anointed in the Hebrew tradition for what he is – King and High-priest – anointed by the Spirit of God as he rose from the waters of the Jordan. So the Christian, rising from the waters of baptism, receives an outward anointing with oil, symbolizing the gift to him of the Spirit of God, and uniting him with Christ in his new vocation. 'The Spirit of the Lord is upon me because he has anointed me . . .' What could be clearer? What more appropriate outward sign than the oil of the olive?

By the third century, a baptismal rite that did not include anointing was unthinkable. Traditions vary about the number of anointings and the significance of each. At Rome,[10] for example, when the vigil is nearly over and the time for baptism is close, the bishop blesses two jars of oil, one for exorcism, and the other called 'the oil of thanksgiving'. Each is taken by a deacon; and the two deacons, each with his jar, sit either side of the presbyter who presides at the font. When the candidate renounces, he is anointed with the oil of exorcism; when he comes up from the font, the presbyter anoints him with the oil of thanksgiving; and the same oil is used by the bishop for the final anointing as he lays on hands (or, as we would say, confirms). Basically it is this pattern that survives in the West and is the norm for the modern Roman rites of initiation. Candidates today are anointed once before baptism and once after; and then a third time when they are brought to the bishop for confirmation. An uncanny consistency in practice, perhaps; but what of theology? What, in other words, does the rite mean or convey?

For this we have to desert the chronicler (like Hippolytus who is simply trying to tell us what happened at Rome in his day) and turn to the preacher. Bishops like Theodore of Mopsuestia, John Chrysostom, Cyril of Jerusalem and Ambrose of Milan are saddled like any bishop of their day with the annual task of explaining the Church's liturgy of initiation to a bewildered and sometimes apprehensive group of converts. For two and sometimes three years a group of kindly, reassuring and competent presbyters, deacons and others have given the basic instruction in Christian belief and living. They have taken the candidates right up to the brink. It is left to the bishop to make some kind of sense (usually after the rites of initiation) of what actually happens at baptism, of what Christians actually experience at the Eucharist. So in many cases, looking back with the candidates on what has been a profoundly moving but eerie experience, the bishops set out in each case to take to pieces the rite and explain its rich symbolism.[11]

First, what Hippolytus calls the oil of exorcism. This is the anointing that takes place in several rites immediately after the candidate has renounced 'Satan and all his works'. This in many ways is a major turning point. The new Christian has made his first decision. There can now be no turning back. John Chrysostom wrote:

> Renouncing him [the devil], they [the candidates] have changed their allegiance and publicly enlisted with Christ. It is for this reason that the bishop anoints you on your forehead and marks you with the seal to make the devil turn away his eyes. He does not dare to look at you directly because he sees the light blazing from your head and blinding his eyes. From that day onwards, you will confront him in battle and this is why the bishop anoints you as athletes of Christ before leading you into the spiritual arena.[12]

Strong stuff! Most would agree. Theodore of Mopsuestia also treats this anointing as the moment of decision. The Christian is marked like a soldier, tattooed indelibly when he enlists; he is also (to mix metaphors) like a lamb, branded by his new owner. The oil glistens on his forehead. The devil takes fright.[13] But there is more to come.

In the Syrian tradition (in which, by and large, pre-baptismal anointing is everything) this first anointing is followed by a total anointing (i.e. the candidate is stripped and oil is poured or rubbed over every part of his or her anatomy).[14] At Milan this is the first anointing, and Ambrose, familiar with athletics in the Greco-Roman world, wastes no time in explaining that this is just what any athlete preparing for wrestling or combat would do. How much more so the Christian preparing to do battle with the forces of evil.[15] This theme of arming for the contest is almost universally accepted by other commentators. But in the Eastern Church there is a deeper significance. Chrysostom sees the total anointing as a defence of every organ of the body against the onslaughts of the devil.[16] Cyril of Jerusalem, after explaining that this flooding with olive oil makes the new Christian part of the true olive tree that is Christ, then goes on to say what one suspects the candidates really want to know – namely that

> the effect [of total anointing] is to disperse every concentration of the cosmic forces arrayed against you . . . for this exorcised olive oil receives through prayer and the invocation of God power so great as not only to burn and purge away the traces of sin but also put to rout all the invisible forces of the Evil One.[17]

As we shall see, this is what blessed or exorcism oil was believed to effect when used on occasions other than baptism – not magic, but certainly very necessary and indeed powerful. Theodore believes the same, but he adds another theological dimension – namely, that total anointing means total salvation (rather like Gregory of Nazianzus' assertion about the incarnations that Christ had to assume a total human nature in order to redeem the lot – 'that which is not assumed is not redeemed'). He wrote:

> You are anointed all over your body as a sign that unlike the covering used as a garment, which does not always cover all the parts of the body, because although it may cover all the external limbs, it by no means covers the internal ones – all our nature will put on immortality at the time of the resurrection and all that is seen in us, whether internal or external, will undoubtedly be changed into incorruptibility according to the working of the Holy Spirit which shall then be with us.[18]

Thus, a little 'Channel-swimmer like', the candidates approached the font and were immersed three times, confessing their faith in Father, Son and Spirit, sometimes in the words of the baptismal creed. They emerged, were clothed in new white garments and, in Syria, went straight into the assembly to be welcomed and to take part for the first time and fully in the Eucharist. In other places – Rome, Milan, Jerusalem, for example – water baptism was followed by a further anointing. 'So you were immersed and you came to the priest,' says St Ambrose. 'What did he say to you? "God the Father Almighty, who has brought you to a new birth through water and the Holy Spirit and has forgiven your sins, himself anoints you into eternal life." See where the anointing has brought you: "to eternal life" he says.' And then, following the Roman tradition (as in, for example, Hippolytus), there is a 'sealing' (presumably another anointing by the *sacerdos* (= bishop)). 'For after the ceremonies of the font,' wrote Ambrose, 'it still remains to bring the whole to perfect fulfilment. This happens when the Holy Spirit is infused at the priest's [i.e. bishop's] invocation' (giving the seven gifts of the Spirit).[19] Cyril of Jerusalem also knows this tradition of a post-baptismal anointing. He wrote that, as Christ after his baptism in the Jordan was 'anointed' by the descent of the Spirit, so Christians, emerging from the font, are anointed with chrism:

> He bathed in the river Jordan and after imparting the fragrance of His Godhead to the waters, came up from them. Him the Holy Spirit visited in essential presence (i.e. personally or hypostatically), like resting upon like. Similarly for you, after you had ascended from the sacred streams, there was an anointing with chrism, the antitype of that with which Christ was anointed, that is of the Holy Spirit. . . . Christ was anointed with the mystical oil of gladness; that is, with the Holy Spirit, called 'oil of gladness' because He is the cause of spiritual gladness. So you, being anointed with ointment, have become partakers and fellows of Christ.[20]

There is much here for the catechist and the father in God. Anointing is for the conflict; anointing is a form of 'sealing' or 'confirming'; anointing is a sign of identification with Christ whereby all those so admitted become *chrestoi* (i.e. Christ's anointed ones); anointing makes Christians 'kings' and 'priests' (those who conquer, those who know God); anointing marks the Christian as belonging to and having enlisted with Christ; anointing is the sign of the coming of the Spirit; anointing with olive oil grafts the Christian into the true olive tree which is Christ. And so we could continue.

A later generation, however, will ask, 'Is anointing essential to the rite of initiation?' If, as some patristic sources suggest, the Holy Spirit is actually given either in the post-baptismal anointing or in the episcopal laying on of hands with anointing (or in both), then it has to be said that a rite of baptism that does not include anointings is in some way deficient.[21] To this it has to be replied first that the contemporary theology of all Christian Churches declares that to pour water on the candidate three times in the name of the Trinity is sufficient to be assured of that person's regeneration, membership of Christ, and ultimate hope of salvation.[22] And second, an examination of some patristic accounts of the ceremonies of baptism reveals that though the post-baptismal anointing is often paralleled with Christ's 'anointing by the Spirit' after baptism in the Jordan, in fact there is throughout this period a very strong theology of the location of the Holy Spirit in the waters of baptism, and an equally strong sense that water baptism imparts the life-giving Spirit as much as any other part of the rite. Theodore, for example, can write:

> After these things . . . you descend into the water which has been consecrated by the benediction of the priest, as you are not baptised only with ordinary water, but with the water of the second birth which cannot become so except through the coming of the Holy Spirit on it. For this it is necessary that the priest should have beforehand made use of clear words, according to the rite of the priestly service and asked God that the grace of the Holy Spirit might come on the water and impart to it the power both of conceiving that awe inspiring child and becoming a womb to the sacramental birth.[23]

The rite – in other words, preparation, promise, water baptism, anointing, reception into the Christian community, welcoming at the Eucharist – is an entirety, a whole. Throughout, God makes us his own; throughout he gives us himself. And all the signs – water, prayer, anointing, blessing, the bread and wine of the Eucharist – are the means and the way to the new life promised to and experienced by those who have discovered the Christian calling.

Anointing and healing

Baptism and healing

Christianity, as has often been said, is a religion of wholeness. Unlike some of its contemporaries in the religious scene of the Roman Empire, it held that the material world was the good creation of a good God, and that its only defects were the result of human sin and what St Paul calls 'the mystery of iniquity'; and that the whole, material and spiritual, body and soul, was redeemable and would ultimately be redeemed. That is why God became incarnate, taking a whole and real human nature in order to redeem the whole of human nature. And it was this whole human nature that he finally redeemed by taking us body and soul through death into the new life of the resurrection.

Christians coming to baptism were told that they were about to enter into this new life.[24] The past was now the past, the misspent youth was over. Something better lay ahead – not necessarily easier, but certainly better, healthier. They were now armed for the task of opposing and defeating the evil in the world, the evil in themselves. And belonging as they did to a world that closely associated disease and sickness with demonic powers, following as they did the Son of God who in his life on earth demonstrated the power of God over evil by healing the sick and raising the dead, it is understandable that they should associate in the first instance God's power to heal with Christ's victory over sin and death, a victory in which they themselves shared through baptism. Baptism, in the language of some of the Fathers, 'stops the rot', bestows incorruption – even immortality.[25] For Athanasius, we are rescued from the downhill path of corruption (*phthora*) by Christ, the Word of God, our Creator who by his personal indwelling puts us back on the path of incorruption (*aphthora*).[26] For Augustine, we are rescued by Christ the Good Samaritan from our hopeless state on the side of life's road, taken to the inn of the Church and supplied with the two sacraments of baptism and the Eucharist.[27] Baptism is the beginning of our redemption; baptism is to do with our healing.

For in a sense the whole 'run up' to baptism is to do with healing and renewal. The past is difficult to shed, there has to be training of mind and body. The Christian has to be fit; he is compared to an athlete, and the anointing is the symbol of this vocation.[28] And it is this association of anointing with life and health and fitness that relates the baptismal anointing to the more complex problems of the sick: those people whom contemporary medicine could not reach, and for whom the Christian community had special care through prayer and what was later to be known as the sacrament of healing. The Lord, after all, as Irenaeus explains, came not to call the righteous to repentance, but sinners instead. 'How then shall the sick be strengthened, or how shall sinners come to repentance? Is it by persevering in the same old course? Surely it is by undergoing a great change and reversal of their former way of life, by which they have brought upon themselves no slight amount of sickness and many sins.'[29]

Health and holiness

The ancient world is rich in stories of healing and healers. Christians who a century ago attempted to prove the divinity of Christ by referring to the miracles he performed would in the first century have had the rug pulled from under their feet by pagan authorities who knew as many and more miracles wrought by others who made less extravagant claims than those Christ's disciples made for him. Since time immemorial, peoples of all civilizations have had recourse to healers. In the Greek world, from Asclepius to Empedocles (the latter had admittedly claimed to be the incarnation of a god) ailments had been cured by religious and cultic means from sores in the foot to arthritis in the hip; the dead had even been raised. Within the Jewish tradition itself, one of the normal responsibilities of the Rabbi was to cast out demons;[30] and the Hebrew Scriptures represent healing by the holy and prophetic as normal and expected. Jesus therefore stands in a well-recognized tradition. Like the prophets and holy men before him, he carries what we should call a self-authenticating authority, his deeds being clearly 'wrought in God', signs of God's power and (in the context of his mission) signs of the kingdom of God. And it seems only natural that when his followers embark on their proclamation of the kingdom, there should be (in Mark's words) 'signs following'[31], that is, healing and the raising of the dead. All this is borne out by Luke's account of the Acts of the Apostles.

It is to be expected therefore that early Christian apologetic should claim that among all their many occupations, Christians are active far more genuinely and realistically than pagans (or indeed heretics) in the healing of the sick. Irenaeus, for example, writing in the late second century, claims that, unlike the Gnostics, 'those who are in truth His disciples, receiving grace from Him, do in His Name perform miracles, so as to promote the welfare of other men, according to the gift which each one has received from Him. For some do certainly and truly drive out devils . . . others still, heal the sick by laying their hands upon them, and they are made whole. Yea, moreover, as I have said, the dead even have been raised up, and remained among us for many years. . . .'[32]

Who did the healing? Who had the gifts? (for the gifts of healing are distinctive and personal). It would be easy to say that the gifts belonged to the apostles and to those whom they authorized – that it was a traditionally clerical affair. But the evidence does not bear this out. Most of the accounts of healing in the first four centuries take us to a holy man, monk or ascetic, desert dweller or pillar saint, only very occasionally a bishop or priest, but in all cases a person recognized by society, Christian and non-Christian, as an authority in matters religious, personal, social and (sometimes) political. Take for example the Abba Benjamin, whose life is described by Palladius in the *Historia Lausiaca*: 'In this mountain of Nitria, there was an admirable man called Benjamin, who had lived uprightly and virtuously till his eightieth year. When he had reached the peak of virtuous living, he was considered worthy of the gift of healing, so that on whomsoever he laid hands or to whom he gave oil that he had blessed, were freed from every sickness.'[33] Benjamin's authority to heal was his recognized holiness of life, though the outward signs used in the healing are prayer, the laying on of hands and anointing.

Palladius tells another story, this time about the Abba Macarius:

But at the time that we were there with St Macarius, there was brought to him from Thessalonica a noble and wealthy virgin who during many years had been suffering from paralysis. And when she had been presented to him, and had been thrown down before the cell of the blessed man, he, being moved with compassion for her, with his own hands anointed her during twenty days with holy oil, pouring out prayers for her to the Lord, and so sent her back cured to her own city.[34]

Similar stories are told by Rufinus about disciples of St Antony healing a man with a wasting disease by total anointing, and by Sulpicius Severus about St Martin pouring holy oil, which he had blessed, down the throat of a paralysed girl, and curing a dumb girl by means of the same kind of infusion. Jerome tells us about Hilarion blessing oil which cured the snakebites of farmers and farmhands during rainfall after a sudden drought; and Rufinus once more relates how John of Lycopolis healed a senator's wife from blindness by sending her a phial of oil blessed by himself. All of these cures are related directly to the outstanding holiness of the healer. But the importance of blessed oil is becoming increasingly apparent.[35]

The blessing of oil

Hippolytus in *The Apostolic Tradition* records that just before the time for baptism the bishop 'gives thanks' over one jar of oil (which is called thereafter 'the Oil of Thanksgiving') and 'exorcizes' another (then called 'the Oil of Exorcism'). But provision is also made for the blessing of oil brought by the people.

'If anyone offers oil', he writes, 'let the bishop give thanks over it in the same way that he gives thanks for the offering of bread and wine; and let him do this not in exactly the same words, but in the same sense, saying: "In the same way, O Lord, may you in blessing this oil, give holiness to those who are anointed with it and to those who receive it, this oil with which you have anointed kings and priests and prophets; and may it give strength to those who taste it, and health to those who use it" '.[36]

We know very little about the use to which this blessed oil was put. Health and healing come last in the list (it is important here to note that Hippolytus writes first about *sanctitas* and only at the very end of his account about *sanitas*). But the fact remains that the oil is offered by the faithful and then, presumably, taken away for private use.

This fits well with the other evidence we have for the use of oil in a private capacity. Sometimes the oil is blessed by a person of recognized authority (a bishop or holy man). We've seen that Sulpicius Severus records that St Martin first blessed oil and then poured it into the mouth of a paralysed girl; he did the same for a girl born dumb.[37] But perhaps more indicative of local custom is the statement that 'the wife of the Count Avitian had sent some oil to Martin that he might bless it (*such is the custom*) so as to be ready when needful to meet different causes of disease.'[38] This taking home of oil for private consumption or application seems to have been widespread. John Chrysostom writes of the benefit of oil taken from church lamps[39] and taken from the martyrs' shrines;[40] others of oil filtered through relics or contained in compartments in crucifixes, sanctified in all these ways for the fundamental purpose of healing and driving away demons.[41] Cyril of Jerusalem is quite convinced that oil, once blessed, is no ordinary oil: 'Beware of supposing' he writes, 'that this ointment is merely ointment. Just as after the invocation of the Holy Spirit the eucharistic bread is no longer ordinary bread but the Body of Christ, so this holy oil in conjunction with the invocation is no longer simple or common oil, but becomes the gracious gift of Christ and the Holy Spirit, producing the advent of his deity.'[42] A powerful remedy, and therefore sought after and used by the faithful and the desperate. Only competent authority could bless (bishop, martyr, holy man); but almost anyone could, in good faith, use and apply.

When we come therefore to more extended prayers for the blessing of oil in the sacramentaries we can expect fuller reference to the needs for which oils were blessed (over and above their use in baptism and confirmation). In *Apostolic Constitutions*, for example, the oil that is offered by the people is blessed as follows:

> Do thou now sanctify this water and this oil through Christ in the name of him that offered or of her that offered, and give to these things a power of producing health and driving away diseases, of putting to flight demons and of dispersing every snare through Christ our hope. . . .[43]

In Egypt, there is an even more explicit prayer:

> We invoke thee who hast all authority and power, the Saviour of all men, Father of our Lord and Saviour Jesus Christ, and we pray thee to send out a healing power of the Only begotten from heaven upon this oil, that it may become to those who are being anointed with it or are partaking of these thy creatures, for a throwing off of every disease, and every infirmity, for a prophylactic against every demon, for a separation of every unclean spirit, for an expulsion of every evil spirit, for a driving out of all fever and shivering fit, and every infirmity, for good grace and remission of sins, for a medicine of life and recovery, for health and soundness in all their parts of soul, body, spirit, for perfect strengthening. O Master, let every Satanic opera-

tion, every demon, every snare of the adversary, every plague, stroke or shaking or evil shadow fear thy Holy Name which we have now invoked and the Name of the Only Begotten; and let them depart from the inward and outward parts of these thy servants.[44]

As in Egypt, so in Syria. The *Testamentum Domini*, a later fourth- or early fifth-century compilation, has a special blessing of oils after the eucharistic liturgy, praying that the oil so blessed may 'deliver those who labour and heal those who are sick and sanctify those who return when they approach to thy faith . . .'[45] Here too, water is blessed for the purpose of healing; Sarepion includes a similar blessing of water ('Let the bishop bless the water or the oil. . . . Do thou now sanctify this water and this oil. . . .'). It is clear too that Christians are being encouraged to resort to this kind of ministration in their sickness rather than to the many alternatives offered in the pagan world. Cyril of Alexandria, for example, says that it is much better to invoke the name of the 'Lord of Sabaoth' than to resort to sorcerers;[46] and Caesarius of Arles says that it is much better to come to the church to receive two 'good things . . . health of body and remission of sins' rather than resorting to 'fountains and trees and diabolical phylacteries and the branding of magical marks on the body and by consulting diviners and soothsayers and fortune tellers.' And then, in another sermon, he continues:

> How much better and more salutary it would be that people should run to the church and receive the Body and Blood of Christ and should with faith anoint themselves and the members of their household with consecrated oil; and according to the statement of the Apostle James, receive not only health of body but also remission of sins.[47]

By the end of the fifth century, therefore, the use of oil, duly blessed or consecrated, for the rites and processes of healing was an accepted part of church life. This must have appeared to those learned in medicine like something of a para-medical provision. It had however a foundation in the rational order and was much more carefully controlled than the more 'back street' alternatives to scientific medicine which flourished for the desperate in the pagan world.

Summary

Of the Christian ministry of healing, therefore, it can be said that:

a) There was a clear authority about who might or might not bless the oils. The oil of the sick in the first five centuries was, so far as we can tell, blessed primarily by the bishop, possibly by a presbyter and occasionally by a holy man of the desert. Other authorities include the relics of martyrs (for example, St Laurence at Rome, through whose remains the faithful poured oil and tapped it out as it emerged, taking it home for healing); crucifixes containing relics and a compartment for the oils; and, at the bottom end of the scale (if absolutely stuck), oil from the lamps in church was considered better than oil from lamps in the street.[48]

(b) The oil could be administered by bishop, presbyter or layman. The evidence suggests that there was a good deal of 'do-it-yourself' anointing during this period. Phials of oil are passed from holy man to distressed woman, from monk-bishop to the terminally sick. From at least the third century onwards oil is brought by the people to the bishop for blessing; and it is taken home for use in any serious necessity. Pope Innocent I in the fifth century tells Decentius, bishop of Eugubium, that oil consecrated by the bishop is 'lawful not for the priests only but for all Christians to use for anointing in their own need or in the need of members of their household.' St James, he continues, writes of presbyters performing the rites of healing; but this (he conjectures) was because bishops would not normally have time to visit all the sick. This does not preclude bishops from blessing the sick and 'touching them with the chrism'. But all Christians may share in this ministry and use the same consecrated oil.[49]

(c) There is a strong connexion in all these early accounts of healing between holiness, renewal of life and repentance. Those who approached the holy man in the desert, would probably tremble before him as he searched their soul, knowing that he would demand some kind of amendment of life or promise before dealing with their sickness. But the long-established connection between spiritual disorder and physical disability meant that the forgiveness of sins was intimately bound up with the grace of healing. As Bede was to write in the early eighth century:

> . . . when they anoint the sick man, they ought to invoke the name of the Lord over him: 'And if he be in sins, they shall be remitted to him'. Many, because of sins committed in the soul, are smitten with bodily sickness or even death. . . . If therefore the sick be in sins and shall have confessed these to the presbyters of the Church and shall have set to work with single heart to relinquish and amend them, they shall be remitted to them'.[50]

(d) The rite is beginning to be considered sacramental. Blessed oil is certainly not ordinary oil. And when Innocent I is asked whether consecrated oil can be given to those who are temporarily excommunicate (i.e. the penitents) he answers 'No', because the rite of healing is a '*genus sacramenti*' (a kind of sacrament) and like the other sacraments should not be given to the excommunicate.

(e) Finally, the provision of oil, duly blessed, for the healing of the sick seems to be more or less universal from the third century onwards, and its actual use and significance more clearly detailed as the centuries progress. There is a curious reluctance during this period to relate the text of James 5 explicitly to any rite of healing. We find this association in both Caesarius of Arles and in Bede, but what to us seems obvious as a clear scriptural warrant is not the peg the Fathers use to hang their theology of anointing and healing. The Fathers believe profoundly in the power of prayer, repentance, exorcism and baptism (with its anointings) to heal the misdirected life and sickness of soul. They believe equally profoundly in the power of prayer, holiness and anointing with oil to heal the sick in both body and soul. But to the end of the patristic period there is no actual rite or form known to us which gathers the presbyters round the bed of the sick and provides a text for their use. No doubt the presbyters did gather, no doubt bishops and faithful also assembled. But there was a breadth, a generous latitude, to the use of holy oil in the age of the Fathers which was only lost when the sacrament of anointing itself became restricted to those whose sickness was deemed incurable and demanded a ritual preparation for purgatory and beyond.

A note on the anointing of the dead

'The dead also are anointed' states Clement of Alexandria in the *Paedagogus*. The anointing of the dead is thereafter nowhere referred to in patristic literature until the *Ecclesiastical Hierarchy* of Dionysius the Areopagite. After describing in considerable detail the rite of consecrating the holy oil (in this case, the chrism) which, by this account, is used in almost all the ceremonies of the hierarchy, he says much about its symbolism but little about its use. From other passages in the *Ecclesiastical Hierarchy* it is clear that the oil is used in initiation (at the point of Confirmation, as understood in the western church) but not for the sick or dying, nor in the rites of ordination. It is however used for the anointing of the dead.

'After the kiss of peace,' he writes, 'the bishop anoints the body of the dead with holy oil. You will remember that in the ceremony of birth from God it is, before baptism, by anointing with holy oil that the initiate is permitted for the first time to participate in the sacred symbol immediately after he has been stripped of his former dress. Now, on the contrary, it is at the end of all that holy oil is poured out over the dead. Then the sacred anointing summoned the initiate to a holy warfare; now the pouring of the oil signifies that in this combat, he has fought to victory.'

Notes

1. Hippolytus, *Philosophumena* 5.21.
2. Clement of Alexandria gives a full but rather disapproving account of the secular use of oil in cooking, cosmetics and medicine, in *Paedogogus* 2.8.
3. cf. Theodore the Studite, *Canones de confessione et satisfactione*, 6.
4. And in churches – cf. *Canones Apostolorum* 3.
5. Examples of all these in Clement, *Paedogogus*, 4.
6. For a study of the oil harvest in North Africa and the association of casual labour for the harvest with the Circumcellions, see W. H. C. Frend, *The Donatist Church*, Oxford 1955. s.v.
7. Augustine, *Enarratio in Psalm* 80.1.
8. Origen, *Hom. in Lev.*, 2.4; *Hom. in Luc.* 10.4, and K. Rahner, *Theological Investigations XV* (ET London 1983), pp. 246ff.
9. Cyril of Jerusalem, *Mystagogical Catecheses* 3.7, referring to 1 John 2.27.
10. Hippolytus, *Apostolic Tradition*, ed. B. Botte, (Munster 1963) p. 47.
11. For a useful account of early Christian preparation for baptism and Lenten instruction by the bishop, see E. J. Yarnold, *The Awe Inspiring Rites of Initiation* (London 1971) (referred to as Yarnold hereafter).
12. John Chrysostom, *Baptismal Homilies* 2.24 (cited in Yarnold op. cit., p. 167).
13. Theodore of Mopsuestia, *Baptismal Homilies* 2.17 (cited in Yarnold, p. 186).
14. Chrysostom, *Baptismal Homilies* 2.24 (cited in Yarnold, p. 167).
15. Ambrose, *De Sacramentis* 1.4 (cited in Yarnold, p. 167).
16. Chrysostom, *Baptismal Homilies* 2.24 (cited in Yarnold, p. 167).
17. Cyril of Jerusalem, *Mystagogical Catecheses* 2.3 (cited in Yarnold, p. 75).
18. Theodore of Mopsuestia, *Baptismal Homilies* 3.8.
19. Ambrose, *De Sacramentis* 2.24 (cited in Yarnold, p. 119); cf. ibid. op. cit. Ambrose, *De Sacramentis* 3.8.
20. Cyril of Jerusalem, *Mystagogical Catecheses* 3.1 (trans. by L. P. McCauley SJ in *The Fathers of the Church* (Washington 1970)).
21. See the note by A. A. Stephenson in McCauley's translation of St Cyril (*The Fathers of the Church*) on *Mystagogical Catecheses* 3.3, 'When is the Holy Spirit given?' pp. 174ff.
22. *Codex Iuris Canonici* 1917, canon 758.
23. Theodore of Mopsuestia, *Baptismal Homilies*, ch. 4, trans. A. Mingana, Woodbrooke Studies VI (Cambridge 1933), p. 54.
24. Much of this is expressed in Cyril of Jerusalem's introductory lecture, *Procatechesis*, trans. L. P. McCauley, *The Fathers of the Church*, I, p. 69.
25. Theodore of Mopsuestia, *Baptismal Homilies*, trans. A. Mingana, Woodbrooke Studies, p. 56. 'It behoves you, therefore, to think that you are going into the water as into a furnace where you will be renewed and refashioned in order that you may move to a higher nature, after having cast away your old mortality and fully assumed an immortal and incorruptible nature.'

26. The argument of the *De incarnatione Verbi Dei*.
27. Augustine, *Sermo* 171.2.
28. Ambrose, *De Sacramentis* 1.4.
29. Irenaeus, *Adversus Haereses* III.5.2.
30. D. Daube, *The New Testament and Rabbinic Judaism* (Oxford 1955), on Mark 1.27.
31. Mark 16.20.
32. Irenaeus, *Adversus Haereses* 2,32.
33. Palladius, *Historia Lausiaca* 12.
34. ibid. 18,11. Macarius was a priest of a place called Cellia.
35. For a still very useful account of individual healers and healings with blessed oil, see F. W. Puller, *The Anointing of the Sick in Scripture and Tradition* (London 1904), pp. 149ff.
36. Hippolytus, *Apostolic Tradition*, ed. Botte, 5, p. 19.
37. Sulpicius Severus, *Dialogus* iii.2.
38. ibid. iii.3.
39. Chrysostom, Hom. 22.6. in *Matth*.
40. Chrysostom, *Panegyrica in Martyres* 2.
41. Eustratius of Constantinople, *Vita Eucychii* 45.
42. Cyril of Jerusalem, *Mystagogical Catecheses* III.3.
43. *Apostolic Constitutions* 8,29.
44. Sarepion of Thmuis, *Euchologion* 17.
45. *Testamentum Domini*, ed. and tr. Cooper and Maclean (Oxford 1902), pp. 77–8.
46. Cyril of Alexandria, *De Adoratione* 6.
47. *Sermo* CCLXV, 3 (in appendix to *Sermones S. Augustini*, PL XXXIX, 2238).
48. See above and entry under Ἔλαιον in G. W. H. Lampe, *A Patristic Greek Lexicon*.
49. Innocent I, *Epistola ad Decentium* 8.
50. Bede, *Historia ecclesiastica Gentis Anglorum*.
51. Text quoted in D. Rutledge *Cosmic Theology: The Ecclesiastical Hierarchy of Pseudo-Denys: an Introduction* (London 1964), p. 199. cf. pp. 119ff. for an account of Dionysius' mystical theology as expressed in his description of the rite of the consecration of holy oil.

7

Anointing in the Syriac Tradition

Sebastian Brock

Introduction

Olive oil plays an important role in all the Oriental Christian rites; but here the Syriac tradition is selected since it alone has the merit of comprising all three ecclesiastical traditions of the Christian East, namely: (i) the Church of the East (often misleadingly called 'Nestorian'), (ii) the Maronite and (until the Middle Ages) the Melkite Churches, both accepting the Council of Chalcedon, and (iii) the Syrian Orthodox Church (often misleadingly called Monophysite, or Jacobite). In the Syriac Churches the oil to be used is always specified as olive oil, and the rich symbolism implicit in the olive and its oil is particularly well brought out by St Ephrem (*d*.373) in his Hymns of Virginity nos 4–7.[1] Although the oil must be pure olive oil, it may be subsequently mixed with a fragrant element, thus constituting 'myron'; until about the thirteenth or fourteenth century this fragrant element was balsam, but subsequently, under the influence of the Coptic practice, based on Exod. 30.22ff., a whole variety of such elements was used. (Elsewhere among the Oriental Orthodox Churches, in those areas where the olive does not grow, oil from other sources may be used; thus, for example, sesame oil among the Armenians.)

Although it is primarily in the context of baptism (where there is a plethora of anointings) that oil is employed, it also features in a number of other liturgical contexts, notably the anointing of the sick, of the newly departed, and in the consecration of churches and altars.

Originally the oil employed would be blessed in the course of a prayer within the service where it was to be used, and in some cases this still applies, but more frequently the oil will have been blessed prior to use by a metropolitan or the patriarch. Essentially in the prayers for the blessing of the oil God is asked to 'sanctify' the oil – that is, bring it into the sphere of the sacred so that the Holy Spirit may act through it (see next paragraph). The oil thus sanctified is called by a variety of different names, such as 'oil (or horn) of anointing', 'oil of prayer', 'oil of grace', 'oil of joy' or 'myron'; in theory, these different terms refer to different uses, but in practice over the course of time there has developed considerable confusion over the terminology, though 'myron' applies only to oil to which some fragrant substance has been added.

Oil and the Holy Spirit

In one of his hymns on the symbolism of the olive and its oil, St Ephrem states that 'this oil is the dear friend of the Holy Spirit, it serves Her, following Her like a disciple' (*H. de Virginitate* 7.6; the Holy Spirit is grammatically feminine in early Syriac literature).[2] The close association between the Spirit and the oil (*meshha*) is further brought out where the relationship between the three Persons of the Trinity is expressed using the terms Anointer (*mashoha*), Anointed (*mshiha* – Messiah, Christ), and Anointment (*meshha*).

In order for the oil to play an effective role as 'friend' and servant of the Spirit, it needs to be 'empowered' by the same Spirit, and thus be brought into the realm of the sacred. Such prayers, requesting the sanctification of the oil, are already found in a baptismal context in the Acts of Thomas (third century); the key phrases in such prayers take on the form of an epiklesis or invocation, as can be seen from the following two examples:

> . . . may Your Power come from the supernal heights and reside in this oil, and may there be depicted in it the mysteries (or, symbols) of your Christ . . . (Maronite baptismal service; the wording reflects Luke 1.35).

> . . . may the grace from the gift of the Holy Spirit . . . come and be mingled in this oil . . . may it reside and tabernacle over this oil, blessing and sanctifying it . . . (Church of the East, baptismal service).

Once it has been thus 'empowered' or sanctified, the oil can in turn become a vehicle for sanctification. As John, Bishop of Mardin in the mid-twelfth century pointed out when talking of the myron,[3] 'The nature of the oil and of the (fragrant) plants, does not possess the power, since the mysteries depicted belong to the Holy Spirit; rather, it is the power and the overshadowing of the Holy Spirit which comes through the pure prayers of the holy bishops over them.'

Baptism

The multiplicity of anointings that characterizes especially the West Syrian baptismal rites (i.e. Syrian Orthodox, Maronite and Melkite) is the result of various duplications that have taken place in the course of the development of the rite. The earliest form of the baptismal rite in the Syrian area was remarkable for the absence of any post-baptismal anointing. Probably in origin the rite had just a single pre-baptismal anointing, known as the *rushma*, or 'mark'. This 'mark' was associated with a number of different meanings,[4] but the two that emerged as the most important seem to have been (i) ownership, with the newly baptized often described as 'lambs' entering the flock of Christ (early texts often see the baptismal 'mark' as replacing the Jewish rite of circumcision); and (ii) adoption as children, authorizing the newly baptized to address God as 'Father'. The 'mark' usually took the form of a cross on the forehead (reflecting the cross-shaped *tau* of Ezek. 9.4, where the Syriac Old Testament indeed has the term *rushma*).

In some areas, perhaps those more exposed to the bathing practices of the Greek world, this pre-baptismal anointing of the forehead was supplemented by a second pre-baptismal anointing, this time of the entire body, coming immediately before the baptism proper.

This pattern of one, or two, pre-baptismal anointings, and no post-baptismal one, was evidently operative in the whole of the Syrian area until towards the very end of the fourth century (though in some places this original practice continued well into the fifth century, or even later). The presence of a post-baptismal anointing is first attested in the Syrian region in the Apostolic Constitutions, and the innovation was no doubt the result of the influence of the liturgical practices of other regions, perhaps especially those of Jerusalem. Since the pre-baptismal anointings were nevertheless kept, a certain amount of ambiguity arose over the meanings and symbolism attached to the different anointings,[5] although the term 'myron' (unknown in the earlier Syriac texts) was exclusively reserved for the post-baptismal anointing.[6]

The structure of the various West Syrian baptismal rites used today was probably more or less fixed by the end of the sixth century, with separate terms used in the formulas accompanying each of the anointings;[7] thus, schematically, we have:

preliminary rites:
first pre-baptismal anointing
> 'N is marked (*metrshem*)'; on forehead;

blessing of font
second pre-baptismal anointing
> 'N is anointed (*metmshaḥ*)'; whole body;

baptism
post-baptismal anointing
> 'N is imprinted (*metṭbaʿ*)'; organs of senses.

(The second pre-baptismal anointing is not present in all the services; thus, for example, it is absent from the Syrian Orthodox 'Tagrit rite' of Iraq, which is also employed in the Syrian Orthodox Church in India. In the Church of the East, however, the anointing in this position is the main one.)

Oil (usually termed 'holy oil' or, in the later West Syrian tradition, 'myron') has yet a further role in the Syrian rites, both Eastern and Western, for some is poured into the font towards the end of the series of prayers requesting the sanctification of the water. The accompanying prayer in the Syrian Orthodox rite links this pouring of the myron on the water with the appearance of the Holy Spirit in the form of a dove over Christ at his baptism, thus emphasizing the close associations in sacred time between the Jordan waters at Christ's baptism and those of the font at Christian baptism. Similar resonances are to be found in the Maronite rite where the priest declares:[8]

> The Myron descends visibly,
> the Holy Spirit invisibly;
> the baptismal font is sanctified
> by Spirit, Fire and Water.

('Fire' and 'Water' will refer to the Jordan water which, according to an early tradition already known to Justin Martyr, caught fire at Christ's descent into it; this water is effectively united in sacred time with the baptismal water.)

Other Syrian baptismal services link the pouring of the holy oil on to the water with the effects that baptism will have; thus in the East Syrian rite the priest proclaims:

> This water is marked, sanctified, and mingled with the holy oil,
> so that it may become a new womb giving birth spiritually in
> baptism . . .

Originally in the Syrian baptismal rites the oil was sanctified by the priest in the course of the service, immediately prior to its use, and this is the pattern still preserved in the Church of the East; it is also found in the oldest forms of the Melkite and Maronite rites.[9]

Subsequently in the West Syrian rites the practice altered, and the oils would be sanctified separately; normally this would be the prerogative of the bishop (the practice of doing this on Holy Thursday was introduced by Bishop Peter of Edessa at the very end of the fifth century).[10] In the canons of John of Mardin (mid-twelfth century) it is specified that the bishop should sanctify the myron once a year, together with the 'oil of anointing' and the 'oil of prayer' (this last for anointing the sick);[11] Barhebraeus (*d.* 1286), however, in his Nomocanon (which is still the standard Syrian Orthodox guide on such matters),[12] limits the sanctification of the myron to metropolitans, the Catholicos or the Patriarch (Nomocanon III.1); he also states that, whereas the sanctification of the myron takes place on Holy Thursday (III.4), the rite for the 'oil of anointing' (i.e. for the pre-baptismal anointings) takes place on Wednesday in mid-Lent (III.5). In his section on the myron Barhebraeus also provides a paragraph (III.3) with instructions for the preparation of 'fragrant oil', using a variety of different fragrant spices; it was this elaborate preparation that subsequently became the norm for myron, and its sanctification the role prerogative of the Patriarch (no longer performed annually).[13]

Anointing of the sick

A common title of Christ in Syriac literature is 'the Wise Doctor, or Physician' who heals both physical and spiritual illnesses. The medium by which this healing is effected is above all in the baptismal oil, the occasion when 'bodies are anointed for forgiveness' (Ephrem, *H. de Virginitate* 7.7). Many early texts indeed associate the spiritual healing from sin that baptism brings about with physical healing as well, and this is still reflected in the phraseology used in connection with the oil in some of the baptismal rites; thus, for example, in the Maronite rite (which contains many archaic features) the deacon prays that the oil, once sanctified, may 'drive out sicknesses, both hidden and manifest'.

This double aspect of the healing properties of oil, duly sanctified, accounts for the use of oil not only for the anointing of the sick (in accordance with Jas. 5.4), but also for its use in some penitential contexts as well.

To judge by scattered allusions, the earliest practice was for the priest to sanctify the oil when required for anointing the sick[14] (the actual anointing could be done by deacons, or, with women, by deaconesses); in the course of the early Middle Ages, however, the 'oil of prayer' would be sanctified beforehand by the local bishop and distributed for use by his clergy. The various collections of canon law regularly distinguish this 'oil of prayer' from the myron used in baptism,[15] but there is disagreement over whether or not it is the same as the baptismal 'oil of anointing'; several earlier texts do separate the two,[16] but it seems likely that in practice this distinction was not always made, and in Barhebraeus' Nomocanon (III.5) it is specifically stated that the oil used for the anointing of the sick is the same as the 'oil of anointing' used in the pre-baptismal anointings.

Towards the end of the Middle Ages a formal rite (of Coptic provenance) was developed in the Syrian Orthodox Church, known as the rite of the Candle (Qandil), during which the oil used is sanctified in the course of a specific prayer. This Rite of the Candle[17] is a long and elaborate service, with a markedly penitential character. In this respect (though not in others) it resembles the East Syrian Rite of Forgiveness,[18] where oil is also used, though there it is specified as being 'the holy oil of baptism'.

Since sickness may also be doctrinal, it is not surprising that anointing with oil (myron in the West Syrian tradition) features in the rite for receiving baptized members of heretical churches – or indeed, baptized members of the Church who have subsequently partaken in magic practices.[19]

In the Eastern Rite Catholic Churches of Syriac tradition (Maronite, Chaldean, Syrian Catholic, and, in India, Syro-Malabar and Syro-Malankara), where a number of liturgical uses of Latin origin have been adopted, the anointing of the sick tends to be replaced by the rite of Extreme Unction.

Other uses

(A) Consecration of churches and altars

The Old Testament practice of anointing altars was taken up again in the Church, and subsequently this was extended to include the walls of a church at its consecration. 'Dionysius the Areopagite' in his *Ecclesiastical Hierarchy* (IV.3.12) knows only the anointing of altars (with myron), but some two centuries later Jacob of Edessa (*d*.708) speaks of myron as 'perfecting churches as houses of God and appointing altars as holy and divine'.[20] Though the anointing of altars and churches is reserved for bishops, it would seem from a sixth-century collection of canons[21] that once a priest could anoint an altar.

(B) Anointing of the departed

The anointing of the dead was a widely attested practice in the ancient Orient, and so it is not surprising that it was taken over by several oriental Churches. In the Syrian Orthodox Church[22] this anointing came in the course of the Middle Ages to be confined to departed bishops, priests and deacons, while in the Church of the East[23] it disappeared from use altogether during much the same period.

(C) Miscellaneous

In the Church of the East oil is also used as an ingredient in making the eucharistic bread.[24]

Finally, it might be noted that the use of oil in ordinations is a Western practice not known to the Syriac churches outside those under Latin influence; nevertheless, in the West Syrian tradition the metaphorical use of the phrase 'anointing of priests' is preserved.[25]

Notes

1. English translation in K. E. McVey, *Ephrem the Syrian: Hymns* (New York 1989), pp. 275–96. For the general background, see S. Brock, *The Holy Spirit in the Syrian Baptismal Tradition* (Syrian Churches Series 9, 1979).
2. See S. Brock, 'The Holy Spirit as Feminine in Early Syriac Literature', in J. Martin Soskice, ed., *After Eve: Women, Theology and the Christian Tradition* (London 1990), pp. 73–88.
3. A. Vööbus, *The Synodicon in the West Syrian Tradition*, II (Corpus Scriptorum Christianorum Orientalium 375–6, 1976), p. 245 (Syriac text), p. 258 (trans.).
4. See especially G. Winkler, 'The Original Meaning of the Prebaptismal Anointing and its Implications', *Worship*, 52 (1978), pp. 24–45.
5. See S. Brock, 'The Transition to a post-baptismal anointing in the Antiochene Rite', in *The Sacrifice of Praise: Studies in Honour of A. H. Couratin* (Ephemerides Liturgicae, Subsidia 19, 1981), pp. 215–25.
6. Following the example set by 'Dionysius the Areopagite' (*Eccl. Hier.* IV), treatises on the myron and its symbolism were composed by several Syrian Orthodox writers from the seventh century onwards; cf. W. Strothmann, *Das Sakrament der Myron-Weihe in der Schrift de Ecclesiastica Hierarchia des Pseudo-Dionysios Areopagita in syrischen Übersetzungen und Kommentaren* (Göttinger Orientforschungen, 1 Reihe: Syriaca, 15, 1977), II. pp. xliii–lx. The two constituents, oil and balsam, are usually said to symbolize the 'composition' of divinity and humanity in Christ (the term corresponds to the Greek *synthesis*).
7. Details can be found in S. Brock, 'Studies in the Early History of the Syrian Orthodox Baptismal Liturgy', *Journal of Theological Studies*, ns 23 (1972), pp. 16–64.
8. A. Mouhanna, *Les rites de l'initiation dans l'église maronite* (Christianismos 1, 1978 = Orientalia Christiana Analecta 212, 1980), p. 257.
9. Translations of the prayers can be found in Brock, *The Holy Spirit in the Syrian Baptismal Tradition*, pp. 93–5.

10. W. Wright, *The Chronicle of Joshua the Stylite* (Cambridge 1882), ch. 32 ('Oil of Anointing').

11. Vööbus, *The Synodicon in the West Syrian Tradition*, II, p. 244 (Syriac text), pp. 257–8 (trans.).

12. There is a Latin translation of the Nomocanon in A. Mai, *Scriptorum Veterum Nova Collectio* X, 2 (Rome 1838).

13. See E-P. Siman, *L'Expérience de l'Esprit par l'Église d'après la tradition syrienne d'Antioche* (Théologie Historique 15, Paris 1971), pp. 97–8.

14. A prayer for this purpose is provided in the *Testamentum Domini*, ch. 24. Oil was also used for healing by hermits; see, for example, Theodoret, *A History of the Monks of Syria*, trans. R. M. Price (Kalamazoo 1985), pp. 77–8, where the hermit Aphraates' patient happens to be a horse.

15. Thus Jacob of Edessa (*d.*708) in Vööbus, *The Synodicon in the West Syrian Tradition*, I. p. 264 (Syriac text), p. 241 (trans.).

16. E.g. Vööbus, *The Synodicon in the West Syrian Tradition*, I, p. 180 (text), pp. 171–2 (trans.); II, p. 244 (Syriac text), pp. 257–8 (trans.).

17. W. de Vries, *Sakramententheologie bei den syrischen Monophysiten* (Orientalia Christiana Analecta 125, 1940), pp. 212, 217–19. There are two recent editions of the Syriac text (St Ephrem's Monastery, Glane/Losser, Holland 1985; and Mar Julius Press, Pampakuda, India, n.d.; the latter contains a facing Malayalam translation); the elaborate nature of the service, however, precludes its frequent use. It might be noted that none of the prayers for the sick in the Syrian Orthodox Manual of Prayers for Priests mentions anointing (*Ktobo da-ṣlawoto d-kohne*, ed. H. Dolapönü (Mardin 1952), pp. 105–9).

18. There is a recent edition, with French translation and a valuable study, by J. Isaac, *Ṭaksa d-Ḥussaya: Le rite du pardon dans l'Eglise syriaque orientale* (Orientalia Christiana Analecta 233, 1989); for the anointing, see pp. 68–9 and 112–13. (There is no surviving East Syrian rite for anointing the sick; see, for example, F. F. Irving, *The Ceremonial Use of Oil among the East Syrians* (Occasional Paper of The Eastern Church Association, ns 4, 1902), p. 8.)

19. An interesting example is provided by canon 19 of the East Syrian synod of AD 554: '. . . When anyone of those who have fallen into this grievous sickness (i.e. of indulging in magic practices) should repent, healing should be offered to him, just as to someone physically sick, by means of the oil of prayer which the priests bless.' For a full translation of the canon, see J. B. Chabot, *Synodicon Orientale* (Paris 1902), pp. 363–4.

20. Section 23 of my edition and translation in *Oriens Christianus*, 63 (1979), p. 36.

21. Vööbus, *The Synodicon in the West Syrian Tradition*, I, p. 164 (Syriac text), p. 158 (trans.).

22. See de Vries, *Sakramententheologie bei den syrischen Monophysiten*, pp. 213–14.

23. See W. de Vries, *Sakramententheologie bei den Nestorianern* (Orientalia Christiana Analecta 133, 1947), pp. 251–2.

24.   See E. S. Drower, *Water into Wine: A Study of Ritual Idiom in the Middle East* (London 1956), pp. 59–60 and 70.
25.   See P. Hofmeister, *Die heiligen Öle in der morgen- und abendländischen Kirche* (Das östliche Christentum nF 6/7, 1948), pp. 162–3.

Select bibliography

W. de Vries, *Sakramententheologie bei den syrischen Monophysiten* (Orientalia Christiana Analecta 125, 1940).

W. de Vries, *Sakramententheologie bei den Nestorianern* (Orientalia Christiana Analecta 133, 1947).

P. Hofmeister, *Die heiligen Öle in der morgen- und abendländischen Kirche* (Das östliche Christentum nF 6/7, 1948).

F. F. Irving, *The Ceremonial Use of Oil among the East Syrians* (Occasional Paper of The Eastern Church Association, ns 4, 1902).

L. L. Mitchell, *Baptismal Anointing* (Alcuin Club Collections 48, 1966).

8

The Use of the Holy Oils in the Orthodox Churches of the Byzantine Tradition

Christine Hall

Oil is used extensively in the liturgical life of the Orthodox Churches. Every Orthodox Christian is an anointed person, for anointing is an integral part of the rites of Christian initiation, the Holy Mysteries of baptism and chrismation.

The oil of baptism, called 'the oil of joy', the 'anointing of incorruption' and 'the life-giving anointing', is blessed during the baptismal rite itself and is used only in that particular celebration of the rite. The holy chrism is blessed by a patriarch or metropolitan with his fellow-bishops on Holy Thursday. It is called 'the heavenly anointing', 'the chrism of [Christ's] Godhead', and 'the seal of the gift of the Holy Spirit'; and, in addition to its use for chrismation, it is used to consecrate altars and antimensia, and to anoint monarchs – although, for obvious political reasons, this last use is becoming more infrequent.

During the Liturgy of the Holy Maslu, olive oil is blessed for the anointing of the sick and referred to as 'the oil of his suffering'. Any oil left over from the anointing is baked into a cake and given to the sick to eat.

Apart from its use in the Holy Mysteries, olive oil has other uses in Orthodox practice. The oil that has burnt in the icon lamps is used by the priest, particularly in the Romanian tradition, to make the sign of the cross on the foreheads of the congregation at the end of the Holy Liturgy and other services. During the four canonical fasts of the year, foods of animal origin (meat, fish, eggs, cheese and milk), wine and oil are generally omitted from the diet. Wine and oil, and more rarely fish, are reintroduced on certain specified days during the fasting periods. Olive oil is also used as a purifier, to wipe the bodies of non-monastic priests and deacons, in preparation for burial.[1] These uses of oil owe their origin to the practices of the early Church.

The oil of baptism and the holy chrism

In accordance with ancient usage, it is Orthodox practice to administer holy baptism and chrismation as an integrated sacrament,[2] to recognize the person thus initiated as a full member of the Church and to admit them, however young they may be, to Holy Communion. Orthodoxy has no rite of confirmation separated from baptism-chrismation, nor is the anointing with the holy chrism normally repeated,[3] as it is in the Roman pattern of Christian initiation. When the Orthodox Church receives a baptized convert (that is, someone who has already been baptized by three total immersions or by the triple pouring of water on the head in the name of the three Persons of the Holy Trinity, but who has not been chrismated), chrismation is usually carried out, together with other parts of the Orthodox baptismal liturgy (notably the exorcisms) which did not form part of the rite by which the convert was baptized.

The baptismal liturgy in current use in the Orthodox Churches is a combination of rites, some of which were separate in earlier usage, as the following outline indicates.

Rite for the making of a catechumen

- Prayers for the making of a catechumen
- Exorcisms
- Declaration (three times) of association with Christ and recitation (three times) of the Niceno-Constantinopolitan Creed by the candidate (or the sponsor, if the candidate is a child)

This rite is essentially a rite of preparation for baptism. It takes place in front of the church doors or in the narthex, because the unbaptized person has not yet been cleansed from original sin and is not yet a member of the Church and a citizen of heaven, whose doors are opened only by baptism. Although concessions are in practice made to different cultural contexts, the rubrics instruct that the candidates should remove their outer clothes and take off their shoes, approaching bare-headed and dressed only in a shirt or tunic. After their baptism, they will be reclothed in the white garment of the illuminated; before it, they 'put off the old man and his deeds', and

imitate Christ who, naked on the cross, triumphed over the princi-
palities and powers.[4] They face the West, from which darkness
comes, for the exorcisms, then the East, where paradise was located,
from which the natural light of the sun comes and from which Christ
the true light, the dayspring from on high, rises, for the declarations
of association with him. In early church practice, catechumens who
had reached the stage of registering their names for baptism were
thereafter frequently assembled in church, so that the prayers of
exorcism might be read over them. Although this has been discon-
tinued as a separate practice, the Molitfelnic urges the priest
officiating at a baptism to take great care over the pre-baptismal rite
and to read the exorcisms slowly, up to eight or ten times,

> because it was the ancient custom of the Church, every day for a
> week, to have these prayers read by the catechizing priests and
> to have them repeated on the eighth day by the bishop or priest
> officiating at the Baptism. . . . We ourselves have seen many
> godly priests reading these prayers three times in their entirety
> and thus baptizing.[5]

Rite for holy baptism and chrismation

Once the candidate is prepared and has been taken from the dominion
of Satan and placed under the power of Christ by the confession of the
true faith, the baptismal rite proper takes place at the font, in the
centre of the church, in the following order:

- Blessing of the water
- Blessing of the oil of baptism
- Threefold signing of the water with the sign of the cross in oil
- Anointing of the candidate with the oil of baptism
- Baptism by three total immersions and emersions
- Clothing in a new garment
- Blessing and presentation of the baptismal candle
- Anointing with the holy chrism
- Encircling of the baptismal table – Epistle – Gospel
- Washing and tonsuring of the newly baptized

It is evident that the use of oil is extensive and integral to the rite.
When the priest has blessed the water of baptism and exorcized it by
three insufflations with prayers, the deacon holds the oil to be used for
the baptism and the priest blesses it by three insufflations in the form
of the cross. The prayer of blessing speaks of the dove who brought
the olive branch to Noah in the ark as a sign of reconciliation and
salvation from the flood; of the gift of the Holy Spirit, through the
olive, to those who were under the Law, and, through its oil, of the
perfecting of those who are under Grace. The priest prays:

103

Bless this oil with the power, the activity and the descent of your Holy Spirit, that it may be anointing of incorruption, armour of righteousness, renewal of soul and body, banishment of every work of the devil . . .

Then, chanting Alleluia at each sign of the cross, the priest makes three signs with oil in the baptismal water, in token of the Holy Spirit who brooded over the face of the waters before the creation of light. The anointing with oil of baptism follows immediately, and the candidate is anointed on the forehead, chest, back, ears, hands and feet, and all the joints.

After the anointing, the priest takes hold of the candidate, holding them upright, facing east, and baptizes them with three immersions and emersions. The newly baptized is then clothed in a new garment, the garment of righteousness, and their sponsor[6] is presented with the blessed baptismal candle, while the following words are sung: 'Most merciful Christ our God, who clothe yourself with light as with a garment, give to me also the garment of light'. The prayer that is then said, before the anointing with the holy chrism, emphasizes the integrity of the initiation rites:

. . . You have been pleased to give to your newly illuminated servant new birth by water and the Spirit and have forgiven all his sins, both voluntary and involuntary . . . give to him also the seal of the holy, allpowerful and worshipful Spirit, and the communion of the holy Body and the precious Blood of your Christ . . .

The newly baptized person is then anointed with the holy chrism. This is a 'holy oil' in the sense that its main ingredient is and must be pure olive oil,[7] although it contains in addition a good proportion of wine and a large number of other ingredients (plants and spices), symbolic of the manifold gifts of the Holy Spirit.

The holy chrism takes three days to prepare[8] and, once blessed on Holy Thursday by the patriarch or metropolitan of each Orthodox Church together with his whole synod of bishops, it is distributed to the priests of each diocese for use during the year.

With the holy chrism, the priest anoints the candidate on the forehead (for the sanctification of mind and thoughts), on the eyes, nostrils, mouth and ears (for the sanctification of the senses), on the chest and back (for the sanctification of the heart and desires), and on the hands and feet (for the sanctification of the ways and deeds of the new Christian). Each time he anoints, he says, 'The seal of the gift of the Holy Spirit'. These words have 2 Cor. 1.21–22 as their basis: 'Remember it is God himself who assures us all, and you, of our standing in Christ, and has anointed us, marking us with his seal and giving us the pledge, the Spirit, that we carry in our hearts.' (JB) This anointing is the antitype of the gift of the Holy Spirit who descended on Christ as he arose from the waters of the Jordan at his own baptism and, since it is what it signifies,[9] it makes the newly baptized a true and complete Christian, a new 'Christ'.

St Cyril's catechetical lectures[10] to the newly initiated of fourth-century Jerusalem make much of this point. 'Now you have been made Christs,' he said, 'by receiving the antitype of the Holy Spirit,' and 'having been counted worthy of this holy Chrism, you are called Christians.' By accepting baptism in the Jordan, Christ 'imparted the fragrance of his Godhead to the waters' and 'he came up from them and the Holy Spirit in the fulness of his being lighted on him, like resting upon like. And to you in like manner . . . there was given an unction . . . and this is the Holy Spirit.'[11] There is also reference in the same source to a real presence and power of the Holy Spirit in the chrism:

> Beware of supposing this to be plain ointment. For, as the bread of the Eucharist, after the invocation of the Holy Spirit, is mere bread no longer, but the Body of Christ, so also this holy ointment is no more simple ointment after invocation, but it is Christ's gift of grace and, by the advent of the Holy Spirit, is made fit to impart his divine nature.[12]

The Holy Mystery of baptism-chrismation usually takes place after the Holy Liturgy, from which consecrated elements are reserved. The sacrament of initiation is completed and crowned by the administration of the Holy Communion to the new Christian, and the Molitfelnic states quite clearly that any priest who does not administer the Holy Communion will, if the new initiate dies before receiving it, be guilty of mortal sin.

The oil of the sick

The Holy Maslu, so called from the Slavonic word for olive oil, is the Holy Mystery of the anointing of the sick. Like the oil for the pre-baptismal anointing, the oil used in this rite is pure olive oil and is blessed, by each of the seven officiating priests, at the service at which it is required. The sevenfold blessing is in token of the manifold gifts of the Holy Spirit (Isa. 11.2–3) and, in the Slav usage, three drops of holy chrism may be added on occasions when it is not possible to assemble the seven priests normally required to officiate. The rubrics allow for the number of priests to be reduced to the trinitarian number, three, or at the very least two. Nevertheless, necessity sometimes dictates that only one priest officiates, an occurrence that the rubrics specifically set out to avoid, in order that no one priest should seem to assume a charism for himself personally and that it should be very clear that the healer is Christ.

The Byzantine rite for the anointing of the sick is long and complex, which is perhaps principally what has led to its infrequent usage in the modern context of high-tech hospitals, in which people anticipate they will get better and where the carrying out of the rite would present a number of practical problems.

In addition to requiring seven priests, the rite includes seven Epistles and Gospels, seven blessings of the oil and seven prayers of anointing. The emphasis on the number seven has been related to various Old Testament texts connected with the manifestation of the mercy of God. For example, Elisha stretching himself seven times over the dead body of the Shunammite woman's child (2 Kings 4.34–35), the blowing of trumpets by seven priests before the fall of Jericho (Josh. 6.13–16) and the sevenfold prayer of Elijah on Mount Carmel, before God gave the rain to end the drought (1 Kings 18.42–45). This last example is itself cited in Jas. 5.17.

In its earlier and shorter form, the anointing of the sick was incorporated into the Holy Liturgy, when needed. It has also been linked with vespers or matins. In its present form, which developed mostly between the twelfth and thirteenth centuries, becoming fixed in the fifteenth, it is celebrated on its own at the request of the sick person, who is required to make their confession beforehand. The Holy Mysteries of anointing of the sick and of confession are regarded in Orthodoxy as extensions of baptismal grace.[13] The complexity of the rite for anointing the sick seems to have stemmed from attempts to give more literal expression to the earlier practice recorded in the Epistle of James (5.14–18). The Holy Maslu normally takes place in church, in the assembly of the faithful, but, when it is necessary for it to take place in the sick person's home, it is customary for the faithful close to the sick person to assemble there.

A bowl of grain or flour and a vessel of pure olive oil, together with seven anointing sticks and seven candles (one for each of the priests), are required for the rite, and its general pattern is as follows.

Rite for the anointing of the sick

- Prayers and psalms
- Sevenfold blessing of the oil by each priest in turn
- Seven Epistles and Gospels, each pair of readings followed by a prayer and an anointing by each of the priests in turn
- The placing of the Gospel on the head of the anointed person
- Prostrations and absolution

Apart from the participation of seven priests, the placing of the Gospel on the sick person's head is another acknowledgement of the fact that the healer is Christ himself. All the priests take hold of the book, and while the other six sing 'Lord, have mercy' quietly, the senior priest prays a prayer which contains the following words:

> It is not my own sinful hand which I place on the head of the one who has come to you in penitence to seek from you, through us, forgiveness of sins, but your strong and powerful hand which is in this Holy Gospel which those who are officiating with me hold on the head of your servant.

On behalf of all the officiating priests, he prays for forgiveness for the sick person, who kisses the Gospel at the end of the prayer. When the concluding litany and prayers have been said, the person who was anointed makes three prostrations, each time saying, 'Bless, holy fathers, and forgive me a sinner'. Each time the priests reply, 'God forgive you and bless you and grant you healing'.

Any oil left over at the end of the service is either used to add to the grain or flour to make a cake for the sick to eat, or is used for burning in lamps in the church or in icon lamps at home.

On the Wednesday in Holy Week, particularly in the Slav and Oriental Orthodox traditions, it is customary to hold a service of general anointing. This is the day on which the Orthodox Church commemorates the Saviour's anointing with perfumed ointment by the woman at Bethany (Matt. 26.6–16 is the Gospel at the Liturgy of the Presanctified on that day). At the service of anointing on Holy Wednesday, the prayer of anointing is said once only, the Gospel is placed on the heads of those nearest, and each person comes to a priest for a short form of anointing or goes to each priest in turn, depending on local custom. Because the Holy Maslu emphasizes the link between forgiveness of sins and the total healing of the person, not just their physical cure, those who are physically healthy may be anointed and this anointing may be repeated. A General Confession is required for anyone who is anointed at a general anointing.

At no time did the sacramental anointing of the sick come to be generally regarded in Orthodoxy as an 'extreme unction' for the dying. As Meyendorff points out, 'Whatever the outcome of the disease, the anointing symbolized divine pardon and liberation from the vicious cycle of sin, suffering and death, in which fallen humanity is held captive.'[14] 'The Church through its presbyters asks for relief, forgiveness and eternal freedom.'[15] In this context, the link between the mysteries of penance, healing and baptism can be more clearly seen. All are given for liberation from the power of sin and evil, for the creation of the new man, conformed to Christ and for incorporation into Christ's own life.

The purpose of sacramental anointing

Anointing with holy oil in the Holy Mysteries of baptism-chrismation and the anointing of the sick needs to be seen against the theological background of its sacramental significance. A very rich symbolism surrounds each anointing, as has been illustrated above and elsewhere in this book. In addition, each anointing has been related by the Fathers and other Orthodox theologians to a particular event in the christification of man.

In a key introductory passage in his work entitled *The Life in Christ*, the fourteenth-century Byzantine theologian-saint Nicholas Kavasilas wrote:

> In the sacred Mysteries, then, we depict his burial and proclaim his death. By them we are begotten and formed and wondrously united to the Saviour, for they are the means by which, as Paul says, 'in Him we live, and move and have our being' (Acts 17.28). Baptism confers being and, in short, existence according to Christ. It receives us when we are dead and corrupted and first leads us into life. The anointing with chrism perfects him who has received [new] birth by infusing into him the energy that befits such a life. The Holy Eucharist preserves and continues this life and health, since the Bread of life enables us to preserve that which has been acquired and to continue in life. It is therefore by this bread that we live and by the chrism that we are moved, once we have received being from the baptismal washing.[16]

'Baptism confers being', and the oil that is to be used for the pre-baptismal anointing is blessed that it may be an 'anointing of incorruption'. New life, the renewal of body and soul and the triumph over evil, are predominant themes in the baptismal liturgy. On man's part there is the unceasing search for a human nature free from the effects of the Fall, the yearning to return to the original relationship for which he was created 'in the image and likeness of God', and on God's part, there is the possibility held out to man of participating in the death and resurrection of Christ, the new Adam, who has recapitulated human nature and is 'the image of the unseen God, the firstborn of all creation'.[17]

'By the Chrism we are moved,' Kavasilas says, in reference to the dynamism set up in the human person by the gifts of the Holy Spirit in chrismation. The Fathers and subsequent Orthodox theologians have perceived the image of God as an actual gift to man, however obscured by sin it may have become. By contrast, they have seen the likeness of God as a potential gift, which man in collaboration with God must work to perfect.[18] Consequently, Orthodoxy allows for the fact that the realization of perfection is achieved in a personally distinctive manner. As Christos Yannaras puts it:

> The Church sees in the personal distinctiveness of each anointed Christian a new possibility for realizing the true life of loving communion, and at the same time an icon of Christ who sets life free and restores it to the fulness of the divine mode of existence.[19]

In the 'unction of royal adoption', there is the seal and confirmation of the 'personal mode of existence inaugurated when nature is made new at baptism', and in its integrated rite of baptism-chrismation, the Orthodox Church holds closely together 'the reality of the death of "the old man" or autonomous individuality and the resurrection of the person into the communion of saints'.[20] There is always the danger that a rite that presupposed a distance of years between baptism and chrismation/confirmation would fragment this sacramental event.

The recovery of the natural

Orthodox anthropology is distinguished by its emphasis on the belief that the true state of human nature is its state at creation. In the light of this assertion, what we commonly call 'human nature' is not the nature conferred on us when we were created in the image and likeness of God, and what we commonly describe as 'natural' is in fact least in accord with our true nature in Christ. As Panayiotis Nellas described it in his most illuminating study, *Deification in Christ*, 'experience proves that the historical reality of man is different from that which we have seen to be defined in the phrase "in the image" '. Nellas attributes this difference to the fact that historical reality is developing in the unnatural situation that man finds himself in as a result of the Fall.[21]

In this context, our first need is to recognize the unnatural situation we are in, and to realize that the natural cannot be found by searching in the unnatural. It can only be found at its real source, and man must make full use of his natural powers to find it.

The garments of skin

To ensure the survival of man after the Fall, God provided for him 'garments of skin' (Gen. 3.21). In expounding this passage of Scripture, the Fathers related the 'garments of skin' to mortality, which has become, as it were, second nature to man since the Fall. In providing these garments, God was 'clothing man in mortality',[22] and 'mortality derived from the nature of beings lacking intelligence was, by God's dispensation, imposed on a nature created for immortality'.[23] Nellas traces the implications of the giving of the garments of skin through the writings of the Fathers, describing the transmutation of life in the image of God into mere survival. Yet together with the gift of garments to ensure the survival of fallen man in his unnatural circumstances, God gave also in the sacramental life in Christ the possibility of the fulfilment of what Nellas calls 'the inherent impetus of the image'. Baptism renews the image obscured by sin, chrismation confers the dynamic gifts of the Holy Spirit which enable man to grow into the likeness of God given to him potentially in creation, and the Eucharist is the only food that will ensure his continuing life.[24]

Sin, death, materiality, the differentiation into male and female, an altered relationship between man and his fellow men and with the whole created order are identified in the writings of the Fathers as results of the fragmentation brought about by the Fall. The fundamental process of reintegration, which they also describe and to which Nellas draws attention, is that of the transformation of the human person, through the Spirit, in Christ. In their insistence on this process, Nellas explains:

> The Holy Fathers, who knew the power of the resurrection and had experienced the freedom of the children of God, out of their love for men do not hesitate to insist on this teaching about the possibility of the resurrection here and now. . . . They do so to show man his real nature and his true majesty in God, while at the same time indicating the paths which lead to it. For this teaching also manifests the fundamental ontological significance which Baptism and the whole of the sacramental, ascetic and spiritual life of the Church has for mankind. All these things do not constitute elements which are added to the nature of man, which one may or may not have according to preference; they form and maintain the essence of man's natural being.[25]

While each of the uses of holy oil in the Orthodox Church clearly has its specific significance just as it has its specifically prepared oil, there is at the heart of all usage a common sacramental purpose. The Church, as the Body of the Christ (the Anointed One), is itself an anointed entity. Incorporation into this Body, effected through the same anointing of the Holy Spirit which the Son of God has himself undergone,[26] restores man to the personhood of communion with God which 'with [his] decline into individuality was corrupted and shattered'. The origin and end of the sacramental life is the restoration of all creation to the realm of the sacred – that is, to the fellowship of the Holy Trinity.[27]

Notes

1. Monastics are signed with the sign of the cross in pure water as a mark of the purity they have already attained in the angelic image.

2. The canon of the Third Regional Council of Carthage (AD 256 or 258) says it is 'necessary for anyone that has been baptized to be anointed, in order that, upon receiving the Chrism, he may become a partaker of Christ'. This is the first canonical mention of the chrism.

    See also canon XLVIII of the Synod of Laodicaea (c. AD 364, though the precise date is disputed): '. . . the illuminated, after baptism, must be anointed with heavenly Chrism, and be partakers of the kingdom of Christ'.

3. 'Note, however, that holy Myron may be administered a second time but only to those who have denied the faith' (note on canon XLVIII of the Council of Laodicaea). The Molitfelnic recognizes the possibility of the effects of chrismation being erased by a life given over to evil deeds (Molitfelnic of the Romanian Orthodox Church, Bucharest 1937, p. 12).

4. St Cyril of Jerusalem, *Catechetical Lectures* XX.2.

5. Molitfelnic, p. 24.

6. Even if the candidate for baptism is an adult, the light is given to the sponsor. In the spiritual life of the candidate, the sponsor is the one who bears the light and the guarantor that he/she will follow the light. The responsibilities of a sponsor never cease, and the particular nature of these responsibilities governs the prohibition in Orthodox canon law of marriage between a sponsor and their godchild.

7. The note to the canon of the Third Regional Council of Carthage insists on this.

8. The note on the interpretation of canon VI of the Regional Council of Carthage (AD 418–19) states that only bishops may prepare the holy myron. They 'can prepare the Myron by themselves but, for the sake of showing obedience and submission to the Patriarch, they assemble in the Great Church and prepare it there'.

9. P. Evdokimov, *L'Orthodoxie* (Neufchâtel 1959), p. 275.

10. St Cyril's authorship of these is in doubt, but alternative suggestions do no more than place the date of composition a few years after him. See F. Young, *From Nicaea to Chalcedon* (London 1983), pp. 128ff.

11. Cyril of Jerusalem, *Catechetical Lectures* XXXI.1.

12. ibid., XXI.3.

13. A Monk of the Eastern Church, *Orthodox Spirituality* (London 1980), p. 144.

14. J. Meyendorff, *Byzantine Theology* (London 1975), p. 199.

15. ibid., p. 199.

16. N. Cabasilas, *Life in Christ* (Crestwood, NJ, 1974), pp. 49–50.

17. Col. 1.15.

18. Gen. 1.26, and see, for example, N. Crainic, *Nostalgia Paradisului* (Bucharest 1940), p. 17ff., and V. Lossky, *The Mystical Theology of the Eastern Church* (Cambridge, 1957), pp. 124–7.

19. Christos Yannaras, *The Freedom of Morality* (Crestwood, NJ, 1984), p. 143.
20. ibid., p. 142.
21. P. Nellas, *Deification in Christ* (Crestwood, NJ, 1987), pp. 43–4.
22. Methodios of Olympus, *On the Resurrection of the Dead* i. 39, quoted in Nellas, *Deification in Christ*, p. 46.
23. Gregory of Nyssa, *On Virginity* 12, quoted in Nellas, *Deification in Christ*, p. 47.
24. There is not space here to do justice to the important theological notion of the garments of skin. The reader is referred to Nellas, *Deification in Christ*, pp. 43–91.
25. ibid., p. 84.
26. Cabasilas, *Life in Christ*, p. 65.
27. For further discussion of the Orthodox view of individuality and personhood in the sacramental context, see *Confession and Absolution*, eds M. Dudley and G. Rowell (London 1990), pp. 128–9.

9

Holy Joys in Store: Oils and Anointing in the Catholic Church[1]

Martin Dudley

> *There before the altar standing*
> *Prays the mitred Pontiff lowly*
> *Duly he performs the rite,*
> *To consecrate the chrism holy.*[2]

The above is a stanza from the early Latin hymn *O Redemptor*, largely
made up of extracts from Prudentius, which found a place in the
Officio in feria V Cenae Domini of the Romano-Germanic Pontifical of
the tenth century. On little evidence, Prosper Guéranger attributed it
to Venantius Fortunatus. Its author is unknown, but the hymn carries
the main themes connected with the Chrism Mass. The first part,
sung as the oil is brought to the altar, speaks of the olive as the emblem
of peace, of the essential relation of the olive tree and the light that
guarantees its fruitfulness, of the need for episcopal consecration and
of the power of anointing in opposing demons. After the consecration,
the second part speaks of renewal effected by anointing and the flow of
grace signified by the oil. The hymn was carried into the Roman
Pontificals of the twelfth and thirteenth centuries and thence to the
Pontifical of Piccolomini and Burchard, of Clement VIII, Urban VIII,
and Benedict XIV, to the revised Holy Week rite of Pius XII, and to
the Roman Missal of 1970. Other parts of the office by which the oils
are blessed and the chrism consecrated have changed, but the use of *O
Redemptor* has remained constant. Through more than nine hundred
years it has expressed the essential theology embodied in the blessing
of oils and anointing and is a witness to a remarkable continuity.

The first extant rites for blessing oils appear in the sacramentaries. The Old Gelasian Sacramentary, whose Roman ancestor was composed between 628 and 715, contains an order for the blessing of chrism in the temporal cycle, in *Coena Domini*. The Gregorian Sacramentary has an order in the Hadrianum version, but not in the Sacramentary of Padua, which also lacks the blessing of the font on Holy Saturday. It is likely to have been a presbyteral version of the sacramentary and therefore presages the separation of episcopal material into a Pontifical from the ninth century onwards, culminating in the Romano-Germanic Pontifical of the tenth century. The blessing of oils thereafter found its place in the Pontifical. In the first true Pontifical, that of the tenth century, Roman and Germanic traditions met and mixed (hence its name), and the Roman practice, which allowed the priests of titular churches to bless the other oils while the Pope alone consecrated chrism, gave way to the Germanic reservation of all three blessings to the mitred pontiff.[3] It was this practice, together with the already current anointings involved in initiation, ordination, consecration of churches, altars, bells and chalices, the crowning of kings and the Church's ministry to the sick and dying, which provided the raw material for the theologians who, in the twelfth century, created and ordered that body of teaching that we call sacramental theology. They sorted out and clarified the various meanings of *sacramentum* and listed those ritual actions that would henceforth be known as sacraments.

There had already been attempts to develop a common understanding of the Church's rites. It was primarily allegorical and came to a sudden blooming early in the ninth century in the *Liber Officialis* of Amalarius of Metz.[4] Amalarius, together with all later liturgical commentators and sacramental theologians of the Middle Ages, followed a principle enunciated by Augustine: 'The sacraments ought to have a certain resemblance to those things of which they are sacraments.'[5] Augustine provided other essential components for the definition of a sacrament: 'A sacrament is a sign of a sacred thing' and 'A sacrament is the visible form of an invisible grace'.[6] When these are combined we have a definition that is clear and universally applicable, such as this given by Hugh of St Victor: 'A sacrament is a corporeal or material element set before the senses without, representing by similitude and signifying by institution and containing by sanctification some invisible and spiritual grace.'[7] The sign was brought about by two elements, words and things, and those things included water, oil, and the like.

Using the water of baptism as an example, Hugh of St Victor explains, in the *De Sacramentis*, the different elements involved in a sacrament. His method can be equally well applied to oil for anointing. Oil has natural qualities that have a certain similitude with the grace of the Holy Spirit. Christ, the Anointed One, instituted, by his own anointing, the signification of anointing for his Church. The word of blessing or consecration is added to the element, and thus, says Hugh, a sacrament is made. Hugh's point needs to be noted: of the water of baptism he says that visible water *is a sacrament* representing from similitude, signifying from institution, and containing spiritual grace from sanctification. The same can be said, in certain circumstances, of oil. We find this already in the Pontifical's sermon: *Oleum vero, quando offertur pontifici, simplex liquor est et speciam habet corporalem, sed post benedictionem sacerdotum transfertur in sacramentum.*[8] Hugh's definition was subsequently found to be inadequate precisely because he insists on a material element and calls it 'the sacrament'. The author of the anonymous *Summa Sententiarum* says that the water and the washing are the *sacramentum* of baptism and the trinitarian invocation is its form.[9] The sign that is a sacrament involves a material element, if needed, together with actions and words. The sacrament as a whole, rather than just the material element, is the efficacious sign of God's grace. Peter Lombard distinguishes a sacrament from any other sort of sign: 'A sacrament brings about the likeness of that reality of which it is a sign. For a sacrament properly so-called is that which is a sign of God's grace and the invisible form of grace in such a way that it evokes the likeness of that grace and constitutes its cause.'[10] Two of the seven sacraments of the new law listed by Peter Lombard, were, essentially, acts of anointing: confirmation and extreme unction. Two others, baptism and ordination, included anointings.

The pattern of sacramental anointings remained constant throughout the period. Amalarius comments on the consecration of three types of oil for three purposes. Employing his allegorical method, he looks for the way in which the visible manifests the invisible. Citing the Epistle to the Romans – 'Ever since the world began God's invisible attributes . . . have been visible to the eye of reason, in the things he has made' – Amalarius seeks that which the olive, its fruit and its oil may reveal. He quotes Isidore of Seville who, in the *Etymologia*, refers to the olive as *arbor pacis insignis* and speaks of the richness of the fruit and the refreshment it brings to the sick. Like the hymn *O Redemptor*, Isidore draws attention to the relationship of the olive and light. Amalarius cites Augustine in Ps. 45: 'The visible oil is for a sign of the invisible oil, for it is in a sacrament, the spiritual oil is invisible.'[11] So as the natural oil brings physical health, Amalarius sees it as the means by which God conveys the spiritual health appropriate to each type of anointing. A sermon found in the Romano-Germanic Pontifical, which clearly derives in part from Amalarius, lists the oils: *oleum pro infirmis et pro populo, oleum principalis chrismatis et oleum ad unguendos catecuminos et neophitos.*[12]

Each of them required a separate mode of consecration and the oil of chrism differed from the others in being a combination of olive oil and balsam. For the anointing of the sick as a sacrament, Amalarius draws his evidence from Mark 6.12–13 and Jas. 5, and has no doubt that it was an apostolic practice. By contrast he says that we do not read of the anointing of neophytes in Scripture, but receive it as an apostolic custom on the authority of the Roman Church. The chrism is rather different and typology rather than allegory is used to interpret it on the basis of the types already given in the consecratory prayer of the Gregorian Sacramentary.[13] Here the olive branch in the dove's mouth is a type of the gift to come (*similitudinem futuri muneris*) and the anointing of Aaron by Moses foreshadows the baptism of Jesus and his spiritual anointing. The addition of balsam to the oil is interpreted in a number of ways and it is specifically linked to the true divinity and true humanity of Christ, together with the unifying power of the divinity exercised on different species.

Hugh of St Victor acknowledged extreme unction as established by the apostles. Dominical institution had not yet become a *sine qua non* of the sacraments. There are two reasons, he says, for its institution: remission of sins and alleviation of sickness. The latter does not necessarily mean alleviation of bodily sickness, for that only comes if it is expedient, but unction received faithfully and devotedly always confers spiritual health. The bulk of Hugh's article is devoted to whether the anointing can be repeated and, as it was increasingly seen as a sacrament of the dying, this became an important question.[14]

By the time John Beleth wrote his *Summa De Ecclesiasticis Officiis* towards the end of the twelfth century, there was no mention of anointing neophytes or catechumens and the three species of sacred oil are *crisma, oleum infirmorum et oleum, quo inunguntur baptizati*.[15] The commentators concerned themselves mostly with chrism and the oil of the sick. Little effort was applied to elaborating a theology of the third oil, which comes to be known for a time as *oleum sanctum* or simply *oleum*, though Benedict XIV again calls it *oleum catechumenorum*. It was used for the anointing on the breast and between the shoulders prior to baptism. This anointing was likened by Ambrose to that given to athletes or fighters; it was preparatory to the receiving of the Holy Spirit. Aquinas, affirming the use of water as part of the very substance of the sacrament of baptism, says that the use of oil and chrism pertain to its solemnity rather than to its substance.[16] These anointings are not essential, he says, but neither are they superfluous for they pertain to the *bene esse* of the sacrament.[17]

By contrast, the anointing at confirmation was counted as essential and St Thomas asks whether chrism is suitable matter for this sacrament.[18] In his reply he picks up a number of points related to Hugh's concept of representation, signification and sanctification. Of representation by similitude, he says, first, that no other oil has the properties that signify the Holy Spirit in the way that olive oil does, for 'the olive tree itself, with branches always green, signifies the newness and mercy of the Holy Spirit'.[19] He then holds that *oleum* means *olive oil* and that other pressed liquids are called oil because of a likeness to *oleum olivarum*. So the oil signifies the grace of the Holy Spirit, and because Christ received this grace in its fullness he is said to have been anointed with the oil of gladness. The balsam that gives it a sweet fragrance extends the effect of the anointing to others, so Paul writes to the Corinthians that 'We are the sweet aroma of Christ.' Aquinas makes an important theological point about Christ who did not himself receive an anointing with oil or give an anointing to the apostles, for there was no need of a material outward sign when he himself received and conferred the spiritual reality. The sign in Jesus' anointing was the Holy Spirit 'like a dove' and for the apostles it was the flames of fire 'for the descent of the Holy Spirit in the form of fire has the same significance as oil except that fire has an active power while oil, as the matter and fuel of fire, is passive'.[20]

From Trent to the code of canon law

Liturgically and theologically, there was little change after Trent, except that, as the Council decreed that the received and approved rites should be used for administering the sacraments, there was an active interest in promoting correct and authentic editions of liturgical books. The canons of 1547 on baptism and confirmation do not mention anointing. The doctrine of Extreme Unction, defined in 1551, refers to the proof texts in Mark and James and teaches that the matter of the sacrament is oil blessed by the bishop, 'because the anointing very aptly represents the grace of the Holy Spirit with which the soul of the sick is invisibly anointed'.[21] The Tridentine teaching is elucidated in the Roman Catechism. Little is made of the anointings at baptism. Of chrism at confirmation, the Catechism says that, composed of oil and balsam and solemnly consecrated by the bishop, chrism is the matter of confirmation, and Dionysius is called as an authority; the same section tells that Pope Fabian testified that the apostles received the composition of chrism from the Lord! The oil is 'by its nature rich, unctuous and fluid' and so can express the fullness of grace.[22] The Catechism also repeats much of the discussion about oil and balsam and the reasons for episcopal consecration that were given by the medieval commentators. A similar pattern is found in the Catechism's teaching on Extreme Unction; the natural powers of oil, given by Isidore and others, are again cited as arguments for the appropriateness of anointing for healing.

The first truly 'official' pontifical was the *Pontificale Romanum* of Clement VIII published in 1595 and subsequently revised by a number of popes. This was intended to replace the many local usages of the Middle Ages. Each edition included the *Officio in feria V Cenae Domini* which was simply inserted, according to necessity, into the Maundy Thursday Mass celebrated by the bishop. Most people, then as now, had never been present at the Chrism Mass. The liturgical reformer Pius Parsch urged every Catholic to be present at least once in a lifetime! The rites involving anointing were found in a number of places: baptism and anointing of the sick in the local volumes called *Rituale*, *Pastorale* or, in England, *Manuale*, which were gradually replaced after Trent by the *Rituale Romanum* which first appeared in 1614; confirmation, ordination of priests, consecration of bishops, dedication of churches, consecration of altars and chalices, the blessing of bells in the *Pontificale*; the Easter blessing of the font in the Missal.

The *Codex Iuris Canonici* of 1917 consolidated the laws concerned with the oils in canons 734–5; many of them had been given definitive form by Benedict XIV. It ruled that the oils used in the administration of the sacraments should be those blessed by the bishop on the immediately preceding Maundy Thursday. Canonists considered the obligation not to use those of an earlier date to be a grave one. The clergy were required to collect their supply of oils from their own ordinary and to keep them, under lock and key, in a special place in the sacristy, baptistry or church. In 1903 the Holy Office had ruled that the oils should not be sent by express or parcel post! If a cleric could not collect them, a good layman was allowed to.[23] Canon 734, section 2, allowed that, according to necessity, a small amount of unblessed olive oil could be added to the blessed oil if the supply was greatly reduced. Canon 945 allowed that the oil for the sick might be blessed by a priest who has obtained a faculty from the Holy See, but such delegation has been frequently denied (e.g. by Pius VI during the French Revolution). The Holy Office ruled, in 1611 and 1842, that a blessing without a faculty would be simply invalid. However, priests of the Oriental Church blessed the oil when administering the sacrament and did so with Rome's approval.[24]

Though there was little change with regard to other anointings, the practice of anointing the sick gradually declined. The Genoese priest Joseph Frassinetti (1804–68) was called the 'Italian Curé d'Ars'. His manual for the parish clergy first appeared in 1863; after nine Italian editions it was translated into English. Well versed in theology, Frassinetti was also blessed with good pastoral sense, and his manual, because it addresses real parochial situations, provides us with a useful picture of nineteenth-century practice. He acknowledges that in the average city parish the priest will know nothing of the condition

118

of the sick until he is called to administer the last rites. From the outset, Frassinetti stresses the need to administer them in good time and warns that relatives, so as not to alarm the patient, delay too long in calling for the priest. He also contrasts the rich and poor. The latter, even when they are not very pious, will welcome the parish priest with pleasure when he comes to visit the sick, and the sick in poor households will not become alarmed when told that they should receive the last sacraments. The former, by contrast, have need of studied discourses 'in order that they might not be frightened at the bare mention of the last sacraments'. Because the relatives are more circumspect, the more affluent classes frequently die without the last rites. Frassinetti reminds young parish priests that those who despise the sacraments during life are generally deprived of them at the hour of death.[25]

On the time for administering Extreme Unction, he follows Alphonsus Liguori and holds that when Viaticum is administered, so should Extreme Unction be. Viaticum may be administered whenever an illness is evidently serious. He holds this view against those who look for a further crisis in the illness or danger of imminent death, because he is convinced of the need for reception of the sacrament before the patient is already past hope. Again Frassinetti points to the unwillingness of the rich to accept the imminence of death and the need for Unction. Sometimes, he writes, the priest ought to be beginning the recommendation of a dying soul, ought to be reciting the *Proficiscere*, and he has not received permission from the family and physician to speak to the dying man about Extreme Unction. Frassinetti lays down a principle:

> Extreme Unction ought not to be administered at the last moment of life, but in every case of serious, and therefore dangerous, illness . . . [the parish priest] ought to teach this doctrine not only in the Church, but when he is visiting the sick: and he should impress it upon the sick persons themselves, upon their relatives, and especially upon the medical attendants.[26]

Commending early administration, he stresses that when the sick receive the sacrament in good time, when they can receive more abundant spiritual advantages from it, many of them recover, but he does not reckon it as a sacrament of healing.

Frassinetti goes on to explain how the anointing should be made. He uses the rite from the Roman Ritual given on p. 185 below. As the person is frequently found to be in a dying condition, the anointing is made swiftly, without the preliminary prayers; these can be recited later if the person survives. When Frassinetti wrote, the question of whether a single anointing would suffice was still unresolved. Grave

119

theologians, he says, are of the opinion that all five senses needed to be anointed for validity's sake, and, as it is extremely easy to do, that is what he recommends.

Dunne's manual for the clergy entitled *The Ritual Explained* appeared in 1928 and is closer in style to the rubrical guides than to a pastoral handbook. His primary concern is with valid administration. The eyes, ears, nose, mouth, hands and feet are anointed. The unctions are double except for the mouth and perhaps the nose: authors vary as to whether the nose should be anointed once, on the extremity, or twice, on each nostril! It is generally held, he says, that unction of just one sense is sufficient for valid reception. The anointing of the feet may be omitted for any good reason. The remaining instructions include the mode of anointing ('The mouth . . . should be firmly closed, and the unction applied to the lips' except in cases of hydrophobia!), the need for sufficient oil, provision of an instrument to be used where there is danger of infection, and the removal of the oil immediately after anointing. The sacrament could be invalid if too little oil was used or too long a pause was made between words. The tenth edition of *Matters Liturgical*, published in 1959, was one of the last manuals revised before the Council. It notes that the parish priest is the ordinary minister of the sacrament which is to be given to those 'who have or have had the use of reason and who are now in danger of death as a result of sickness or old age'. The anointing cannot be repeated in the same illness. The question of a single anointing in case of necessity is resolved. Except in the case of grave necessity, the anointing must be performed by the hand of the priest and not by means of an instrument.

Liturgically, the post-Tridentine process was one of rubrical refinement. Pastorally, there remained the necessity of ministering to the sick, but, as time went on, there were fewer of Frassinetti's pious poor and less demand for the sacrament. The bourgeois had come to fear death and everything associated with it. Pius XI and Pius XII, in their encyclicals and addresses on priesthood, stress that there will always be the sick to assist and comfort with the last sacraments and the dead for whom to celebrate funeral rites, but the division between the sacraments for the dying and the rites for the dead had become blurred. Viaticum and unction were but a preamble to the Requiem Mass.

The Liturgical reform of Pius XII

By the decree *Maxima Redemptionis Nostrae Mysteria* of 16 November 1955 Pope Pius XII established a restored order for Holy Week. Two principles governed the reform: scrupulous faithfulness to the best liturgical traditions and sensitivity to pastoral interests.[27] The Chrism Mass was a product of that reform. It retained, almost unchanged, the texts for blessing the oils, but provided an entirely new Mass formulary drawn primarily from the Gelasian Sacramentary. The Mass used texts from Exod. 30.25,31; Ps. 88[89].2; Ps. 27[28].7–8; Ps. 44[45].7–8; Jas. 5.13–16 and Mark 6.7–13. The prayers for blessing and consecration were carried on unchanged from the Pontifical. It is true, as Pius Parsch observed, that few modern Masses could rival in beauty and excellence the new Chrism Mass, yet it showed at once that the various, and perhaps ultimately incompatible themes involved – priesthood, healing, the sacramental power of chrism, the anti-demonic power of the oil of catechumens – only stayed together with difficulty. The Mass was a great improvement on previous practice which had the rest of the Maundy Thursday rites – procession of the sacrament, stripping and washing of altars, washing of feet – as well. The bishop, as *O Redemptor* declares, is about to pay his debt by consecrating the chrism. He is assisted by twelve priests, seven deacons and seven subdeacons. The collect states that God uses the ministry of priests (*sacerdos*) to regenerate his people. The Epistle tells the sick to call the *presbyteros ecclesiae*. The Gospel, though it concludes with the anointing of the sick, is about the sending out of the apostles. The blessing of chrism refers to its use for anointing the priesthood, but the priestly language is ambiguous and, given that the prayer then refers to baptism, it probably ought to be construed as the common priesthood. At the second level, the Epistle and Gospel are about the healing anointing, but then the blessing of the oil of the sick is a very low key affair compared with the consecration of chrism. The Gelasian Preface stresses the sacramental function of chrism and the dignity conferred by baptism and anointing (this immediately before blessing the oil of the sick) and the Preface of Blessing links Old Testament anointings with the anointing of Jesus at his baptism and the anointing of believers. It should not surprise us that the post-Vatican II reform changed both emphasis and structure, but the direction in which the change went is remarkable.

Anointing in the reformed rites of the Roman Catholic Church

The *Ceremonial of Bishops*, issued in Latin in 1984 and in English in 1989, is almost the last book in the liturgical revision decreed by the Second Vatican Council. By its nature, as a ceremonial handbook for bishops, masters of ceremonies and others, it presents, in a particular perspective, the entire reformed liturgy. Chapter 7 of it, devoted to the Chrism Mass, contains a summary of the use of holy chrism and the other oils:

> The holy chrism consecrated by the bishop is used to anoint the newly baptized, to seal the candidates for confirmation, and to anoint the hands of presbyters and the heads of bishops at their ordination, as well as in the rites of anointing pertaining to the dedication of churches and altars. The oil of catechumens is used in the preparation of catechumens for their baptism. The oil of the sick is used to bring comfort and support to the sick in their infirmity.[28]

This is a very short and business-like statement and that may explain why it lacks the more Christocentric and figurative language of other liturgical texts, though, even when compared with other similar statements, such as those about abbots[29] or altars[30] it must be considered too limited in its expressions. The liturgical texts we shall now survey use much richer language.

Chrism

In the reforms that followed the Second Vatican Council the relation of liturgical and sacramental rites to Christ was made explicit. The attention given to the oil of the sick at the Chrism Mass by Pius XII's reforms was transferred to the chrism itself. The bishop's Mass at which the oils are blessed, ordinarily celebrated on Maundy Thursday morning, is called the *Missa Chrismatis* and it is concelebrated with the diocesan college of presbyters. The *Ceremonial* explains the reasons for this:

> Presbyters are brought together and concelebrate this Mass as witnesses and co-operators with their bishop in the consecration of the chrism because they share in the sacred office of the bishop in building up, sanctifying, and ruling the people of God. The Mass is therefore a clear expression of the unity of the priesthood and sacrifice of Christ, which continue to be present in the Church.[31]

But the remarkable change was the addition of the renewal of priestly promises. Maundy Thursday is, of course, permeated with themes deriving from the Last Supper. The tradition shows that if you try to give all of them adequate liturgical expression the liturgy becomes confusing and unwieldy. The reasons for the present practice are partly theological and partly liturgical. The oils were blessed on Maundy Thursday because they would be needed for the Easter Vigil. Maundy Thursday is, however, the day, *par excellence*, (in spite of Corpus Christi) of Eucharist and priesthood. As a secondary function of chrism is its use at ordinations, it is reasonable, given the presence of priests at the Chrism Mass, to make the link firmer, by giving expression in the renewal of vows and in the proper preface, entitled *De sacerdotio Christi et de ministerio sacerdotum*, to the nature and calling of the ministerial priesthood. The primary function of chrism, that of anointing at baptism and confirmation, might suggest an alternative reading already present in the texts: that which stresses the royal, priestly and prophetic nature of the people of God. It might be argued that this is affirmed at the Paschal Vigil, with the renewal of baptismal promises, but the omission in the new rite of the pouring of chrism into the font breaks an important symbolic link.

The prayer to bless the oil of the sick is normally incorporated into the eucharistic prayer of this Mass, before the doxology, though it may, for pastoral reasons, be used separately. The blessing of the oil of catechumens and the consecration of chrism follow the prayer after communion. The former involves a simple prayer but the latter is much more elaborate and is concelebrated.

There are two alternative consecratory prayers, termed (A) and (B). In the first of them the baptism of Jesus is seen as the fulfilment of the prophecy of David, in Ps. 45, that the Christ would be anointed with the oil of gladness. In a slightly didactic tone, the prayer goes on to say that chrism takes its name from Christ and that it has been used to anoint priests, kings, prophets and martyrs. A similar point, though omitting martyrs, is made in the introduction to the rite.[32] Both prayers make reference to the royal, priestly, and prophetic work of Christ. The royal and priestly nature of Christ's anointing, though not its prophetic character, is found in other texts. The Preface of the Chrism Mass says 'By your Holy Spirit you anointed your only Son High Priest of the new and eternal covenant', and the Preface of the Baptism of the Lord speaks of the Spirit 'seen as a dove' anointing Jesus 'with joy as the Christ'. The last liturgical celebration of the year, Christ the King, declares still more boldly: 'You anointed Jesus Christ, your only Son, with the oil of gladness, as the eternal priest and universal king'.[33]

During the consecration, the anointing at baptism is deliberately linked to Christ's own anointing. Chrism is 'a sign of life and salvation' (A) and 'a sign and source' (B) of God's blessing. The anointing that uses it is equated with the anointing with the Spirit. This anointing, with chrism and Spirit, transforms the baptized into the likeness of Christ and gives them a share in his royal, priestly, and prophetic work. (B) The latter idea is repeated in the baptism rite:

> He now anoints you with the chrism of salvation. As Christ was anointed Priest, Prophet, and King, so may you live always as a member of his body, sharing everlasting life.

Reference to the Spirit is only found at confirmation when, making the sign of the cross in chrism on the forehead of those to be confirmed, the bishop says:

> N., be sealed with the Gift of the Holy Spirit.

Both priests and bishops are anointed at their ordination. The hands of priests are anointed with chrism, after being vested in chasubles, as they kneel before the bishop. *Veni, Creator Spiritus* may be sung. The bishop says:

> The Father anointed our Lord Jesus Christ
> through the power of the Holy Spirit.
> May Jesus preserve you to sanctify the Christian people
> and to offer sacrifice to God.

Anointing is an integral part of the rite of dedicating a church. The notes to the rite link the anointing of the altar with chrism to its being a symbol of Christ, the Anointed One. The anointing of the church – that is, of the so-called consecration crosses on the walls – signifies that it is given over entirely and perpetually to Christian worship. There are to be twelve or, for good reason, four, such crosses as a 'symbol that the church is an image of the holy city of Jerusalem'.[34] The only words spoken during the anointing, in which the entire altar table is anointed, together with the crosses, are those said by the bishop:

> We now anoint this altar and this building. May God in his power make them holy, visible signs of the mystery of Christ and his Church.[35]

The oil of catechumens

The oil of catechumens is blessed at the Chrism Mass if its use has been retained by the conferences of bishops. The introduction to the rite of blessing says:

> By the oil of catechumens the effect of baptismal exorcisms is extended. Before they go to the font of life to be reborn the candidates for baptism are strengthened to renounce sin and the devil.

But episcopal conferences were given explicit permission to omit the anointing with the oil of catechumens in the Rite of Christian Initiation of Adults and in the Baptism of Children.[36] J. D. Crichton states that the retention of the rite depends on cultural factors and stresses that it is wholly inappropriate if it conveys nothing to the recipients or to the participating community.[37] The Rite of Christian Initiation of Adults (RCIA) also allows, for pastoral necessity, the blessing of the oil by a priest and provides a form for it (see Chapter 14). When the oil of catechumens is used, the person is anointed on the breast or both hands or, if desired, on other parts of the body, and the following words are said:

> We anoint you with the oil of salvation
> in the name of Christ our Saviour;
> may he strengthen you with his power,
> who lives and reigns for ever and ever.

When children are baptized, the anointing follows a prayer of exorcism because 'it expresses the liberation of the child from the power of sin'. Anointing is always omitted if there are a large number of children and the priest simply prays over the children with hands extended.

The Catholic Church's teaching about the oils is summed up in the rite for blessing a repository in which they are kept, contained in the *Book of Blessings*, originally issued in 1970 and revised to conform with other liturgical texts in 1985. Its more powerful theological language creates a contrast with the rather prosaic piece from the *Ceremonial of Bishops* with which we began this survey, and it may be wondered whether the fifteen years that separates the books has been marked by a tendency towards rubricism. In the preparation to the rite, the minister says:

> God manifests his grace through the sacramental signs he has entrusted to his Church. By the anointing with oil, the sick are strengthened and healed, the catechumens are empowered to resist Satan and to reject sin and evil, the baptized are sealed with the gifts of the Spirit, and the ministers of the Church are sanctified in God's service. Through the use of these holy oils may God's grace be poured forth always upon the Church.[38]

The prayer of blessing, specifically citing the healing, comfort, and sanctification bestowed on those anointed in God's name, asks that the holy oils will 'confirm our unity in faith and prayer with our bishop' and all the members of the Church and be 'effective signs' of God's love.

The theology of oil and anointing after Vatican II

Three factors may be distinguished in the theology of anointing presented in the reformed rites. The first is the explicit reference to Christ as the anointed one and the relation of the baptized to Christ. The second is the way in which the three oils function as effective signs. The third is the varied forms of anointing.

The controlling biblical texts for Christ as the Anointed One used in the liturgy are Isa. 61 ('The Spirit of the Lord is upon me because he has anointed me . . .'), Acts 10.38 ('You know how God anointed Jesus of Nazareth with the Holy Spirit and with power'), used at the baptism of Christ and at the Mass of Easter Day, and Luke 4.18, with its quotation from Isa. 61, used as the Gospel at the Chrism Mass and at initiation. Among the Psalms, Ps. 45 takes pride of place: 'therefore God, your God, has anointed you above your fellows with oil, the token of joy'. Ps. 88 is also used at the Chrism Mass. Three other anointing texts receive little or no attention: Acts 4.27 ('. . . your holy servant Jesus whom you anointed') is read in course on the Monday of the second week of Easter; 2 Cor. 1.21 ('And if you and we belong to Christ guaranteed as his and anointed, it is all God's doing; it is God also who has set his seal upon us and, as a pledge of what is to come, has given the Spirit to dwell in our hearts') on the seventh Sunday in ordinary time (Year B); and Heb. 1.9, which quotes Ps. 45 as a reference to the Son of God, not at all. Liturgically, these texts provide a point of reference only for the anointing with chrism that identifies the person or thing being anointed with Christ.

There are three areas that require further clarification, points at which the full logic of the meaning given to chrism by its relation to Christ has not been carried through. The introduction to the rite of blessing of oils calls chrism a sign. As Christians are, by baptism, plunged into the paschal mystery of Christ, so they become sharers in his royal and prophetic priesthood. By confirmation, Christians receive the spiritual anointing of the Spirit now given to them. The two anointings – after baptism and at confirmation – are given different meanings, but it is difficult to see how the participation in Christ's work and the gift of the Spirit can be separated, but the rites do separate them. In the RCIA, the newly baptized are told prior to anointing, that, born again in Christ, they have become members of Christ and of his priestly people, and that they will now, when anointed, share in the outpouring of the Holy Spirit. The problem here is a more general one regarding initiation and is too large to be explored here. A related problem concerns the relation of the common priesthood and that of the ordained. The Chrism Mass readings stress common priesthood, though it is the promises of the ministerial priesthood that are renewed. The consecration of chrism asks that the baptized, when anointed, may be granted 'royal, priestly, and prophetic honour'. The preface refers to the one priesthood of Christ, received when he was anointed, which continues in the Church. It affirms Christ's gift of the dignity of a royal priesthood to his own people prior to his call of men to share his sacred ministry 'by the laying on of hands' rather than by anointing. It seems a little odd that Pope Paul VI should have linked the consecration of chrism, drawing its meaning from Christ himself and with its primary use being at initiation, to the renewal of priestly promises, when anointing is a very small part of the ordination rite. The necessity of concelebrating the consecration of chrism, with the presbyters as witnesses and co-operators, together with the theological content of the consecratory prayer, places a stress on chrism that seems out of proportion to its significance in the life of the Church. There are echoes, and not just faint ones, of the role of the hierarch and of chrism as they are found in the writings of Pseudo-Dionysius.

There are contrasts and parallels between the consecration of chrism and the blessing of water for baptism at the Easter Vigil. The Missal still calls it 'blessing of water', but elsewhere it is called more precisely the blessing and invocation of God over baptismal water.[39] Comparing the new prayer for blessing the water with the old, which had a number of ritual actions within it and concluded with the pouring into the water of some of the oil of catechumens and of chrism, Alex Stock finds that it has abandoned the link between blessing and the fruitful transmission of power.[40] He believes that the earlier rite looked uncomfortably like magic and so needed to be 'modernized' – that is, brought into a contemporary philosophical framework. The consecration of chrism has not been modernized to the same extent, though certain features of the Pian rite, including the elaborate and public preparation of the balm and the breathing over the chrism, are now optional, and the commixture and threefold salutation *Ave, sanctum Chrisma* have been abandoned. That the chrism, kept throughout the year, is transformed and 'charged' remains obvious in a way that it no longer is with the baptismal water, which will only be kept, at most, until the end of the Easter season. The obvious points of contact between the blessing and the consecration are the references to creation (the Spirit breathes on the water/the earth produces fruit trees; the olive gives oil), the flood (sign of baptism/Noah's olive branch as a sign of a greater gift to come – baptism and anointing), the baptism of Jesus (foreshadowed by the washing and anointing of Aaron), and the more general references to salvation. The difference comes in what God is asked to do. In the blessing of the water he is asked 'by the power of your Spirit give to the water of this font the grace of your Son' and 'send the Holy Spirit upon the waters of this font'. In the consecration of chrism he is asked to bless the oil, to fill it with the power of the Holy Spirit, and to make it a sign of life and salvation (A) and to make it a sign and source of his blessing (B).

Commenting on the *Summa Theologice* 3a, 72, 3 ad 3, in which Aquinas says that 'physical matter is not capable of grace as a subject, but only as the instrument of grace', James Cunningham observes that 'the power of the Holy Spirit resides in the consecrated chrism no more than the power of Christ in the baptismal water. It is in use of both sacramental elements that they become effective ministers of grace.'[41] That sacraments and other sacramental elements are given for use is not to be denied, but there is clearly a difference between unblessed water and that which is blessed, and unconsecrated oil and the holy chrism.

Of course, 'sign' takes us to the heart of sacramental theology. That a sign is also a source of blessing makes it efficacious. The signification is reinforced, and created for non-olive based cultures, by the recitation of the 'holy history' of the olive and its oil. There is already a natural signification, as well as an evocative and expressive one, so that we must say that the holy chrism is that type of sign which is a symbol drawing us into the life and work of Christ the Anointed One. Its meaning comes not from a specific dominical 'do this', as in the case of baptism and Eucharist, but from a symbolic connection to Christ made by way of the controlling biblical texts. Chrism would therefore fulfil the conditions of a sacrament set out in George S. Worgul's definition: '[Sacraments are] symbols arising from the ministry of Christ and continued in and through the Church, which when received in faith, are encounters with God, Father, Son, and Holy Spirit.'[42]

It would also conform to Michael G. Lawler's definition:

> A sacrament is a prophetic symbol, established by and modelled upon Christ the symbol of God, in and by which the Church, the Body of Christ, proclaims, realizes and celebrates for believers who place no obstacle that presence and action of God, which is rightly called grace[43]

if 'established by' Christ is not understood in terms of direct dominical institution, but by Christ establishing a pattern to be replicated in the Church, his body. Lawler reminds us that the current analogical extension of the word 'sacrament' picks up a traditional Catholic theme that the grace of God is mediated by created reality; something specifically stated in the consecration of chrism. It involves a return to the position prior to the technical definition of 'sacrament' in the twelfth century when a wide range of created realities were acknowledged as sacramental of relationship to God.[44] It would, however, fall severely short of Tad Guzie's definition:

> A sacrament is a festive action in which Christians assemble to celebrate their lived experience and to call to heart their common story. The action is a symbol of God's care for us in Christ. Enacting the symbol brings us closer to one another in the church and to the Lord who is there for us.[45]

As oil is used in rites where other actions – washing, laying on of hands – are more important, it lacks its own continued distinctive festive action. Nevertheless, though we should acknowledge that Guzie's emphasis is increasingly prevalent, Worgul and Lawler express a more traditional Catholic sacramental theology, and chrism looks like a sacrament. Has there been a change in the language used about chrism which makes it look more like a sacrament? Certainly the reformed rites place a greater stress on it. Oil, according to one liturgical manual of 1961,[46] is 'a symbol for the imparting of grace' and is symbolic of the Holy Spirit, but this is clearly not the same as saying that it is a 'sign and source' or that it is itself filled with the Holy Spirit. It is surely the regained sense of the people of God as a royal and priestly people that has brought about this shift in significance for anointing and hence for the holy chrism.

Notes

1. As the history and theology of anointing the sick has been extensively dealt with in the last twenty-five years, this chapter is concerned primarily with liturgical practice and theological ideas about the blessing of oil and anointing in general. The anointing of the sick in the reformed Roman rite is considered in Chapter 14. The following books and articles relate primarily to it. The older textbooks are still useful, notably P. E. Palmer, *Sacraments and Forgiveness* (London 1960); B. Poschmann, *Penance and the Anointing of the Sick* (London 1963), although only 24 pages out of 257 are devoted to anointing; and P. De Letter's article in *Sacramentum Mundi* (London 1968), 1, pp. 37b–40a, which begins with the statement, 'The sacramental anointing of the sick today holds little pastoral appeal'! There are a number of significant historical studies:

   A. Chavasse, *Étude sur l'onction des infirmes dans l'église latine du iiie au xie siècle; i. Du iiie à la réforme carolingienne* (Lyons 1942).
   P. Murray, 'The Liturgical History of Extreme Unction', in *Studies in Pastoral Liturgy*, ii (Dublin 1963). (This is based on the second unpublished section of Chavasse's study.)
   H. B. Porter, 'The Origin of the Medieval Rite for Anointing the Sick', *Journal of Theological Studies*, ns, VII (1956), pp. 211–25.
   H. B. Porter, 'The Rites for the Dying in the Early Middle Ages', (*Journal of Theological Studies*, ns, X (1959), pp. 43–62 and 299–307.

   There is much good material in the following entries (listed in order of appearance) in P. E. Fink, ed., *The New Dictionary of Sacramental Worship* (Collegeville, MN, 1990), pp. 1161–89:

   J. M. Schellman, 'Sick, Anointing of, Frequency of'
   C. W. Gusmer, 'Sick, Communal Anointing of'

The Oil of Gladness

C. W. Gusmer, 'Sick, Communion to the'
J. M. Schellman, 'Sick, Ministry of the'
J. Glen, 'Sick, Pastoral Care of the' (with bibliography)
J. M. Schellman, 'Sick, Sacrament of, Ministers in'
L. J. Richard, 'Sickness, Christian View of'

C. W. Gusmer has written extensively and definitively on the subject. In addition to the entries in Fink and his standard work *And You Visited Me: Sacramental Ministry to the Sick and Dying*, revised edn (New York 1989), reference should be made to 'Liturgical Traditions of Christian Illness: Rites of the Sick' in M. J. Taylor, ed., *The Sacraments: Readings in Contemporary Sacramental Theology* (New York 1981), pp. 225–40, and to 'Anointing of the Sick' in J. A. Komonochak, M. Collins and D. A. Lane, eds, *The New Dictionary of Theology* (Collegeville and Dublin 1990), pp. 21–7.

The theology of anointing is considered by K. Rahner in *The Church and the Sacraments* (London 1963), esp. pp. 112–17, and in *Meditations on the Sacraments* (London 1977), pp. 79–93. The relation of the sacrament to the charism of healing is carefully analysed by T. Talley, 'Healing: Sacrament or Charism?' in M. J. Taylor, ed., *The Sacraments: Readings in Contemporary Sacramental Theology* (New York 1981), pp. 241–52.

The following should also be consulted:

T. Coyle, *Christian Ministry to the Sick*, (London 1986). This is a very readable pastoral companion to the new rites.
Liturgical Conference Saint-Serge, *Temple of the Holy Spirit: Sickness and Death of the Christian in the Liturgy* (New York 1983). This collection, from the French original of 1975, is concerned with East and West; it includes papers by Bernard Botte, Adrian Nocent, Jordi Pinell, Ambrose Verheul and Cyrille Vogel.
J. J. Ziegler, *Let Them Anoint the Sick* (Collegeville 1987). This is an historical study intended to answer the question of extending the ministry of anointing to deacons and laypeople.

2.   This is the full text of the hymn. The anonymous translation was widely circulated early this century. A modern version of the hymn, translated from the Latin by Bishop Richard Rutt, appears in the *New English Hymnal*, no. 512.
Part I

O Redemptor, sume carmen temet concinentium.

*O Redemptor

Audi Judex mortuorum,
Una, spes mortalium,
Audi voces proferentum
Donum pacis praevium.
*O Redemptor

O Redeemer of mankind! receive the hymn of them that sing your praise.

*O Redeemer

Hear us, Judge of dead and living,
Hope of mortals, hear us singing.
Hear us, emblematic tribute
From the peaceful olive bringing.
*O Redeemer

Arbor foeta alma luce
Hoc sacrandum protulit:
Fert hoc prona praesens turba

Salvatori saeculi.
*O Redemptor

Stans ad aram, immo supplex
Infulatus pontifex
Debitum persolvit omne
Consecratio chrismate.
*O Redemptor

Consecrare tu dignare,
Rex perennis patriae,
Hoc olivum, signum vivum,
Jura contra daemonium.
*O Redemptor.

Part II
Ut novetor sexus omnis
Unctione chrismatis,
Ut sanetor sauciata
Dignitatis gloria.
*O Redemptor

Lota mente sacro fonte

Aufugantur criminia:
Uncta fronte sacrosancta
Influunt charismata.
*O Redemptor

Corde natus ex Parentis
Alvum implens Virginis,
Praesta lucem, claude mortem
Chrismatis consortibus.
*O Redemptor

Sit haec dies festa nobis
Saeculorum saeculis:
Sit sacrata, digna laude,
Nec senescat tempore.
*O Redemptor

Fruit of light the tree did yield
That gave this hallowed store:
Worshipping the world's Redeemer,
This we offer and adore.
*O Redeemer

There before the altar standing
Prays the mitred Pontiff lowly:
Duly he performs the rite,
To consecrate the chrism holy.
*O Redeemer

Consecrate thou, Christ eternal,
King of heaven our home,
This our chrism, a living Seal
Against the powers of doom.
*O Redeemer.

That by this most sacred unction
Either sex may be renewed,
And our wounded glory rescued
Through the Spirit's plenitude.
*O Redeemer

First the hallowed fountain's waters
Cleanse the soul from taint of sin,
Then with oil the brows anointed,
And all graces flow within.
*O Redeemer

Son of the eternal Father,
Virgin-born, afford us light:
Who receive this holy unction:
Save us from Death's gloomy night
*O Redeemer

May this day of festal gladness
Keep its holy joys in store.
Dignified with joyful praises,
Blooming now and evermore.
*O Redeemer.

3. A. Chavasse, *Le Sacramentaire Gélasien* (Paris 1958).
4. P. Rorem, *The Medieval Growth of Liturgical Symbolism* (Nottingham 1986), p. 21.
5. Augustine, Epist 98,9; *Summa Sententiarum* 4.1; Peter Lombard, Bk 4, Dist 1, IV; Rorem, *The Medieval Growth of Liturgical Symbolism*, p. 24; Amalarius, *Liber Officialis* 2:14; the edition by J. M. Hanssens (Vatican City 1948–50) has been used here.

6. E. R. Fairweather, ed., *A Scholastic Miscellany: Anselm to Ockham* (Philadelphia 1966), p. 338.

7. R. J. Defarrari, trans., *Hugh of St Victor on the Sacraments of the Christian Faith* (Cambridge, Mass. 1951), p. 155.

8. *Pontificale Romano-Germanicum*, XCIX, 301, pp. 8–10; the edition by C. Vogel and R. Elze (Vatican City 1963, 1972) has been used here.

9. Thomas Aquinas, *Summa Theologice* (Oxford 1975), 56, p. xvii.

10. ibid.

11. Enarratio in Ps. XLIV, 19, PL 36, p. 505.

12. *Pontificale Romano-Germanicum*, XCX, 301, pp. 3–5.

13. *Sacramentum Gregorianum* 77.

14. Hugh of St Victor, *De Sacramentis*, Book 2, Part 15.

15. John Beleth, *Summa de ecclesiasticis officiis*, 95, pp. 14–15; the edition by H. Douteil, *Corpus Christianorum continuatio Medievalis*, 41–41A (Turnhout 1976) has been used here.

16. Thomas Aquinas, *Summa Theologice*, 3a, 66,10 ad 2.

17. ibid., ad 4.

18. Thomas Aquinas, *Summa Theologice*, 3a, 72,2.

19. ibid., ad 3.

20. ibid., ad 1.

21. Denzinger-Schönmetzer *Enchiridion* (Rome 1976), 1695.

22. J. A. McHugh and C. J. Callan, trans., *Catechism of the Council of Trent for Parish Priests* (London 1934), p. 203.

23. P. J. Lydon, *Ready Answers in Canon Law* 4th edn (New York 1954), p. 434.

24. J. A. Abbo and J. D. Hannan, *The Sacred Canons* (St Louis and London 1952), 2, p. 66, note 1.

25. J. Frassinetti, *The New Parish Priest's Practical Manual* (London n.d.), p. 309.

26. ibid., p. 324.

27. *The Assisi Papers: Proceedings of the First International Congress of Pastoral Liturgy Assisi-Rome, September 18–22, 1956* (Collegeville 1957), p. 152.

28. *Ceremonial of Bishops*, s. 274. Publication details of liturgical books cited here are given in the Notes to Chapter 14.

29. ibid., s. 667.

30. ibid., ss. 918–21.

31. ibid., s. 274.

32. *The Sacramentary*, p. 1015.

33. *The Sacramentary*, Preface of Christ the King.

34. *Dedication of a Church and an Altar*, p. 19.

35. ibid., p. 36.

36. Rite of Christian Initiation of Adults, *The Rites*, Introduction IV,65, 7; Baptism, Introduction V, 24,2.

37. *Rite of Christian Initiation of Adults: A Study Book* (London, St Thomas More Centre 1988), cf. pp. 89–90 and 172.

38. *Book of Blessings*, p. 486.

39. Baptism for Children, *The Rites*, p. 219.

40. A. Stock, 'The Blessing of the Font in the Roman Liturgy', in M.

Collins and D. Power, eds, *Blessing and Power, Concilium 178* (Edinburgh 1985), p. 50. See also D. Serra, 'The Blessing of Baptismal Water at the Paschal Vigil in the Post-Vatican II Reform', *Ecclesia Orans*, VII-1990, 3, pp. 343–68.

41. Thomas Aquinas, *Summa Theologice* (Oxford 1975), 57, p. 198, note 9.
42. G. S. Worgul, *From Magic To Metaphor* (Lanham, MD, and London 1985), p. 128.
43. M. G. Lawler, *Symbol and Sacrament* (New York 1987), p. 51.
44. ibid., p. 47.
45. T. Guzie, *The Book of Sacramental Basics* (New York 1981).
46. L. Eisenhofer and J. Lechner, *The Liturgy of the Roman Rite*, (Edinburgh and London 1961).

10

The Sacramental Use of Oil in Anglicanism and the Churches of the Reformation

Geoffrey Rowell

In the medieval Church in the West the sacramental use of oil was part of the rites of baptism, confirmation, ordination and the unction of the sick – a rite which, by the later Middle Ages, had become in practice 'Extreme Unction', a sacramental anointing before death, rather than a sacrament of healing. In addition, following Old Testament practice, kings were anointed at their coronation. The upheavals of the Reformation resulted in the virtual disappearance of anointing in both the Church of England and in the practice of the Churches of the Reformation in Europe. The one place where anointing did survive was in the coronation rite, not only in England, but also in Denmark and Sweden.

The Reformation attack on what were considered superstitious ceremonies, combined with a demand for clear, scriptural warrant for any sacramental practice, meant that the use of oil and chrism in baptism, confirmation and ordination was repudiated. The anointing of the sick, for which explicit scriptural authority (Mark 6.13 and Jas. 5.13–14) might be claimed, fared little better. In England, Cranmer's 1549 Prayer Book provided a form for anointing in the Visitation of the Sick. It appears as an appendix to the rite, prefaced with the rubric: 'If the sick person desire to be anointed, then shall the priest anoint him upon the forehead or breast only, making the sign of the cross.' The limitation of the anointing to the forehead and breast contrasts with the sevenfold anointing of the Sarum rite. The prayer that accompanies the anointing asks that 'as with this visible oil' the

134

body of the sick person 'outwardly is anointed', so God may grant that the soul 'inwardly may be anointed with the Holy Ghost, who is the spirit of all strength, comfort, relief and gladness'. This is followed by petitions for God to restore the sick person to bodily health, 'if it be his blessed will', and for release from all 'pains, troubles and diseases, both in body and mind', concluding with a request for God's mercy and forgiveness and the gift of 'ghostly strength by his Holy Spirit' to resist and overcome all temptations and the assaults of the devil. In Cranmer's second Prayer Book of 1552 unction has disappeared, it being one of the things criticized by Martin Bucer, who asked, in relation to anointing generally, 'Where is our command to regard chrism as a sacrament?'[1]

In Sweden, the *Manual* compiled by Olavus Petri – 'the first vernacular Prayer Book to appear in a modern language',[2] published in 1529, and finally in 1593 becoming the 'use' of the whole realm – includes unction in the rite for the visitation of the sick. Although in his *Little Book on the Sacraments* (1528) Petri had mentioned baptismal unction as something that could remain useful, when administered with the intention not of conferring grace but as a reminder of baptism, no rite of either confirmation or baptismal anointing finds a place in Petri's *Manual*. Both in the prologue and epilogue to his *Manual*, Petri discusses the place of anointing, following the Lutheran line that it is one of the *adiaphora* – 'things indifferent' – yet cautious about magical and superstitious interpretations.

'We have,' Petri writes:

> many Ceremonies and customs, when the sacraments are celebrated, which the sacraments themselves could well be without. Thus we use salt, Chrism, Oil, lights and white robes in baptism; in former days they were wont to use, milk, honey or wine in baptism; which customs were for the adornment of baptism, rather than for any special efficacy. For baptism in itself is equally good if such Ceremonies are omitted, for neither were they in use in Christendom at the beginning.[3]

On these grounds, baptismal anointing and chrismation are omitted from the *Manual*.

As far as unction for the sick is concerned, Petri justifies his provision of a form for anointing by way of concession to human weakness. Because of abuses, in which unction has been made into 'a passport or a ward between the devil and the [sick person's] soul', an anointing 'unto death and not unto life, . . . it were a good thing, following the scriptures, that such anointing should be left out.' The apostles anointed as a sacrament of healing, it was 'bodily medicine'. That, therefore, provided some justification for its retention. 'One must be indulgent to the infirm, and teach them how they should regard the anointing, so that they do not ascribe to it more efficacy than is due.'[4] Petri reaffirms this in his epilogue, adding in a comprehensive spirit:

> If there should be anyone who hath in mind to minister anointing as an outward sign of the inward unction of the Holy Ghost, as doth happen in the chrismal unction at baptism, let him do according to his mind, though the scriptures agree not with him . . . in such minor matters I do not desire to make dispute.[5]

In his order for 'The Visitation, Shriving, Communion and Anointing of the Sick', Petri prefaces the anointing with an extensive rubric. If the sick person desires to be anointed the priest is admonished to give him instruction about its meaning, reminding him 'that salvation standeth in Jesus Christ and in no other creature in heaven or upon earth'. He is not to depend upon the anointing but on the grace and mercy of God. Anointing is only 'according to ancient custom, which hath its source in the use of the apostles' time':

> When they were wont to visit them that were sick, they took with them precious ointment or water, which was effectual to strengthen the sick person's member after that they anointed it therewith, and heartily prayed to God for him that was sick, that he would grant him his health again; so that the unction was used with the intent to restore him that was sick to health; they did not anoint him with the intent that he should die; nor did they give him such anointing as a viaticum, as hath now for a long time been taught without reason or truth.[6]

Petri provides for a sixfold anointing – of eyes, ears, nostrils, lips, hands and feet – each anointing being done with a standard formula adapted to the particular sense: 'Almighty God, who hath visited thee with sickness, confirm thy sight' (for the anointing of the eyes). The prayer that follows grounds the anointing in Christ's ministry and commission:

> O Lord Jesus Christ, thou who for the health and salvation of us all didst come into this world here below, and was made man; thou who didst teach and preach the way of salvation, and restore to health many and countless men who came to thee with all manner of sickness; thou who didst give the same power and commandment to thy chosen apostles, so that they did go forth and preach the kingdom of heaven, anoint the sick with oil, and make them whole again: vouchsafe now likewise to restore this our sick brother (sister), who hath been anointed with oil; confirm and restore his [her] sick and impotent members, and

pour thy Holy Spirit into his [her] heart, that he [she] may serve thee with a sound body according to thy holy commandment, and afterwards together with all Christian men come to thy eternal kingdom . . .[7]

This prayer is a major reconstruction of the prayer following anointing in the medieval rite. Petri's sixfold anointing is an increase on the medieval Swedish practice, in which the breast, the throat and the shoulders were anointed. The curious reference in the rubric to the apostles anointing with water is thought by Yelverton to be a reference to *Apostolic Constitutions* 7.22, where in discussing the anointing with oil before and after baptism, there is the comment that 'if there be neither oil nor ointment, water is sufficient both for the anointing and the seal', though this does not seem a very likely reference as Petri's rubric explicitly refers to apostolic practice in visiting the sick, which is not mentioned in the *Apostolic Constitutions*.[8]

Petri's emphasis in his rite is on the prayer of faith and on healing, of which anointing with oil is a permitted, though not necessary, sign. In this he is in line with Luther's critique of Extreme Unction in *The Babylonian Captivity of the Church*. Luther denies that unction is a sacrament, and that it is Extreme Unction: a rite for those on the brink of death. The fact that scriptural authorization is found in the Epistle of James, 'the epistle of straw', as Luther called it, does not commend it. No apostle, only Christ, could institute a sacrament and there is no mention in the Gospels of Extreme Unction. Even if James were to be followed, the emphasis falls on 'the prayer of faith' and anointing with oil is for recovery not viaticum. As practised by the Catholic Church, the sacrament is not efficacious – 'scarcely one in a thousand is restored, and then no one thinks it is by the sacrament, but by the help of nature or medicine'.[9] More telling, for Luther, is the reference in Mark 6.13 to the apostles anointing with oil and healing many who were sick. This was apostolic practice, but it belonged to the first age of the Church and is now obsolete. So, Luther concludes, 'we should class Extreme Unction among those "sacraments" which we ourselves have instituted, such as the blessing and sprinkling of salt, or holy water':

We cannot deny that any creature whatever may be sanctified by the word and by prayer, a fact taught by the apostle Paul (1 Tim. 4,5). Similarly, we cannot deny that forgiveness and peace are given through Extreme Unction. This however, does not take place because it is a sacrament divinely instituted, but because he who receives it, receives it believing that forgiveness and peace are now his.[10]

Calvin likewise believed that healing following anointing belonged to the miraculous gifts that accompanied the first preaching of the gospel and that had now ceased within the Church; thus he condemned the Roman practice of blessing oil and anointing 'half-dead carcasses' – this was not what was meant by the practice described by James.[11] Unction, Calvin sharply commented, was 'a mere hypocritical stage play'.[12]

The lack of dominical authority for the use of oil, and its distortion into a sacrament of the dying, are reiterated themes in Reformation writing both in England and on the Continent. Bucer's contention that unction was 'neither ancient, nor commended by any precept of God or laudable example of the saints; but has been introduced by a distorted imitation of an apostolic act, of whose imitation the ministers have manifestly neither a mandate nor a faculty',[13] was echoed in many subsequent writings. Bishop Jewel in his *Treatise on the Sacraments* denied that James intended to inaugurate a universal order and practice. He objected to the rites for blessing oil, that addressed the oil – '*Ave, sanctum oleum*, Hail, O holy oil' – and prayers that the Spirit might dwell in the oil:[14]

> Would you think that St James gave courtesy by bowing his body, and saying *Ave* to the oil? Did he speak words of conjuration to drive away the evil spirit? Would he ever say that oil doth heal both body and soul? Or that remission of all sins is given by anointing?[15]

In his reply to Harding, Jewel defended the removal of baptismal anointing on the grounds that it was not apostolic. James Calfhill castigated those who sought salvation in the chrismatory – they would be 'sure to lose it in Christ . . . salvation shall not be got out of an oil-box'.[16] Bishops Grindal and Horn writing to the Swiss Reformer, Bullinger, in 1567, reported that 'the Church of England has entirely given up the use of [prayers in] a foreign tongue, breathings, exorcisms, oil, spittle, clay, lighted tapers, and other things of that kind, which by the act of parliament are never to be restored'. They added that they entirely agreed with the Swiss reformer, that 'women neither can nor ought to baptize infants on any account whatever'. (The Reformation was not often favourable to the ministry of women!)[17] In his 1576 Articles of Enquiry, Grindal asked whether the parson used 'any oil and chrism, tapers, spittle, or any other popish ceremony in the ministration of the sacrament of baptism'.[18] Objections to oil were often part of a wider repudiation of the sacramental use of material things, as we see in the comments of Bishop James Pilkington of Durham, a Marian exile and staunch Protestant, who asked in his commentary on Haggai:

What can their holy ashes, holy palms, holy crosses, holy bells, holy cream, relics, moulds, chalice, corporas, fire, candles, beads, or that which is that most holy relic, their oil, wherewith they anoint their shavelings, priests and bishops, do?

There is no creature which can give that holiness to another which is in itself; this thing belongs to Christ alone.[19]

Anointing was the inward anointing of the Spirit; the external rite, while it may have been appropriate to the very first age of the Church, where the Lord confirmed the gospel by miraculous signs, was now no longer needed. In the seventeenth century Herbert Thorndike thought the revival of anointing a theoretical possibility, but Jeremy Taylor thought it wrong for a small group to revive it without the warrant of the Church of England as a whole. In *Holy Dying*, Taylor writes that God has appointed no distinct sacraments for the dying, but has provided common ministrations for all. 'The Holy Ghost, that *anointing from above*, descends upon us in several effluxes, but ever by the ministries of the church':

> *Our heads* are anointed with that sacred unction in baptism, not in ceremony, but in real and proper effect; our *foreheads* in confirmation, *our hands* in ordination; *all our senses* in the visitation of the sick; and all by the ministry of especially deputed and instructed persons.[20]

Outward anointing is unnecessary to those who receive through these ministrations the inward anointing of the Spirit, 'whose blessed unction from above, is comfort, light, and fire of love'.[21]

Given that this was the all but universal attitude towards the use of oil, it is interesting to note the occasional exception even within the English Puritan tradition. In the seventeenth century, in a congregation of Independents in exile at Arnhem in the Netherlands, anointing with oil was introduced:

> In that Church also the Doctrine of extreme Unction was so far brought back, that they began to annoint their sick with oyl; taking it as an ordinance of Christ, and a kind of sacrament for the people, at least a holy ceremony: no less of a divine Institution than Ordination and imposition of hands were for Officers.

John Goodwin, the pastor of the congregation, wished to restore it among the Independents in England, judging that, although Protestants had been right to protest at the Roman abuse of unction, in rejecting it they had gone too far, 'even denying it to have that use of restoring the sick as a seal of the promise and an indefinite means to convey that blessing, which God in mercy hath appointed it to be'.[22]

Later on in the eighteenth century, anointing with oil was revived by the General Baptists, along with the love-feast and foot-washing.[23]

Less surprisingly, anointing was revived in the worship of the Nonjurors, in their 1718 liturgy. 'Anointing with Oil,' the preface stated, was 'not only supported by primitive practice', but commanded by St James – not, however, as Extreme Unction, but as a sacrament of healing and recovery.[24] The 1549 order is restored to its place at the end of the order for the visitation of the sick, and a prayer for blessing oil is provided:

> *Then the Priest shall take some sweet oil of olives, and, putting it in a decent vessel, he shall stand and consecrate it according to the form following*:
> O Almighty Lord God, who hast taught us by thy holy Apostle Saint James to anoint the sick with oil, that they may attain their bodily health, and render thanks unto thee for the same; look down, we beseech thee, and bless and sanctify this thy creature of oil, the juice of the olive: grant that those who shall be anointed therewith, may be delivered from all pains, troubles, and diseases both of body and mind, and from all the snares, temptations, and assaults of the powers of darkness . . .[25]

In the revised office of confirmation the sign of the cross and anointing with chrism were restored, the bishop being directed to 'anoint everyone with the Chrism or ointment, making the sign of the cross upon their forehead, and saying: "N., I sign thee with the sign of the cross, I anoint thee with Holy Ointment" '. A form is provided for the bishop to consecrate the chrism.[26] Some sixteen years later in 1734, Thomas Deacon, by then consecrated as a non-juring bishop in Manchester, published *A Compleat Collection of Devotions*, compiled on the principle that Christians should 'submit to all the doctrines, practices, worship, and discipline . . . of the ancient and universal Church of Christ from the beginning to the end of the fourth century'.[27] His model was the 'Clementine' liturgy found in the *Apostolic Constitutions*. The 1718 order was reprinted with a few amplifications suggesting that the bishop, assisted by a deacon, should consecrate the oil after the recitation of the Nicene Creed in the Eucharist. The oil is to be kept safely and priests may apply to the bishop for oil to use in their ministry. In his catechetical exposition of unction, Deacon maintains that it is 'as the outward unctions of the Church are emblems of the inward unction of the Holy Ghost' forgiveness and spiritual strength are mediated by anointing conjoined with the prayers of the priest for the sick. The outward ceremony is designed 'to render those prayers effectual'.[28]

If the sacramental use of oil had all but vanished in England after the Reformation, there was one significant and important exception:

the anointing of the monarch in the coronation rite. Kings as well as priests were anointed in the Old Testament – they were the Lord's Anointed. In Western Europe the earliest record of anointing a European king appears to have been that of Wamba or Bamba of the West Goths, who was anointed king by Quirigio, Archbishop of Toledo, in 673. In England Egferth of Mercia was anointed in 785, and the pontifical of Egbert provides for the anointing of the king. By no means all Christian kings were anointed, and in the later Middle Ages anointing was the special mark of the kings of England, France, Jerusalem, Sicily, and (after 1309) Scotland, together with the Holy Roman Emperor. The kings of England and France were distinguished by being anointed with chrism as well as with holy oil. In France the king was anointed with the oil kept in the *Saint Ampoule*, which was said to have been brought from heaven by a dove at the prayer of Saint-Rémy for the baptism of Clovis. In the coronation rite a drop of oil was taken from the *Saint Ampoule* with a golden needle and mixed with the chrism before the king was anointed seven times.[29]

At the end of the reign of Henry VIII, when chrism and oil were still being used in baptism and confirmation, the *Rationale of Ceremonial* justified the use of chrism in the following terms:

> It signifyeth principally the Imperial and priestly dignity of Christ and his anointing with the spiritual unction of the Holy Ghost above all creatures, and secondarily the defacing and abolishing of all the consecrations of the old law which were dedicate in oil, and therefore in Cena Domini the old oil is burnt and destroyed and new consecrated, signifying thereby, the new regeneration of Christ, and the holy inunction which we have by his spirit, and it admonisheth us of our state and condition which we have by Christ, for as of Chrisma Christ is named, so of Christ we be called Christians. In figure whereof kings, priests and prophets were anointed to put them in remembrance also of brightness of conscience and sweet odour of fame to God's glory and edifying of their neighbour.[30]

Edward VI was anointed according to the Latin rite, 'in the brest, in the midst of his back, on his two bowghts of his arms, and on his head making a cross; and after making another cross on his head with holy chrism'.[31] Mary Tudor, alarmed lest the oil used for Edward VI's coronation (which had come down from the time of Henry IV) should have lost its efficacy as a result of the breach with Rome, obtained a fresh supply through the Imperial ambassador, which had been blessed by the Bishop of Arras. The chrism was used for the coronation of Elizabeth I, which was the last English coronation to be in Latin. The Queen complained of the chrism that it 'was grease and smelt ill'.[32] A new chrism was prepared for the coronation of Charles I on Candlemas Day 1626. The recipe for this has survived: the 'cream', or chrism, was made from an infusion of orange and jasmine flower oil in 'oil of been', distilled rose and cinnamon oil, benzoin, ambergris, musk and civet.[33] James II's apothecary, James St Amand, prepared an 'exceeding rich and fragrant oil' for the coronation of James and Mary of Modena, for which he was paid £200.[34] A similar formula to the chrism of Charles I has been used in English coronations ever since.[35] The Stuart kings were anointed in six places: William and Mary on the crown of the head (now placed first instead of last), the breast, and the palms of the hands. At the coronations of William IV and Victoria the anointings were reduced to two: on the crown of the head and on the palms of the hands.[36]

For the coronation of Charles I the oil was blessed by William Laud, then Bishop of St Davids, in place of the Dean of Westminster (who was almost invariably a bishop who held the deanery in conjunction with a diocese). The formula is a short Latin prayer asking that the oil with which the king is to be anointed may be blessed by God so that the king may be sanctified by the Spirit, live devoutly in God's presence, and in happiness among all men. Archbishop Sancroft's prayer for the blessing of the oil at the coronation of William and Mary is in English and asks that the oil may be blessed, with which the king and queen are to be anointed and consecrated:

> And, we beseech thee, O holy Father, plenteously to pour out upon them both all the Gifts and Graces of the Holy Ghost, which thou didst of old confer upon thy chosen Servants by this Ministry, through Him who was anointed with the Oil of Gladness above his Fellows, Jesus Christ, thy Son, our Saviour.[37]

The order for anointing itself was truncated in the case of James II, for whom the whole order was shortened because of the suscepti-bilities of a Roman Catholic monarch being crowned by an Anglican archbishop. In the fuller form for Charles I's coronation, after the litany, and the prayers for the blessing, protection and guarding of the king in his office, the Archbishop begins the anointing with the *Sursum Corda*. This is followed by a preface form prayer, rehearsing the mercy of God in the dove with the olive branch which notified the end of the flood; in the consecration of Aaron, and in the making of 'Priests and Kings and Prophets to govern thy People Israel' by 'the effusion of the oil':

> We beseech thee, Almighty Father, that by the fatness of this thy creature thou wilt vouchsafe to bless and sanctify this thy servant Charles, that in the simplicity of a dove he may minister

peace unto his people; that he may imitate Aaron in the service of God; that he may attain the perfection of Government in Counsel and Judgement and that by the anointing of this Oil thou mayest give him a countenance always cheerful and amiable to the whole people.[38]

The anointing of the king's hands was done with the words, 'Let these hands be anointed with holy Oil, as Kings and Prophets have been anointed, and as Samuel did anoint David to be King.' A similar and somewhat shorter formula appears in the coronation order for William and Mary, where it is spoken at the first anointing on the crown of the head, and a brief sentence of blessing is added at the anointing of the breast and hands.[39] In the 1626 order two prayers follow the anointing. The first asks that Christ, who was anointed by the Father 'with the oil of gladness above his fellows', might 'by his anointing, pour down upon [the king's] head the blessing of the Holy Ghost and make it enter into the bowels of thy heart, that so by this visible gift thou mayest receive invisible grace'. The second petitions that by the anointing of holy oil the king's heart may be kindled with the love of God's grace.[40] In Bishop Henry Compton's order for the coronation of William and Mary, the anointing is followed by a reference to the anointing of Solomon, which has already appeared in the anthem sung before the anointing in this and earlier orders: 'As Solomon was anointed King by Zadok the Priest, and Nathan the Prophet; so be You anointed, blessed, and consecrated'. Wickham Legg suggests that by the insertion of the word 'consecrate' here and in the prayer for the blessing of the oil ('Bless this Oil . . . and sanctify these thy chosen Servants . . . who . . . are now to be anointed, and consecrated King and Queen of this Realm'), Compton was attempting to compensate for the omission of the prayers before the anointing, in which the archbishop prayed for God's blessing on the king, 'whom in lowly devotion we do consecrate', prayers that had been omitted in the reduced rite for James II's coronation.[41]

The anointing of the sovereign endured as the sole use of oil in the Church of England from the Reformation until the Oxford Movement, but even then there was little in the way of the revival of anointing until quite late in the day. Professor Charles Gusmer, in his study of the ministry of healing in the Church of England, expresses surprise that so little notice has been taken in studies of the Oxford Movement of efforts to revive the anointing of the sick. But Gusmer himself can only point to a short discussion by Alexander Forbes, Bishop of Brechin, in his commentary on the Thirty-nine Articles (1867), an essay by John Henry Pye, *Ought the sick to be anointed?*, published in the same year, and an 1881 catechism on anointing by Charles S. Greueber. In addition, there are forms for anointing of the sick published by Pye, Brother Cecil of the Society of St Joseph, and the order provided by the *Priest's Book of Private Devotion*, which first appeared in 1872 and went through various revisions.[42] The Protestant controversialist, Walter Walsh, ever alert to record the spread of popish practices in the Victorian Church of England, is only able to offer among his examples of ritualist teaching a prayer from the *Day Office of the Church* for exorcizing oil.[43] The anonymous *English Catholic's Vade Mecum* (4th edn, 1874) simply reprints the form of anointing from the 1549 Prayer Book.[44] In F. G. Lee's 'Guide for the reverent and decent celebration of Divine Service, the Holy Sacraments, and other Offices', *The Manuale Clericorum* (1874), the priest is directed to use the order from the 1549 Prayer Book. Lee noted in the appendix that the three oils were formerly consecrated by bishops on Maundy Thursday. Now that this was no longer the case, the right of blessing reverted to the priest, who had 'an inalienable *power to consecrate* – for he performs the highest sacerdotal act when he says "HOC EST CORPUS MEUM" '. Blessing of oils was not an essential part of the bishop's office.[45]

Bishop Forbes of Brechin, the first Tractarian bishop, certainly believed it was, and not only blessed oil himself but supplied episcopally blessed oil to those known to him in various parts of the country who required it. It was Forbes who administered unction to the dying Sister Katherine of the Sisterhood of the Holy Cross in 1850 – the first recorded anointing of the sick in the Church of England, apart from the Nonjurors, since the Reformation.[46]

On Maundy Thursday 1894, Archbishop Benson was present at Florence as a private visitor for the Holy Week and Easter ceremonies, and attended the consecration of the oils – surely the first Archbishop of Canterbury to witness this since the Reformation. Despite Benson's considerable liturgical knowledge, his reaction was typically Protestant:

> Bishop seated in hideous mitre down on his cope, looking east. Chapter round him in three sides of a square, Archdeacon beside him; after each oil was compounded and consecrated, each Canon approached and singing three times in higher and higher key 'Ave Sanctum Chrisma' or 'Ave Sanctum Oleum', kissed the lips of the vessel containing it, and breathed on it.
>
> This seems to be 'Sacerdotalism' if you like. But it is difficult to penetrate alien ideas.[47]

With the turn of the century, F. W. Puller of the Cowley Fathers delivered a series of lectures on anointing of the sick, which were subsequently published. Having provided a scholarly study of the biblical roots of anointing of the sick, and its subsequent development in the early and medieval Church, Puller urged the restoration of unction in the Church of England. It had scriptural warrant; supernatural healing was to be expected in the Church, and Puller knew 'of very remarkable recoveries which have followed on the administration of Unction to the sick, by priests belonging to our own branch of the Church'; official recognition of anointing would strengthen belief in the power of prayer, and would enable the Church to offer a sacramental ministry to those who were seeking healing from faith-healers. Puller in particular mentioned 'the Peculiar People', a sect particularly strong in Essex, who were founded in London in 1838 and practised anointing in lieu of medical treatment.[48] Puller's lectures, together with Percy Dearmer's advocacy, and provision of liturgical forms in the 1907 edition of *The Parson's Handbook*, provided the important impetus that led to the official recovery of anointing of the sick in the Church of England. Puller believed that it was for the bishops to decide whether they would reserve the right of consecrating oils to themselves, or whether they would depute it to a priest, as in the East.[49] In Dearmer's form, which became the basis of the subsequent official forms, the consecration of the oil by the priest was adapted from the Nonjurors' liturgy, the prayer of anointing was a version of the 1549 prayer, and a concluding collect was taken from the Greek *Euchologion*.[50] John Wordsworth, the Bishop of Salisbury, a noted liturgist, believed there to be 'no sufficient precedent or reason' for restricting the blessing of the oil of the sick to a bishop, and hoped that, were anointing to be given official sanction, care would be taken to avoid: '(1) any appearance of locally and permanently transferring Divine power and presence into the *creatura olei*; (2) the consequent requirement that the Bishop should be a sort of spiritual apothecary, keeping a store of unguents of divers kinds'.[51] In a subsequent direction, Wordsworth ordered that oil should be blessed by the priest for the occasion; that 'the anointing should be on the forehead, or on the forehead and the palms of the hands'; and that 'all the oil should be consumed'.[52]

After the First World War the Lambeth Conference of 1920 appointed a commission on the ministry of healing, which reported in 1924. The commission urged that prayer and sacrament should be used in conjunction, suggested that 'religious methods' were most appropriate 'where moral or intellectual difficulties have contributed to the disorder', and concluded that ministry 'more immediately directed to the complete restoration of the patient' might then be used. 'This may take the form of Unction (i.e. anointing with oil by a priest), or of Laying on of hands (either by a priest or a lay person), or of both.'[53] It was hoped that, with this encouragement, unction might find a place in the Revised Prayer Book, but the bishops wished to wait until the Lambeth Conference of 1930 had had an opportunity to consider it. The revised order for ministry to the sick in the

1928 Prayer Book therefore only made provision for the laying on of hands.

One of the leading proponents of a restored rite of unction was Prebendary Charles Harris, from the Anglo-Catholic wing of the Church. Harris, whose own personal ministry to the sick was notable (he claimed in his Canterbury Convocation speech of 1931 to have 'anointed and laid hands on thousands of people during the last twenty-five years'),[54] successfully carried a motion in the Lower House of the Convocation of Canterbury requesting the bishops to provide a rite for unction of the sick. Such a service was to be 'drafted with due consideration for ancient precedent and for modern pastoral experience and therapeutic psychology', the rites being tailored 'not only to the physically infirm, but also to mental and nervous sufferers'.[55] Harris played a major part on the drafting committee subsequently set up by the bishops. In the subsequent debates there was anxiety among some bishops about the encouragement of superstitious uses of oil. The Modernist Bishop Barnes of Birmingham declared that the approval of any form of unction would be a 'retrograde step towards religious barbarism'.[56] The supporters of unction carried the day and in 1935 a form of Administration of Holy Unction was approved by the Canterbury Convocation for 'provisional use in the Province subject to diocesan sanction'. Two forms are given in 'The Order of the Hallowing of Oil', which might be performed by either a bishop or a priest. In his major article on 'The Visitation of the Sick' in the 1932 symposium, *Liturgy and Worship*, Harris had argued that, although it was more fitting for a bishop to consecrate the oil, there were ample precedents for a priest doing so:

> An Anglican priest need have no hesitation in consecrating his own oil, when episcopal oil is difficult to obtain; but he should ordinarily use oil supplied by his own Bishop, partly out of respect for his office as the chief minister of the Sacraments, and partly from psychological considerations, episcopal oil having undoubtedly much greater 'prestige' in the eyes of patients than the oil of a simple priest.[57]

Harris also suggested that when it was desirable 'that auxiliary daily anointings should be performed by the husband, wife, or nurse of the sick person, or by some authorized sick-visitor, or by the patient himself, oil in sufficient quantity should be blessed by the priest'. Harris also implies that he would hope for a more copious application of oil than the exiguous way in which unction was contemporarily administered, citing the words of Matthaeus Galenus:

> [Unction] was not formerly performed so sparingly as now; but the whole body was smeared and anointed. Not only were the

organs of the senses anointed, but all the parts in which the disease lurked, and that sometimes for seven successive days . . .[58]

It is noteworthy that the coronation anointing was always 'on the crown of the head' and with a sufficiency of oil, which necessitated a linen coif being worn by the newly anointed monarch.[59] Harris was also concerned that unction should be seen as a remedial, therapeutic ministry, appropriately used in cases of mental as well as physical illness. Unction should be performed 'while the patient is in a relaxed, tranquil and receptive condition of mind' and should continue daily – or very frequently – until the patient is decidedly better.[60] Harris also proposed that in 'grave cases of sexual obsession . . . the *quasi-exorcistic* use of Unction' may well be 'extraordinarily effective':

> In all the graver sexual cases, Unction should be used. Treatment, if successful, should conclude with a final administration of Unction for the purpose of *the solemn reconsecration of the Temple of the Holy Ghost*. Before its administration in this sense and for this purpose, St. Paul's teaching that the human body is the temple of the Holy Ghost should be strongly impressed on the mind of the patient; and I Cor.vi.19–20 should be read. This method of administering Unction is a valuable safeguard against relapse.[61]

Harris notes that unction with special reference to the remission of the sins of lust was known in medieval England, the Sarum Manual providing for anointing on the loins in the case of the man and the navel in the case of a woman, for this purpose; the York Manual providing for an anointing of the navel for both sexes.[62]

The 1935 Canterbury order provided two forms for the 'hallowing of the Oil', one based on a prayer from the Sarum Pontifical, the other a version of the Nonjurors' liturgy. The Sarum prayer is less explicitly a direct blessing of the oil than the one based on the Nonjurors' form, which asks God 'to bless and sanctify this oil'. The Sarum prayer asks that

> by the operation of the Holy Ghost, the Comforter, this oil may avail for the healing of all infirmities. To all who receive it, and put their trust in thy mercy, may this anointing be a heavenly medicine, a spiritual remedy, an inward and abiding unction, unto the strengthening and healing of soul and mind and body, and the renewal of the indwelling of the Holy Ghost in thy living temple.[63]

Anointing was to be done with the right thumb in the sign of the cross on the forehead of the sick person. The Convocation of York followed

Canterbury in providing a form for unction in 1936. In other parts of the Anglican Communion, forms for unction had been provided in America (1928), Scotland (1929), and were to be provided in South Africa (1954) and Canada (1962). Gusmer's 1974 study of the development of the ministry of healing in the Church of England includes a number of later unofficial texts, though before the form of anointing authorized in *Ministry to the Sick* (1983). In this form unction is moved from the point after communion which Harris and the 1935 service had thought appropriate, to a point following the ministry of the word and general confession. A rubric states that anointing 'should be used more sparingly than the laying on of hands, and is especially appropriate for use when a sick person is at a time of crisis'. The provision of the canons is noted that 'the priest "should use pure olive oil consecrated by the bishop of the diocese or otherwise by the priest himself" ', but no form is given for the priest to do this. In the same way, the Synod refused to authorize a form for blessing oils on Maundy Thursday, despite eucharistic propers having been provided in the *Alternative Service Book 1980*. The 1979 American Prayer Book provides a form for the priest to bless the oil for anointing the sick, and there is a rubric stating that in cases of necessity a deacon or layperson may perform the anointing using oil blessed by a bishop or priest. The prayer for blessing oil refers to Mark 6.13 and not to James. ('Send your Holy Spirit to sanctify this oil; that, as your holy apostles anointed many that were sick and healed them, so may those who in faith and repentance receive this holy unction be made whole.') Anointing is by the sign of the cross on the forehead. The Canadian *Book of Alternative Services* (1985) has an introductory note stating that the laying on of hands and anointing 'provide the moment when the prayer of the Church for the healing power of God is made specific and particular in relation to the sick person'. 'It is also a sign of forgiveness and consequently of reconciliation in and with the Christian community.' Anointing may be performed by laypersons authorized by the bishop. All use oil blessed by the bishop. The warrant is again given by reference to the gospel, but unfortunately by linking anointing with the laying on of hands it appears to suggest clear gospel warrant for Jesus anointing, as well as the twelve.

In recent years American Protestantism has seen a number of revivals of anointing of the sick. In the Lutheran tradition provision is made for anointing in the *Occasional Services* published as a companion to *The Lutheran Book of Worship* (1982). This may be either in a setting of corporate worship, or at home or in hospital. After the laying on of hands in silence, the minister may 'dip a thumb in oil, make a sign of the cross on the forehead', and pray that, as the apostles anointed and healed many who were sick, so the Spirit may be given to the one anointed with oil that he or she 'may in repentance and hope be made whole'. A rubric states that, 'The oil for anointing is olive oil, to which an aromatic ingredient such as synthetic oil of cinnamon or oil of bergamot may be added.' The *Book of Worship* (1986) of the United Church of Christ and the Presbyterian *Holy Baptism and Services for the Renewal of Baptism* under the title 'Renewal of Baptism for the Sick and Dying' contain forms of anointing.[64]

There is no doubt that anointing of the sick has been the major area of growth in the use of oil among the churches of the Anglican Communion and also, to a more limited extent, among some of the Reformed churches. In an attempt (1) to assess when oils were first blessed in the Church of England, (2) to ascertain what form was used, and (3) to judge the extent of the increase of the use of oil at baptisms and confirmations following the rubric permitting its optional use in the *Alternative Service Book*, enquiries were made of all diocesan bishops and cathedrals. A small handful of dioceses, under the influence of sympathetic bishops, had blessed oil before 1960, another ten began to do so in the 1960s, about another ten began to do so in the 1970s, and there now seems to be blessing of oils publicly by the bishop – almost invariably at a Maundy Thursday Eucharist – in all dioceses. The influence of the reformed Roman Catholic Holy Week order, with the renewal of priestly vows at the Chrism Mass, has been powerful. A signficant number of replies indicated that the use of oil had increased – the amount consecrated being between 3.5 and 4.5 litres. Most of this increase was attributed to the more widespread use of oil for anointing the sick, where those influenced by the charismatic movement have frequently taken this into their practice. The use of anointing at confirmation seems to have grown fairly slowly, though significantly so in some dioceses – particularly where the bishop has encouraged it. Sodor and Man is the only diocese in the Church of England where its use at confirmation is now universal and widely accepted.[65]

One further Christian tradition making use of oil should perhaps finally be noted. In the nineteenth century the Catholic Apostolic Church grew out of the charismatic movement inspired by Edward Irving and, under the influence in particular of J. B. Cardale, developed a richly symbolic liturgical life in which anointing figured significantly. A full form was provided for the anointing of the sick, with a prayer of blessing of oil to be used in case of necessity. The gift of the Spirit is asked, to 'bless + this oil to the mystical healing, through thy divine power, of the body and soul of this thy servant'. Anointing is in the name of the Trinity, and with a petition that 'all pain, infirmity and sickness may be expelled' from the body and the soul 'delivered from all corruption and power of sin'.[66] In the rite for the consecration of an angel (bishop) the candidate is anointed with chrism by the consecrating apostle, who seals the candidate with the cross, and consecrates him to the office of an angel, praying that he may be imbued 'with the mystical anointing of the Holy Spirit'.[67]

Looking back over the four centuries since the Reformation on the use of oil among Anglicans and Protestants, it is clear that, beginning in the last century and continuing in this, the old Reformation polemic against the supposed superstition of the use of a material substance like oil to express and be an effectual sign of God's grace has largely ceased to carry weight. In England the continuous use of oil for anointing kings was throughout this time a limited though significant witness. Small groups occasionally felt compelled by scriptural warrant to restore the use of oil for healing, but only in this century has it become increasingly accepted. The Welsh poet, David Jones, in an important essay, 'Art and Sacrament', wrote of how our bodiliness affirms the essential sacramentality of our being, a sacramentality that was given the most powerful affirmation of all, when, taking human flesh, God 'placed himself in the order of signs'. Thus Jones writes:

> Theology regards the body as a unique good. Without body: without sacrament. Angels only: no sacrament. Beasts only: no sacrament. Man sacrament at every turn and all levels of the 'profane' and 'sacred', in the trivial and in the profound, no escape from sacrament.[68]

The Reformation with its exaltation of the word, and its suspicion of the spiritual power of matter, was in danger of forgetting it. The poet Edwin Muir, on discovering the inseparable link between incarnation and sacrament, reflected on the practical denial of this in his Scottish Calvinist background:

> How could our race betray
> The Image, and the Incarnate One unmake
> Who chose this form and fashion for our sake?
>
> The Word made flesh here is made word again,
> A word made word in flourish and arrogant crook.
> See there King Calvin with his iron pen,
> And God three angry letters in a book,
> And there the ideological hook
> On which the Mystery is impaled and bent
> Into an ideological instrument.[69]

As in the incarnation the word is made flesh, so in God's healing and consecrating grace the outward anointing of oil is made the effectual sign of the inward anointing of the Holy Spirit.

Notes

1. D. F. Wright, *Common-Places of Martin Bucer* (Appleford 1972), p. 224.
2. E. E. Yelverton, *The Manual of Olavus Petri* (London 1953), p. xi.
3. ibid., p. 63.
4. ibid., p. 64.
5. ibid., p. 108.
6. ibid., p. 87.
7. ibid., pp. 88–9.
8. ibid., p. 48, note 2.
9. M. Luther, 'On the Babylonian Captivity of the Church', in J. Dillenberger, ed., *Martin Luther: Selections from his Writings* (New York 1961), p. 352.
10. ibid., p. 355.
11. cf. I. Calvini, *Opera Selecta*, V, pp. 452–5, cited in C. W. Gusmer, *And You Visited Me* (New York 1984), p. 33.
12. J. Calvin, *Institutes*. iv. 19, 18
13. Bucer, *Censura*, cited in C. W. Gusmer, *The Ministry of Healing* (Alcuin Club Collections, 56, Greak Wakering 1974), p. 71.
14. J. Jewel, *Works* ii (Parker Society, XXI, Cambridge 1847), p. 1136.
15. ibid.
16. J. Calfhill, *Works* (Parker Society, XXX, Cambridge 1846), p. 218.
17. *Zurich Letters*, i (Parker Society, VII, Cambridge 1842), p. 178 (Letter xxv).
18. E. Grindal, *Remains* (Parker Society, IX, Cambridge 1843), p. 160.
19. J. Pilkington, *Works* (Parker Society, III, Cambridge 1842), p. 164.
20. J. Taylor, *Holy Dying*, V.i (*The Whole Works of . . . Jeremy Taylor*, London 1822, IV, p. 505).
21. H. B. Porter, *Jeremy Taylor, Liturgist (1613–1667)* (Alcuin Club Collections, no. 61, London 1979), pp. 115–16; John Cosin's translation of the *Veni Creator*.
22. W. Horton Davies, *The Worship of the English Puritans* (Westminster 1946), p. 245.
23. W. Horton Davies, *Worship and Theology in England: From Watts and Wesley to Maurice, 1690–1850* (Princeton and London 1961), p. 128.
24. Gusmer, *Ministry of Healing*, p. 75.
25. Cited in ibid., p. 76.
26. T. Lathbury, *A History of the Nonjurors: Their Controversies and Writings, with Remarks on Some of the Rubrics in the Book of Common Prayer* (1845), p. 495.
27. H. Broxap, *Thomas Deacon: A Biography* (Manchester 1911), p. 173.
28. Gusmer, *Ministry of Healing*, p. 77.
29. For this, and further details of the anointing of the last pre-Revolutionary king of France, Louis XVI, see J. McManners, 'Authority in Church and State: Reflections on the Coronation of Louis XVI', in G. R. Evans, ed., *Christian Authority: Essays in Honour of Henry Chadwick* (Oxford 1988), pp. 280–1.

30. C. S. Cobb, *The Rationale of Ceremonial 1540–1543* (Alcuin Club Collections, XVIII, London 1910), pp. 14–15.
31. C. Wordsworth, ed., *The Manner of the Coronation of King Charles the First of England* (Henry Bradshaw Society, London 1892), p. 32 note.
32. ibid., p. xxi note.
33. ibid., p. 4; p. xxi note, where 'oil of been' is identified as either oil from the ben-nut of the Indian horse-radish tree (*moring pterygosperma*), or sesame oil.
34. ibid., p. xxi note.
35. cf. J. D. Jamieson, 'The Anointing of the Queen, Some Notes on the Coronation Oil', *The Pharmaceutical Journal* (30 May 1953), pp. 404–5 and 415.
36. J. Wickham Legg, *Three Coronation Orders* (Henry Bradshaw Society, XIX, Westminster, 1900), p. 144.
37. Wordsworth, *The Manner of the Coronation*, pp. xix–xx and note. This form disappears in the order for Queen Anne's coronation (cf. Wickham Legg, *Three Coronation Orders*, p. xxiii).
38. ibid., pp. 30–1.
39. Wickham Legg, *Three Coronation Orders*, p. 22.
40. Wordsworth, *The Manner of the Coronation*, pp. 34–5.
41. Wickham Legg, *Three Coronation Orders*, pp. 22 and xxii; L. G. Wickham Legg, *English Coronation Records* (Westminster 1901), p. 255. The prayer for the consecration of the monarch followed that in the medieval coronation rite found in the fourteenth century *Liber Regalis* (cf. p. 89).
42. Gusmer, *Ministry of Healing*, pp. 80–5, passim.
43. W. Walsh, *The Secret History of the Oxford Movement* (5th edn, London 1899), pp. 407–8.
44. *English Catholics Vade Mecum* (4th edn, London 1874) pp. 135–6.
45. *The Manuale Clericorum* (London 1874) pp. 162, 236–7.
46. T. J. Williams and A. W. Campbell, *The Park Village Sisterhood* (1965), pp. 68–9.
47. A. C. Benson, *The Life of Edward White Benson, sometime Archbishop of Canterbury*, II (London 1899), p. 241.
48. F. W. Puller, *The Anointing of the Sick in Scripture and Tradition with some considerations on the Numbering of the Sacraments* (1904), pp. 300ff.
49. ibid., pp. 302 and note, 381–2.
50. Cited in Gusmer, *Ministry of Healing*, p. 94.
51. E. W. Watson, *Life of Bishop John Wordsworth* (London 1915), p. 312.
52. ibid., p. 313.
53. C. Harris, in W. K. Lowther Clark, *Liturgy and Worship* (London 1932), pp. 473–5.
54. F. L. Cross, *Darwell Stone, Churchman and Counsellor* (Westminster 1943), p. 214.
55. Gusmer, *Ministry of Healing* p. 99.
56. ibid., p. 101.
57. Lowther Clark, *Liturgy and Worship*, p. 485.
58. ibid., p. 496 note.
59. The anointing 'on the crown of the head' was still the usage at the

coronation of Queen Elizabeth II in 1953, though the linen coif has disappeared, presumably with oil being used more exiguously.

60. Lowther Clark, p. 522.
61. ibid., p. 528.
62. ibid., p. 491 note.
63. Gusmer, *Ministry of Healing*, pp. 103–4.
64. Gusmer, *And You Visited Me*, pp. 39–40.
65. Discussion of the diocesan forms of service for blessing of oil will be found in the liturgical texts section. It is also interesting to note that this growth in the sacramental use of oil in the Church of England has coincided with the growth of aromatherapy.
66. *The Liturgy and other Divine Offices of the Church* (London n.d.), pp. 524–5.
67. ibid., p. 450.
68. D. Jones, *Epoch and Artist* (London 1959), p. 167. The phrase 'he placed himself in the order of signs' is quoted by Jones from the French Jesuit theologian, Maurice de la Taille, ibid., p. 179.
69. E. Muir, 'The Incarnate One', *Collected Poems* (London 1960), p. 228.

11

The Sacrament of Anointing Administered in Hospital

Norman Autton

How wonderful it is, is it not, that literally only Christianity has taught us the true peace and function of suffering. The Stoics tried the hopeless little game of denting its objective reality . . . and the Pessimists attempted to revel in it . . . but Christ came, and he did not really explain it; he did far more, he met it, willed it, transformed it, and he taught us how to do all this, or rather he himself does it within us, if we do not hinder the all-healing hands . . . in suffering we are very near to God (Friedrich von Hugel).

The picture

Sickness has a habit of taking us all unawares, and seldom do we seem prepared for it. It has little respect for time and no concern for circumstance; there can be no standard or stereotyped reaction, no rigid rules or regulations. We seem cut off from the ordinary routine of everyday life in a hospital ward; no longer are we actively involved in 'the trivial round' or the 'common task'. Sickness somehow alienates us and we 'lose our place'; we become all too aware of the seeming chasm between 'the world of the sick' and 'the world of the well'. Being a hospital patient may be too personal and individualistic a matter for either advice or generalization, but it very soon reveals to us what we are and who we are spiritually as well as physically. If our religion is one of mere formal and rigid observance, it will indeed be

154

sorely tested. Should we be one of those numerous people like Hetty in George Eliot's *Adam Bede*, 'who have had Godfathers and Godmothers, learned their catechism, been confirmed, and gone to church every Sunday, and yet for any practical result of strength in life or trust in death, have never appropriated a single Christian idea or Christian feeling', we shall find it extremely difficult to derive any degree of spiritual help during a period in a hospital ward.

What a difference it makes when we know that we shall never have to suffer alone, but we always suffer in Christ. Behind all our pain and suffering there is a God who not only cares, but who shares. The victory gained is not so much *over* pain as *through* pain. Between the love of God and the problem of pain stands the cross of Christ, reconciling, healing and redeeming. No longer will pain or suffering be a predicament when we recognize God through his Holy Spirit immanent in our lives and present in our pain; *faith* rather than *explanation*, *confidence* rather than *diffidence*, will be the watchwords. 'Now is my soul in turmoil and what am I to say? Father, save me from this hour? No, it was for this that I came to this hour. Father, glorify thy name' (John 12.27–28).

As Christians it is our duty to help overcome our sickness, thus bringing good out of evil – to struggle rather than succumb. In the words of Teilhard de Chardin: 'The Christian is not to swoon in the shadow, but to climb in the might of the cross.' It is our duty to take every reasonable step to get well, using all that is best of the resources of both church and medicine. It is only thus that we grow through suffering.

One of the main resources offered by the Church is the great healing sacrament of anointing with oil, which can be administered by the hospital chaplain or, with his permission, the patient's own parish priest. Much of the loneliness or seeming isolation in sickness is overcome when we realize that by use of the Church's sacraments we are united not only with our own parish church, but with the whole Body of Christ. We are as Christians always 'in the church, with the church, and for the church'.

The preparation

The priest

The administration of the sacrament will require much personal preparation. The priest cannot pray and prepare others unless he himself is endeavouring to the best of his ability to be an open and receptive channel of God's healing grace. The contagion of his own personal spiritual life will speak far more meaningfully than any words he may utter: 'The glory which you gave me I have given to them' (John 17.22).

At all times the priest's preparatory prayers will be as his Lord's, short and simple; always in the name of Jesus Christ, and seeking their fulfilment 'through Jesus Christ our Lord'. The remembrance of the sick patient to be anointed, by name, will make his preparation more personal and penetrating: 'Simon, Simon . . . I have prayed that your faith may not fail' (see Luke 22.31; cf. Mark 5.9; Rom. 1.9; Eph. 1.15, 16). Sick people, especially those who are facing crisis, often experience a deep sense of loneliness and frustration: 'Sir, I have no one . . .' (John 5.7), 'Why this waste?' (Matt. 26.8) and prayer becomes increasingly difficult particularly with the onset of pain or weakness. Such personal prayer on their behalf by the priest and his worshipping community symbolizes true sympathy and identification. Together they will be meeting with Christ about the sickness of another. Like the four friends of the Gospel story (Mark 2.1–5), they will lay the patient's needs at the feet of their Lord, leaving him there in perfect confidence and trust.

An important part of the hospital chaplain's ministry will be to build up full confidence in and co-operation with the doctors, nurses, and all who are ministering to the needs of the patient. They should also be informed about the anointing, and the full meaning and significance of the sacrament explained, so that their own understanding, and prayerful support will be forthcoming. It will be pointed out in preparation that the form of healing will be in God's hands for it is not ours to direct or to demand. Rather, in faith the patient needs to be content to respond firmly and convincingly with others who have sought Christ's help in affliction: ' "Do you believe that I have power to do what you want?" "Yes, Sir", they said. Then he touched their eyes and said, "As you have believed, so let it be" ' (Matt. 9.28–29).

Prayers of preparation by the priest will also include periods of stillness and silence. 'Speak, Lord, for thy servant heareth' is a petition which can so easily be reversed. Silent prayer and meditation at the bedside will instil calmness and courage. 'In quietness and confidence will be your strength'. 'Thou will keep him in perfect peace whose mind is stayed on thee'. The priest in the hospital ward must take pains to see that such a mode of prayer is a period of *living silence* and not of *dead stillness*.

The patient

There will be those patients who are already familiar with the sacraments and who are living within the mystical body of Christ, the Church, through regular prayer, worship and reception of the sacraments. Others who are less familiar with the healing ministry of the Church will need a fuller and more thorough understanding of the sacrament, should their physical and emotional state allow. It cannot be overemphasized that the patient should have a clear appreciation of the significance of anointing with oil, together with a sincere desire for its use. Time spent by the sick person in preparation will of necessity have to be flexible. It needs must vary with each patient as well as with the urgency of the circumstances.

Where conditions allow, the patient may be encouraged to read (or have read to him) passages of Scripture that speak of prayer and penitence, of hope and of healing, of praise and thanksgiving. They should be read slowly, intelligently and meaningfully. 'Did not our hearts burn within us as he talked with us . . . and explained the scriptures to us' (Luke 24.32). As well as reading, the patient will be listening: listening to Christ speaking through the pages of the Gospels; in this way the reader will be holding, as it were, a dialogue with Christ. It is only then that Christ's word becomes a lantern unto our feet and a light unto our paths (Ps. 119.105). A helpful selection of Psalms and Readings is found in the Appendix (pp. 50–60) of 'Ministry to the Sick', Authorized Alternative Services.

Sickness so quickly saps energy, and creates emotional tenseness and spiritual lethargy, all of which have an effect upon our prayer life. Consequently, the simpler and shorter the patient's prayers are the better, and the more direct and positive petitions are the more effective they become. Such preparatory prayer will place ourselves at God's disposal so that he can do with us and in us what he himself wills for us. In our prayers we shall try to unite ourselves with the crucified Christ, offering ourselves and our sufferings – feeble, weak and sick instruments though we are – as channels through which his work of redemption might be wrought. Such prayers will be set against the background of the praying of the whole Body of Christ and they will form part of the prayers of the whole Church. 'This is how you should pray; *OUR* Father . . .' (Matt. 6.9). The sick person will not be praying as an isolated individual but as a corporate member of the Church of Christ.

A sense of penitence will be very necessary, for forgiveness and healing are closely linked. There can be either a formal or general confession which will be a requisite if the patient is to approach the sacrament in the right frame of mind. 'Go, sin no more,' said our Lord to those whom he healed. Absolution is granted by the authority of the priest who acts not only for God, but also on behalf of the fellowship of the Church to which all belong.

Hope will enable us to place ourselves whole-heartedly in his care, submit ourselves to his love, and resign ourselves to his wisdom. Instilled with hope and expectancy there will be no demand for a particular blessing, but rather the assurance that peace and joy will most certainly be ours.

The procedure

The anointing is most commonly administered during periods of crisis, prolonged pain and chronic illness, and before surgery (recalling that there is no such thing as a 'minor' operation to the patient concerned). There may be long periods of deterioration or weakness, and situations in which there appears to be little hope of physical recovery. General practice seems to be that the sacrament is used sparingly, and the sacramental act of the laying on of hands (which forms an important part of the sacrament of anointing) is deemed more suitable for frequent administration. It appears wise to be guided by good sense and sound pastoral experience.

It is usually administered in the context of the sacrament of Holy Communion (see 'Ministry to the Sick', Authorized Alternative Services, pp. 29–34), but should this not be practical it may form part of morning or evening prayer, or of the office of compline. In other circumstances it is of course administered on its own.

A small bedside table or locker should be made available in the hospital ward, prepared similarly as for the reception of Holy Communion (should the anointing take place within the rite). On the white cloth will be placed the stock containing the hallowed oil, together with some cotton wool in a glass bowl. The oil will have been blessed by the bishop for use (traditionally each Maundy Thursday), but the priest himself may bless it before the anointing if necessary. He will dip his thumb in the holy oil at the appropriate part of the service, and make the sign of the cross on the forehead of the sick person, using these or similar words: 'N, I anoint you with oil in the name of our Lord Jesus Christ. May our heavenly Father make you whole in body and mind, and grant you the inward anointing of his Holy Spirit, the Spirit of strength and joy and peace. Amen.'

The following prayer, or some other appropriate one, may be said:

> The almighty Lord, who is a strong tower to all who put their trust in him, be now and evermore your defence, and make you believe and trust that the only name under heaven given for health and salvation is the name of our Lord Jesus Christ. Amen.

The priest will afterwards wipe the patient's forehead with the cotton wool, and also cleanse his own thumb and fingers. Where appropriate he will then resume the Holy Communion at 'The Peace' (Holy Communion Rite A, sections 30,31; Rite B, sections 24,25); the cotton wool will be burnt after use.

Canon B 37 provides that the anointing should be made on the forehead with the sign of the cross, but other parts of the body may be anointed in addition to the forehead. This symbolic act will be carried out slowly, reverently and with dignity, for it will remind the sick person of the passion of Christ, and the definite feel of the holy oil marked in the form of a cross will inspire confidence and strengthen faith. In this sign we can offer up ourselves and our pain and suffering and that of others to Christ, not as a magic symbol but as an assurance and pledge of his presence with us: 'Hold thou thy cross before my closing eyes, shine through the gloom, and point me to the skies.'

Silence may be kept at appropriate points within the liturgical order at the discretion of the priest. After receiving the sacrament, the sick person may wish to relax, rest and express thanks. The anointing will be seen as granting healing and hallowing grace to withstand the many evil influences that prove a great strain and create such stress to body, mind and spirit in times of sickness. Its prime purpose is the strengthening of the spirit rather than the sole physical improvement of the body (although this may often occur as a result). The benefits of the sacrament will almost certainly include the hallowing of the spirit, the quieting of the mind, and the allaying of fear and anxiety, all of which can help the patient to face up to the trials of sickness with renewed strength and inner calm.

The sacrament may be administered away from the ward and in the hospital chapel should the patient be ambulant or be able to be brought in a wheelchair. The chapel will provide more accommodation should family, friends, and members of medical and nursing staff be present. The corporate nature of the sacrament is thus emphasized and the rite itself carried out in an atmosphere of peace and quiet away from the busyness and hurly-burly of a normal hospital ward.

At the discretion of the priest, very sick children, those patients who are unconscious or not in their normal state of mind, may be anointed, for the faith, penitence and prayers of the faithful will uphold and strengthen them. In cases of dire emergency a simple form such as the following may be used: 'By this holy anointing may the Lord forgive you whatever you have done amiss. Amen.'

Finally, it should be stressed that the administration of the sacrament of anointing is not confined in its usage to any niceties of 'churchmanship' or 'specialized ministries'; rather, it is to be used by every parish priest as part of his normal pastoral ministry.

Pastoral care

Should the patient remain in hospital for a period of time, subsequent pastoral care will be exercised by the chaplain. If there is an early discharge home, the chaplain will commend the sick person to the parish priest so that ongoing support and encouragement can be given. What consolation will be granted by the knowledge that one is being sustained and strengthened by the thoughts and prayers of other members of the Body of Christ, by the faithful worshipping community, by the prayer group and individual friends. Such prayers offered on our behalf can give us new impetus, invigorating our whole outlook, and often radically changing the course of our illness for the better. The awareness that 'two or three have met together' on our behalf 'will grant us strength and power through his spirit in our inner being' (Eph. 3.16).

The priest will encourage the patient to continue to make acts of faith, hope and love that 'we may so pass through things temporal, that we finally lose not the things eternal'. By abandoning our whole selves to the fulfilment of God's purposes within us, we are kept 'both outwardly in our bodies and inwardly in our souls'.

After the anointing the sick person may achieve a speedy recovery of health. More often, though, healing will be gradual and a steady physical improvement noted. At other times a wonderful sense of peace and joy will be granted to the patient without perhaps any significant physical restoration, yet he will be enabled to offer his pain and weakness in union with the redemptive work of Christ and become obedient to the mystery of God's will. No suffering is ever wasted for it can be used for higher purposes, as Christ himself, 'son though he was, learned obedience in the school of suffering, and, once perfected, became the source of eternal salvation for all who obey him' (Heb. 5.8). There will be occasions, too, when complete healing may only come through death itself.

The norm of the ministry of healing is the full co-operation of church and medicine as they work together for the wholeness of man. The command of our Lord to heal was a general summons to his whole Church, and not only to those of the ordained ministry. In pastoral care of those who have been anointed the chaplain works alongside the consultant, the parish priest with the general practitioner. As healing is part of the total gospel, so its fulfilment includes priest and laypeople exercising together a corporate ministry. Healing involves not so much the faith of an individual sufferer, but rather the faith of the whole Church offering to God the co-operation that is an essential element for the working out of his acts of salvation. It is St Paul in 1 Cor. 13 who points us to 'the best way of all': the ongoing corporate ministry of the Christian congregation, which is 'patient, kind and envies no one . . . as never selfish . . . keeps no score of wrongs . . . delights in the truth . . . [has] no limit to its faith, its hope, and its endurance', as the true healing power given through his body, the Church.

12

The Oil of Gladness for Wholeness: Hospice Ministry and Anointing

Maureen Palmer

Life as a whole never takes death seriously. It laughs, dances, and plays, it builds, hoards and loves in death's life. Death the 'great adventure' has become 'king of terrors' (Rabindranath Tagore).

Death is a unique event that comes to us all. During this century medicine has become so orientated towards prevention and cure that the dying patient is regarded as a failure. This attitude was very apparent when a 75-year-old gentleman with a bowel cancer was told by his surgeon, 'By this operation I can make an attempt to save you.' The gentleman concerned, a man with a strong faith, retorted indignantly, 'But I am already saved!' The surgeon was nonplussed. Medical comments such as 'There is nothing more we can do!' or 'The case is hopeless' illustrate the view that death is a failure.

Sheila Cassidy has written:

We have to learn a new way of practising medicine, a staying of the hand, allowing people to die a gentle death *today* instead of resuscitating them to live another painful week or die a more difficult death tomorrow. And of course, if we are to stay our hand rather than fight on we must explain why – to the family, to the nurses, to our colleagues, perhaps even to our patients.[1]

The hospice movement has revolutionized this 'clinical failure' attitude to death and now it is less likely that we speak in hushed tones and push the dying into side wards, where they are out of sight. The

161

hospice movement has tried to encourage the dying to 'live to the full today'.

Hospice medicine is different: there is no expensive technology, no drips or tubes, but there is superb nursing care, there is comfort, drugs to relieve pain and reassurance both of patients and relatives. Above all, there is that precious commodity, time: to listen, and to let patients and relatives ask their questions. Good hospice care involves everyone associated with it, from the kitchen staff to the medical director, but it is costly, not only in monetary terms but also in terms of emotional energy and self-giving from all involved. Terminal care must be the integrated care of the whole person – body, mind and spirit – and the spiritual help that may be given to people who are terminally ill can assist not only in preparation for the death of the patient, but also in the acceptance of the situation by relatives and friends alike.

In today's world we expend an enormous amount of time and energy in preparation for life's events: antenatal preparation, preparation for school, for work, for marriage, for retirement; we prepare for the spiritual events of life – baptism and confirmation – but we seldom prepare anyone for death. Indeed, death is the 'taboo' subject of our age. Often we will not even mention the word. Instead we say, 'He has fallen asleep' or 'He has passed away' – anything rather than say 'He has died'. However, the whole of our life is a preparation for the life in eternity when we shall live close to God – in his nearer presence and in his greater light. It is the time when the mystery of our existence will be solved and when the glass will be cleared so that we no longer see through it darkly, but rather face to face. Viewed in this light, death is exciting – for 'the best is yet to be'.

A 24-year-old girl was heard to remark, 'I'd much rather die of cancer than be killed in an accident. How awful not to have the time to say "Goodbye".' When one knows that the illness is terminal, there is time to prepare for the event of death and here the sacrament of anointing is of such value. One needs preparation not just to get the affairs in order, but also to get the spiritual life in order. Just a short time left to live . . . it may signify the loss of everything that was hoped for, but it could mean the gentle coming to terms with one's mortality. It may mean anger or resentment and the question 'Why me?' or it may mean the acceptance that our life span is finite. For many it will mean anguish at the relationship that will be broken or cut short, but it may also mean reconciliation and living life to the full.

Anointing and laying on of hands is commanded in the epistle of James:

> If one of you is ill, he should send for the elders of the church,
> and they must anoint him with oil in the name of the Lord and

pray over him. The prayer of faith will save the sick man and the Lord will raise him up again; and if he has committed any sins, he will be forgiven.[2]

In the early Church the healing of physical illness was always seen as a manifestation of the Spirit's power, as James indicates, but as the Church grew more worldly, it lacked strength of prayer and the courage of its conviction. The resultant lax attitude led to a lack of awareness of the healing power of Christ. The Church also became preoccupied with sin and ordinary people had a heightened belief in the miraculous and superstitious; fantasy took the place of sound theology. One of the results of such an outlook was that sin and illness became so connected that the ministry of healing, and particularly anointing, was not given so much to ensure wholeness in this life, but rather a good existence in the next. This had the result that anointing for healing became anointing for remission of sins at death. In more recent times anointing with oil has been reinstated as an important part of the sacrament of healing; not only healing of the disease, but in the true meaning of the word *sozo* – meaning to save, to reconcile, to make whole.

In terminal illness anointing is being increasingly used not as viaticum, but very much in the much wider meaning of the term, much as stated in the 1549 Prayer Book. 'The Visitation of the Sick' is remarkably avant-garde and recognizes the value of anointing when it states:

> As with this visible oil thy body is anointed: so our heavenly Father Almighty God, grant of his infinite goodness, that thy soul inwardly may be anointed with the Holy Ghost, who is the spirit of all strength, comfort, relief and gladness.[3]

The prayer continues to petition God for the restoration of bodily health and the release from 'all pains, troubles and diseases, both in body and mind'. The dying, and those who keep vigil with them, need the strength, comfort and courage given by the Holy Spirit in order to be able to surrender with gladness. Often people who have a terminal illness turn to God, perhaps having neglected their relationship with him for years, and anointing can be the seal of that newly restored and rich relationship. It is used to signify the assurance of God's presence and forgiveness, wholeness of life, reconciliation and surrender, as the following example shows.

Stanley was an active, newly retired man with many plans for the future. He was a man of faith, a man of prayer, a church warden. On his own admission he was looking forward to the freedom of retirement to paint, to read, to spend more time with his wife and to devote more of his life to God. Then the blow fell. Only six months after his retirement he was found to have inoperable cancer. He and his wife together went through all the classic stages of such a discovery: the denial; 'they must have made a mistake'; the anger and 'Why me?'; and finally the sadness of acceptance. Stanley took time to read and study the Book of Job, which was another man's experience of bad news and progressive pain and suffering, of loss of independence, of loss of a carefree and hopeful future. Out of the study and the accompanying pain, Stanley asked his parish priest to hear his confession and to give him the sacrament of unction. It was soon after that initiative that Stanley began to attend regularly the day centre of the local hospice. There the laying on of hands and sacrament of unction formed a very important part of the spiritual life of the hospice – not only for the patients, but also for relatives and staff. Stanley's perception of anointing, and indeed of healing, altered considerably in his last months and he would say, 'Give me the oil of gladness for wholeness' as he came to see his death as an adventure into the unknown realms of God's presence. Of course, the days were sometimes sad, and it was hard for his wife to accept his death in the way he looked for it. Some three years after his death his wife was able to write, 'Stanley always called the oil of anointing the "gladness for wholeness" but when he died it was for me a bitter draught. Now, looking back three years, I believe I have grown through the experience of his death and the oil (which my parish priest still gives me) has become the oil of gladness for acceptance.'

The oil of assurance

It is natural to fear death or, often more accurately, the process of dying. Questions as to how one will cope with pain, with loss of independence, with preparation for those left behind, make the prospect frightening; thus the dying person needs reassurance, time to talk and adjust, support from all with whom he comes into contact. Despite this, dying is a very lonely business, for whatever the support given at the point when one comes face to face with the reality of death, one stands alone, and the loneliness can be terrifying both for the patient and for those closest to him. Such loneliness is expressed by C. S. Lewis in his reflection on the death of his wife, H:

> It is incredible how much happiness, even how much gaiety, we sometimes had together after all hope was gone. How long, how tranquilly, how nourishingly, we talked together that last night!
> And yet, not quite together. There's a limit to the 'one flesh'. You can't really share someone else's weakness, or fear, or pain. What you feel may be bad. It might conceivably be as bad as

what the other felt, though I should distrust anyone who claimed it was. But it would still be quite different . . .

We both knew this. I had my miseries, not hers; she had hers, not mine. The end of hers would be the coming-of-age of mine. We were setting out on different roads. This cold truth, this terrible traffic-regulation ('You, Madam, to the right – you, Sir, to the left') is just the beginning of the separation which is death itself.[4]

The oil is, firstly, an assurance of the presence of God and of his love:

Nothing therefore can come between us and the love of Christ, even if we are troubled or worried, or being persecuted, or lacking food or clothes, or being threatened or even attacked. As scripture promised: For your sake we are being massacred daily, and reckoned as sheep for the slaughter! These are the trials through which we triumph, by the power of him who loved us. For I am certain of this: neither death nor life, no angel, no prince, nothing that exists, nothing still to come, not any power, or height or depth, nor any created thing, can ever come between us and the love of God made visible in Christ Jesus our Lord (Rom. 8.35–39 JB).

Nothing can separate us from the love of God. The agonies of the loss of independence, the impending parting from the loved ones, are all helped by the assurance in the oil that Christ stands beside us, that his love was so great that he died for us.

There is a need for people to look back at the story of their lives and see that they have achieved, that they have been loved, that the little deaths of a normal life have been coped with. The saddest people are those who look back and see that their life has been meaningless, that the world has no purpose. Dag Hammarskjold expresses the need for reassurance: 'What I ask is absurd: that life shall have a meaning. What I strive for is impossible; that my life shall acquire a meaning.'[5]

The majority of people do believe that life has been meaningfully lived and they need the assurance to believe that 'the best is yet to be'. The anointing gives that reassurance.

The oil of wholeness

'Do not seek death. Death will find you. But seek the road which makes death a fulfilment.'[6]

In terminal illness there comes the time when the decision is made to stop all treatment and patients are often then at a very low ebb.

They feel broken; frequently they are full of anger: with their doctors, with their family and with God, and the anger with God may make them feel very guilty. They feel there is nothing left for them but to 'wait for death'. The oil of anointing can encourage them to live each day as it comes, so the days become 'last days' full of laughter and joy rather than 'lost days' where the patient lives in regret that days are numbered. It may allow people to seek the road that makes death a fulfilment. Hospice care encourages patients to do today exactly what they feel they can do, and never put off anything that they can do, however small, until tomorrow. Many people have unfinished business to do: a visit to the family in America; a trip to see Worcester play and win a cricket match; to learn to paint or express their feelings about their illness in poetry. One man had worked hard all his life and had left his children in his wife's care; his route to wholeness included learning to bath and feed his baby grandson. For each person the route to wholeness will be different, but the anointing for wholeness is a prayer to live day by day. Having learned to take each day as it comes, the true wholeness allows us to say: 'This is the day made memorable by Yahweh; what immense joy for us' (Ps. 118.24).

The oil of reconciliation

But now in Christ Jesus, you that used to be so far apart from us have been brought very close, by the blood of Christ. For he is the peace between us, and has made the two into one and broken down the barrier that kept them apart, actually destroying in his own person the hostility caused by the rules and decrees of the law (Eph. 2.13–15 JB).

Whatever one is in life, is certainly what we are in death, so the first priority is to learn to love oneself. All through life one causes pain and sorrow to others, sometimes inadvertently, sometimes purposely. This has to be faced, and in facing the hurt of others we learn to know and love ourselves; we learn to live with our strengths and weaknesses and to acknowledge the hurt and pain of others. The oil of reconciliation can be a great help to us; for as we share the oil, we share in the darkness and in the sharing there is healing of the hurt both of ourselves and of others.

Marion was a widow, a very lonely, frightened and sad lady. She had few visitors, and those that came were superficially bright and always reassured her that 'she looked better': a charade she went along with. One day with great diffidence she asked to make her communion, although she was clearly uncomfortable about her request. She then began to speak of the real 'death' that she had died when her only daughter, a brilliant physicist, had married an Asian lawyer. Marion was horrified by the marriage: she refused to admit her future son-in-law to the house; she refused to attend the wedding; and she saw the whole episode as a failure on her part to provide for her the sort of home she wanted. Now that she had admitted she was dying she wanted to say 'I'm sorry' and to be reconciled. With some difficulty the daughter was contacted and she came to visit – there was a mixture of fear, resentment and sadness, but she brought with her her husband and small daughter. She told us that Mother had always had such high standards that she was always slightly afraid of her, and that the marriage had been a wonderful liberation for her. She went in alone to see Marion, and two hours later she emerged to collect her husband and daughter to introduce them. It was hard for them all: the harsh and hurtful words could not be unsaid, and the silence of five years stood between them. A few days later Marion requested that she and her daughter might share the Eucharist and the chaplain suggested that anointing might be a tangible way of sealing the forgiveness and the reconciliation that they had each given and received. In the event, the anointing was done and Marion died a few days later, with her granddaughter asleep beside her, and her son-in-law and daughter reading to her from the Psalms.

The oil of anointing for reconciliation liberated the whole family: it allowed Marion rebirth of the relationship before her death, and it allowed her daughter and son-in-law the knowledge that they were forgiven for the hurt caused. They were all then able to accept Marion's physical death.

The oil of surrender

Finally, there is nothing left to do but to say: 'Father, into your hands I commit my spirit' (Luke 23.46).

In a television interview not long before his death, David Watson said, 'We must make the radical change from (intellectually) being willing to be in heaven but (emotionally) wanting to be on earth, to wanting to be in heaven but being willing to stay on earth until death comes.'

There is an enormous distinction between surrender and resignation. Resignation means 'to sign off', to resign from function, whereas surrender means such trust and confidence that you can put yourself unreservedly, joyfully, by an act of freedom into the hands of the loving God who made you, whatever happens, because you are sure of him as you are sure of nothing and nobody else.

'No one takes it [my life] from me; I lay it down of my own free will,' Jesus said (John 10.18). This statement in the discourse of the

Good Shepherd and the prayer in the Garden of Gethsemane –
'Nevertheless, let your will be done, not mine' – is pure surrender of
Jesus into the hands of his Father. So the oil of surrender allows the
sick person to 'let go' while not destroying his courage or dignity, for a
man who cannot rise to cope with small things may rise to great acts of
courage and love when faced with his death.

The oil of surrender becomes also a 'thanksgiving' for both the sick
person and the family. For the family it is often the thanksgiving that
the suffering is almost over, that the person is going to glory, while for
the person himself it may be that he re-echoes the words of Dag
Hammarskjold:

> – night is drawing nigh—
> For all that has been – Thanks!
> To all that shall be – Yes![7]

Notes

1. S. Cassidy, *Sharing the Darkness* (London 1988), p. 15f.
2. Jas. 5.14–16 JB
3. *The First and Second Prayerbooks of King Edward VI*. (London, Everyman) p. 264
4. C. S. Lewis, *A Grief Observed* (London 1961), p. 13f.
5. D. Hammarskjold, *Markings* (London 1964), p. 14.
6. ibid., p. 136.
7. ibid., p. 87.

13

The Revival of Oils in Contemporary Culture: Implications for the Sacrament of Anointing

Rebecca Abrams and Hugo Slim

The resurgent use of oils in the latter half of this century has largely taken place in the secular sphere, but the process and outcome of this secularization of oil has profound implications for the role of the sacrament of oil in today's Church. In this chapter we make a preliminary exploration of the increased use of oil in secular society and the appropriation of its sacramental image by the health and beauty industries. We then consider both the beneficial and harmful effects of contemporary applications of oil; and examine the significance of this trend for contemporary Christianity.

The use of oils has traditionally been associated with the warmer climates and more sensual cultures of Mediterranean and Eastern civilizations. The abundance of olive groves and spices in such areas means that oils have always played a prominent part in the life of Eastern peoples. In the last ten years, however, the use of oils has become increasingly widespread in the colder, less sensual civilizations of Western Europe and North America. In Britain today, for example, it would not be an exaggeration to talk about the massification of oils. They are used extensively and applied in a variety of ways, as bath oils, sun oils, massage oils, aromatherapy oils, incense oils, hair oils, and skin care oils.

The enormous rise in the use of oils by the predominantly Protestant cultures of Northern Europe and America may not simply be the result of richer economies and increasing contact between east and west, north and south. It may also represent part of a spiritual sea change in these northern countries. Increasing disillusionment with the orthodoxies that have claimed to safeguard their physical and spiritual wellbeing has prompted people to move away from both orthodox medicine and orthodox religion. Instead a growing number of people are experimenting with a variety of 'alternative' treatments for physical ailments, and in the same way, have increasingly abandoned the precepts of orthodox religion to explore a variety of new spiritual cures.

In both spheres – religion and health – the drive has been towards a more 'holistic' view of life and person, a view that combines rather than separates body and soul, one that rejoices in the whole person. In this context, it is not perhaps surprising that one traditional Christian sacrament that has made an enormous come-back is oil: the most sensual, the most luxurious of the sacraments, and the one most associated with healing and making whole. Of all the sacraments, oil is the one that takes most account of our outward bodies. In keeping with this, many contemporary secular applications of oil, such as massage and aromatherapy, are aimed at uniting the body and mind by soothing both at once.

Oils and health

Oil has become increasingly widely used as people strive to take their health care and well-being back into their own hands. It has become an important ingredient in people's determination to treat themselves. Shops like the Body Shop and Neal's Yard sell an extensive range of different oils: concentrated essential oils, base oils, and oils ready mixed in a variety of combinations related to their function. Particular oils are considered to have particular healing properties. Lavender, for example, is recommended for nervous conditions, pine for bronchitis, thyme for fatigue and ylang-ylang for high blood pressure.

Three aspects of this health-centred oil industry are distinctive. First, many of the oils are used in treating diseases that are considered to be specific to contemporary Western society: stress, anxiety, tension and fatigue. These common problems are the ones that medical orthodoxy has been least able to respond to effectively. Secondly, using oils involves people in the process of diagnosis. Indeed, self-diagnosis is a vital part of the appeal, and arguably the efficacy, of using oils in this way. The preliminary to buying the right oil is to ask the questions, 'How do I feel?' and 'What do I want?' The individual thereby takes control of his or her health and emotions, rather than handing the responsibility to a professional. Thirdly, oils are felt to be safe. They are welcomed for being natural and not having the side effects or other sinister associations of many pharmaceutical drugs. People are familiar with oils. They react positively and instinctively to them and are not afraid of them. This profoundly held belief has been shaken somewhat in recent months by reports in several national newspapers concerning the risks of using essential oils in certain contexts, for example, during pregnancy. The result has been a tightening up of guidelines and recommendations for the use of oils. Manufacturers and suppliers of oils have been understandably keen to play down the possible risks, and the public by and large seem happy to be reassured. The conviction that what is natural is good seems to be a resilient one.

The great majority of the health applications of oils today *are* safe, it would seem. Furthermore, they are empowering and responsive to people's actual and perceived needs, and may provide an outward way of restoring inner health.

Significantly, much of the prescriptive and marketing language used to describe these oils is drawn from sacramental language. Oils, we are told, 'revitalize', 'refresh', 'renew', and 'restore'; they contribute to a sense of 'wellbeing'. In general, most of the health uses of oils are beneficial and seem to answer people's needs. The various home-based applications, and the more professional therapies that use oil, allow people to slow down, to recognize their condition, to combine mental and physical care and, quite literally, to soften up. Most people who use oil in this way are engaged in a healing, or 'wholing', process that can often make an important and continuing contribution to their lives.

Oils and cosmetics

However, such a positive use of oils is not the whole story in today's world. The bulk of the world's oils are not used as part of a new and liberating health process. Instead, they are sold as part of the $20 billion a year cosmetics industry. In this context, they play a sinister part in sustaining what Naomi Wolf has called 'The Beauty Myth'.[1] This is the myth that asserts that women are created second-class beings and should therefore endeavour to perfect themselves, chiefly through achieving physical beauty. The Beauty Myth is 'the belief that equates femaleness with pollution'[2] and urges women to go to every length to cleanse and purify themselves. It is this myth, Wolf believes, that renders women dangerously preoccupied with their beauty and purity to the extent that they become impotent to challenge their secondary status in society.

Of specific relevance to this chapter is the study that Wolf has made of the marketing of cosmetic oils and creams, and the place they take up in women's lives. She draws attention to the religious, often sacramental language that is employed in the marketing of cosmetics, and refers to the cosmetic oils and creams as the new 'holy oils'. However, as she makes clear, these are not oils that heal. While the use of cosmetic oils *per se* need not necessarily be as deleterious as Wolf suggests, the language used to promote the use of these modern-day lotions and potions would certainly seem to play on women's insecurities. The potential results of using cosmetic oils are described in near-messianic terms by marketing gurus, despite the proven scientific limitations of these products. The effect that can be more easily charted is the psychological one on women themselves, who may find themselves not within reach of the promised salvation, but caught in an ever-increasing cycle of inadequacy and despair. Wolf compares the beauty industry to a religious cult that preys on women and eventually hypnotizes them, forcing them to become obsessed with their figure, their complexion, their age, their eating habits and their skin care. She comments that this obsession 'is the kind of self-scrutiny which used to be reserved for the soul',[3] but which is now transferred to (and possibly reserved for) the body – and almost exclusively *women's* bodies. The result, in Wolf's thesis, is that many women end up doing battle with their bodies, and despising and often harming their physical self. The part oils play in this process is therefore in stark contrast to the healing and holistic role made for it in alternative health practices and traditional Christian anointing.

While the use of cosmetic oils may be enjoyable, the cosmetic industry and the language it employs can be said, for the most part, to create false needs and unrealistic expectations, asserting the possibility of perpetual youth and unwrinkled skin. It implies that women are unclean and decaying, and then claims that its product can purify and protect. One oil will 'revitalize' and 'cleanse', another will 'give new life', one will 'renew', while another assures women that they will be 'reborn'. In this context, the appropriation of sacramental language is alarming. The emphasis is on setting ridiculous physical standards and maintaining permanent dissatisfaction. As Wolf says, 'The holy oils industry is a megalith that for forty years has been selling women nothing at all.'[4]

Wolf goes on to show how the 'holy oil industry' encourages women to gain the physical nourishment they need through oils and lotions rather than food. The Beauty Myth conspires to deny them their rightful food intake and instead oils are claimed to 'nourish' women, to 'feed' their skins with extraordinary concoctions of olive oil, honey, banana extract, peanut oil, passion fruit . . . The nutrition metaphor extends to women's emotional lives too, where oils will 'comfort' and 'cherish' them, and provide the 'loving' and 'special care' that may be lacking in their lives.

172

Wolf's analysis of the beauty industry is on the whole convincing and shows that, as cosmetics, oil are being misrepresented as in some way sacramental. The use of oils as cosmetics for women is not born out of the fact that people want to rejoice in their bodies and feel whole. Instead, the very idea of modern cosmetics implies a dissatisfaction and rejection of the body. The emphasis is on patching it up, trying to stop the rot – a rot that men, for the moment, do not seem to have. Such a use of oils is built on self-denial and a notion of women that is incompatible with contemporary Christian teaching.

Renewed relevance for the sacrament of oil

The increasing role of oils in people's secular lives is bound to influence the way they view the sacred use of oil. This has important implications for the Church today and for any current reassessment of the sacrament of anointing. For 8,000 years the religious and secular uses of oil have developed side by side. The ancient Egyptians and Greeks, the Chinese and the Romans all nurtured the sacral function of oil while also respecting the wide range of practical applications of oil in everyday life. This single substance therefore assumed a vital third role as a bridge between the secular and the sacred spheres of human activity. However, a major part of Christian tradition has engendered negative attitudes towards the body and a desire to subdue the physical that has corresponded with a reverence for the unencumbered soul. This trend has gathered pace in the last 200 years, and is perhaps, most graphically demonstrated in the female population where potentially life-threatening disorders such as anorexia and bulimia are reckoned to affect over 50 per cent of British and American women, of whom as many as 90 per cent at any one time are expressing physical dissatisfaction by dieting.[5]

Paradoxically, this 'flesh loathing' has succeeded in gradually marginalizing the realm of the spirit: deprived of the means of easy passage between these two states of body and soul that the secular and sacred applications of oil permitted, the individual has been forced to choose. Since choice between these two essential realms is reductive at the profoundest level, the result has been a slow and painful atrophying of body and spirit. The Jungian analyst Bani Shorter suggests that 'Ritual does not die though it can be neglected, trivialised, misused and to some extent ignored. Yet if desacralised and cut off from psychic awareness, its motive force, the image of the Holy, reverts to unconsciousness, while existing observances become repetitious and sterile.'[6] The gradual disappearance of ritual uses of oil in the past, in both secular and sacred realms, has brought about a general impoverishment of both, as well as profoundly depriving the individuals who are denied access to these vital rituals.

The last decade has witnessed an encouraging change: a concerted drive to reinstate the body as central to human existence, rather than an obstacle to it: a determination to celebrate physicality. The 1980s brought a surge of interest in health clubs, work-outs, aerobics classes and jogging. While these contain remnants of a puritanical and punitive past, they have been accompanied by a gentler enthusiasm for vegetarianism, massage and aromatherapy, what could be termed 'body loving' activities. It is in the revival of these touch-oriented trends that one can find theological significance. Aromatherapy, writes one practitioner and devotee, has the power 'to revive, to restore, to heal the body'. It goes on: 'An aromatherapy massage . . . does nothing less than bring new life to the body.'[7] Resurrection is here: physical, spiritual, literal and symbolic.

However ambiguous contemporary secular uses of oil may appear, they nevertheless contain signs of an authentic spiritual yearning to reunite body and soul as well as a developed appreciation and experience of oils. This provides a new and unprecedented opportunity for the revival and development of the sacramental use of oils within contemporary Christianity. Oil may be again, as it always was, a bridge that spans the banks of spirit and flesh, a sacrament that reconciles the two within the human heart and mind.

Conclusions

If the Church is to re-examine the sacrament of oil, it is important that it takes the secular revival of oils into account. In some contexts associated with health, the appropriation of sacramental language is part of a vital and restorative use of oils. In other contexts, most notably the massive cosmetics industry, sacramental language associated with oils and creams is being abused as part of a wider process of oppressing women and contributing to anxiety and despair. A new sacramental theology of oil must expect to be read and interpreted from this already wide and differing experience of oils in today's culture – some positive, some negative.

New sacramental practice using oil in the Church should build on people's already positive experience of oils. Sacramental practice relating to oil should aim to be broadly based and empowering, keeping the benefits of oil in people's own hands. As the sacrament that most relates to the sense of touch and healing, it should be embraced as that which above all reclaims the body and rejoices in the whole person.

Notes

1. Naomi Wolf, *The Beauty Myth* (London 1990).
2. ibid., p. 90.
3. ibid., p. 100.
4. ibid., p. 109.
5. Jane Ogden, *Fat Chance: The Myth of Dieting Explained* (London and New York 1992).
6. Bani Shorter, 'If Ritual Dies', lecture no. 231 (The Guild of Pastoral Psychology, 1988).
7. Judith Jackson, *Aromatherapy* (London 1987).

14

Rites for the Blessing of Oils and Anointing: The Western Tradition

Martin Dudley

The rites of the Roman Catholic Church, immediately before and after Vatican II, and those of the Anglican churches and the Lutheran churches in the United States and Canada are given here. For each group, these are divided into (A) the blessing of oil, (B) the anointing of the sick, and (C) other anointings. Editorial notes are enclosed in brackets [].

The pre-Vatican II Roman rite[1]

The reform of Holy Week by Pius XII in 1955 provided a new Chrism Mass, but the prayers of blessing and consecration were carried over from the section *De Officio in feria V Cenae Domini* of the post-Tridentine *Pontificale Romanum*. The prayers are largely based on the Gelasian Sacramentary, though a number of variations, introduced when the texts were incorporated into the twelfth-century Roman pontifical, were retained.

(A) *The blessing of oil*

Blessing of the oil of the sick
[This blessing precedes the
words *Per quem haec omnia* in
the canon of the Mass. The

176

bishop leaves the altar and comes to sit at a table set before the altar. He faces both table and altar. When the oil has been placed on the table, he stands, wearing the mitre, and says the exorcism:]

Exorcizo te, immundissime spiritus, omnisque incursio satanae, et omne phantasma. In nomine + Patris, et + Filii, et Spiritus + Sancti; ut recedas ab hoc oleo, ut possit effici unctio spiritalis ad corroborandum templum Dei vivi; ut in eo possit Spiritus Sanctus habitare, per nomen Dei Patris omnipotentis et per nomen dilectissimi Filii ejus Domini nostri Jesu Christi qui venturus est judicare vivos et mortuous, et saeculum per ignem.
R. Amen.

Unclean spirit, I exorcize you and with you every assault of Satan, and every false illusion in the name of the + Father, and of the + Son, and of the Holy + Spirit; depart from this oil, that it may be made a spiritual unction to fortify the temple of the living God, that in it the Holy Spirit may dwell through the name of God the Father almighty, and through the name of his most beloved Son, our Lord Jesus Christ, who will come to judge the living and the dead and the world by fire.
R. Amen.

[The bishop removes his mitre, and continues with the blessing:]

V. Dominus vobiscum
R. Et cum spiritu tuo.

V. The Lord be with you.
R. And with your spirit.

Emitte, quaesumus, Domine, Spiritum Sanctum tuum Paraclitum de caelis in hanc pinguedinem olivae, quam de virido ligno producere dignatus es, ad refectionem mentis et corporis; et tua sancta + benedictione, sit omni hoc unguento caelestis medicinae peruncto tutamen mentis et corporis, ad evacuandos omnes dolores, omnes infirmitates, omnemque aegritudinem mentis et corporis, unde unxisti

Send forth, we pray you, Lord, your Holy Spirit, our Advocate from heaven upon this rich juice of the olive which you have been pleased to bring forth out of a green tree for the solace of soul and body: that by your holy blessing + whoever is anointed with this ointment of heavenly strength with which you anointed priests, kings, prophets and martyrs, may receive protection of soul and body for deliverance from all

177

The Oil of Gladness

Sacerdotes, Reges, Prophetas et Martyres: sit Chrisma tuum perfectum, Domine, nobis a te benedictum, permanens in visceribus nostris. In nomine Domini nostri Jesu Christi.

[The Mass continues.]

The Holy Chrism
[After the last ablutions, he returns to the table. The bishop, without mitre, rises and blesses the balm or balsam.]

V. Dominus vobiscum
R. Et cum spiritu tuo.

Deus, mysteriorum caelestium et virtutem omnium praeparator, nostras, qaesumus, preces exaudi, hanc odoriferam sicci corticis lacrimam (quae felicis virgae profluendo sudorem, sacerdotali nos opimat unguento) acceptabilem tuis praesta mysteriis, et concessa benedictione + sanctifica. Per Dominum nostrum Jesum Christum Filium tuum, qui tecum vivit et regnat in unitate Spiritus sancti Deus, per omnia saecula saeculorum.
R. Amen.

Oremus.

Creaturarum omnium, Domine, procreator, qui per Moysen famulum tuum permistis herbis aromatum fieri praecepisti sanctificationem unguenti; clementiam tuam suppliciter deposcimus, ut huic unguento, quod radix produxit stirpea,

pains, all infirmities and all sickness of soul and body; may it be, Lord, your perfect chrism, blessed by you for us, abiding in our whole being: in the name of our Lord Jesus Christ.

V. The Lord be with you.
R. And with your spirit.

O God, the author of heavenly mysteries, and of all virtues, we entreat you to hear our prayers: that these fragrant tears of dry bark (which trickling down from a fruitful branch supply us with a rich ointment for the anointing of the priesthood) may be made acceptable to you for your sacraments, and sanctify + them by giving your blessing. Through Jesus Christ your Son our Lord who lives and reigns with you in the unity of the Holy Spirit, God, for ever and ever.
R. Amen.

Let us pray.

O Lord, the creator of all things, by your servant Moses you commanded the hallowing of ointment made with the mixture of aromatic herbs; we humbly implore your mercy that you would bestow the grace of your Spirit and the fullness of

spiritualem gratiam largiendo, plenitudinem + sanctificationis infundas. Sit nobis, Domine, fidei hilaritate conditum; sit sacerdotalis unguenti Chrisma perpetuum: sit ad caelestis vexilli impressionem dignissimum; ut quicumque baptismate sacro renati isto fuerint liquore peruncti, corporum atque animarum benedictionem plenissimam consequantur, et beatae fidei collato munere perenniter amplientur. Per Dominum nostrum Jesum Christum Filium tuum, qui tecum vivit et regnat in unitate Spiritus sancti Deus, per omnia saecula saeculorum.
R. Amen.

+ consecration on this ointment, drawn from a growing plant. May it be seasoned for us, Lord, with joyous faith; make it a lasting chrism for the anointing of the priesthood; make it worthy to be used in impressing the sign of your heavenly standard; that whoever after being born again by your holy baptism, shall be anointed with this ointment may obtain the fullness of your blessing in body and soul, and ever be enriched by the blessed faith given to them. Through our Lord Jesus Christ.
R. Amen.

[The bishop receives the mitre, and then mixes the balm, on a paten, with a little of the oil from the vessel containing the oil for the Chrism, saying:]

Oremus Dominum Deum nostrum omnipotentem, qui incomprehensibilem unigeniti Filii sui sibique coaeterni divinitatem mirabili dispositione verae humanitati inseparabiliter conjunxit, et cooperante gratia Spiritus Sancti, oleo exsultationis prae participibus suis linivit, ut homo, fraude diaboli perditus, gemina et singulari constans materia, perenni redderetur, de qua exciderat, hereditati; quatenus hos ex diversis creaturarum speciebus liquores creatos Sanctae Trinitatis perfectione + benedicat, et benedicendo +

Let us beg our Lord God almighty, who inseparably united the incomprehensible Godhead of his only-begotten and co-eternal Son unto a true humanity, and by the grace of the Holy Spirit anointed him with the oil of gladness above his fellows, in order that man who is made of two substances united in one, and who had been undone by the fraud of the devil, might be restored to the everlasting inheritance from which he had fallen; that he may bless + with the fullness of the blessing of the Holy Trinity these liquids which are derived

179

sanctificet, concedatque, ut simul permisti unum fiant; et quicumque exterius inde perunctus fuerit, ita interius liniatur, quod omnibus sordibus corporalis materiae carens, se participem regni caelestis effici gratuletur. Per eumdem Dominum nostrum Jesum Christum Filium tuum, qui cum eo vivit et regnat . . .
R. Amen.

from different species of creatures, and that he will sanctify + them by his blessing, and grant that being mingled together they may become one; and that whosoever shall be outwardly anointed therewith, may be so inwardly anointed that being freed from all contamination of bodily matter, he may rejoice in being made a partaker of the Kingdom of heaven. Through the same our Lord . . .
R. Amen.

[The bishop, followed by the twelve concelebrating priests, breathes three times in the form of a cross over the chrism. The bishop continues with the exorcism:]

Exorcizo, te, creatura olei, per Deum Patrem omnipotentem, qui fecit caelum et terram, mare et omnia quae in eis sunt, ut omnis virtus adversarii, omnis exercitus diaboli, omnisque incursio, et omne phantasma satanae eradicetur, et effugetur a te; ut fias omnibus qui ex te ungendi sunt, in adoptionem filiorum, per Spiritum Sanctum. In nomine Dei + Patris omnipotentis, et Jesu + Christi Filii ejus Domini nostri, qui cum eo vivit et regnat Deus, in unitate ejusdem Spiritus + Sancti, per omnia saecula saeculorum.
R. Amen.

Creature of oil, I exorcise you by God the Father almighty, who made heaven and earth, and the sea and all in it, that all the power of the enemy, all the host of Satan, and all the assaults and illusions of the devil may be rooted out and chased away from you; may you be to all who are anointed with you the means of their adoption as sons through the Holy Spirit. In the name of God the Father + almighty, and of Jesus + Christ, his Son, our Lord, who being God, lives and reigns with him in the unity of the same Holy Spirit, world without end.
R. Amen.

[The mitre is removed and the bishop chants the Preface:]

V. Dominus vobiscum.
R. Et cum spiritu tuo.
V. Sursum corda.
R. Habemus ad Dominum.
V. Gratias agamus Domino Deo nostro.
R. Dignum et justum est.

V. The Lord be with you.
R. And with your spirit.
V. Lift up your hearts.
R. We lift them to the Lord.
V. Let us give thanks to the Lord our God.
R. It is fitting and proper so to do.

Vere dignum et justum est, aequum et salutare, nos tibi semper, et ubique gratias agere: Domine, sancte Pater, omnipotens aeterne Deus: Qui in principio, inter cetera bonitatis tuae munera, terram producere fructifera ligna jussisti, inter quae hujus pinguissimi liquoris ministrae olivae nascerentur, quarum fructus sacro chrismati deserviret. Nam et David prophetico spiritu gratiae tuae sacramenta praenoscens, vultus nostros in oleo exhilarandos esse cantavit: et cum mundi crimina diluvio quondam expiarentur effuso, similitudinem futuri muneris columba demonstrans per olivae ramum pacem terris redditam nuntiavit. Quod in novissimis temporibus manifestis est effectibus declaratum, cum baptismatis aquis omnium criminum comissa delentibus, haec olei unctio vultus nostros jucundos efficit, ac serenos. Inde etiam Moysi famulo tuo mandatum dedisti, ut Aaron fratrem suum prius aqua lotum per infusionem hujus unguenti constitueret sacerdotem. Accesit ad hoc amplior honor, cum Filiis tuus Jesus Christus Dominus

It is truly fitting and proper, right and profitable to salvation, that we should always and everywhere give thanks to you, Lord, holy Father, almighty everlasting God: for in the beginning among the rest of your bounteous gifts, you commanded the earth to yield fruit-bearing trees, among which was the olive which produces this rich juice for making holy chrism. Hence it was that David, foreknowing by a prophetic inspiration the sacraments of your grace, sang that our faces were to be made glad with oil: and when of old the sins of the world were expiated by the flood, a dove announced that peace was restored to the earth by bearing an olive branch, the type of the gift to come, which in these latter days has been manifested; for after the waters of baptism have washed sins away, this anointing of oil gives us joy and peace. Hence, too, you commanded your servant Moses to ordain his brother Aaron priest by pouring oil upon him, after he had been cleansed with water. A greater honour still was that when your Son, our Lord Jesus Christ, bade John

The Oil of Gladness

noster lavari se a Joanne undis Jordanicis exegisset, ut Spiritu Sancto in columbae similitudine desuper misso, Unigenitum tuum, in quo tibi optime complacuisse, testimonio subsequentis vocis ostenderes, et hoc illud esse manifestissime comprobares, quod cum oleo laetitae prae consortibus suis ungenudem David propheta cecinisset. Te igitur deprecamur, Domine, sanctc Pater, omnipotens aeterne Deus, per eumdem Jesum Christum Filium tuum Dominum nostrum, ut hujus creaturae pinguedinem + santificare tua + benedictione digneris, ut Sancti + Spiritus ei admiscere virtutem, cooperante Christi Filii tui potentia, a cujus nomine sancto Chrisma nomen accepit, unde unxisti Sacerdotes, Reges, Prophetas et Martyres: ut sit his qui renati fuerint ex aqua et Spiritu Sancto, Chrisma salutis, eosque aeternae vitae participes, et caelestis gloriae faciat esse consortes.

baptize him in the waters of the Jordan, you sent upon him the Holy Spirit in the form of a dove; so that by a voice bearing testimony you might designate your only-begotten Son, in whom you were well-pleased, and might prove, beyond all doubt, that this was the fulfilment of what the prophet David had foretold, when he sang that he was to be anointed with the oil of gladness above his fellows. We therefore pray you, holy Lord, almighty Father, eternal God, through the same Jesus Christ, your Son, our Lord, that you would be pleased to + sanctify by your + blessing this oil, your creature, and infuse into it the virtue of the + Holy Spirit, through the co-operating power of Christ, your Son, from whose name it has taken its own of chrism, with which you anointed the priests, kings, prophets and martyrs. May this oil be to them who are born again from water and the Holy Spirit, a chrism of salvation making them partakers of life everlasting, and co-heirs of heavenly glory.

[The final sentence is said, not sung.]

Per eumdem Dominum nostrum Jesum Christum Filium tuum, qui tecum vivat et regnat in unitate ejusdem Spiritus Sancti Deus, per omnia saecula saeculorum.
R. Amen.

Through the same Jesus Christ, your Son, our Lord, who lives and reigns with you and the Holy Spirit, God, for ever and ever.
R. Amen.

[The bishop pours the
combined balm and oil into the
vessel containing the chrism,
saying:]

Haec commixtio liquorum fiat omnibus ex ea perunctis propitiatio et custodia salutaris in saecula saeculorum. R. Amen.	May this mingling of liquids bring to all anointed with them mercy and safe protection for ever and ever. R. Amen.

[The bishop salutes the chrism
three times, each on a higher
note. The salutation is repeated
by the priests, who genuflect.]

Ave, sanctum Chrisma.	Hail, Holy Chrism!

[The mouth of the vessel is
kissed. The bishop receives the
mitre and then, followed by the
priests, he breathes on the oil of
catechumens in the same way as
they did on the chrism. The
bishop says:]

Exorcizo te, creatura olei. In nomine Dei + Patris omnipotentis et in nomine Jesu + Christi, et Spiritus + Sancti, ut in hac invocatione individuae Trinitatis, atque unius virtute Deitatis, omnis nequissima virtus adversarii, omnis inveterata malitia diaboli, omnis violenta incursio, omne confusum et caecum phantasma eradicetur et effugetur, et discedat a te; ut, divinis sacramentis purificata, fias in adoptionem carnis et spiritus, eis qui ex te ungendi sunt, in remissionem omnium peccatorum; ut efficiantur eorum corpora ad omnem gratiam spiritualem accipiendam sanctificata. Per	Creature of oil, I exorcise you, in the name of God the + Father almighty, and in the name of Jesus + Christ, and of the Holy + Spirit, that by this invocation of the undivided Trinity and by the power of the one Godhead, all the most wicked powers of the enemy, all the inveterate malice of the devil, every violent assault, every disorderly and dark illusion, may be rooted out and chased away and dispelled from you: that hallowed by the divine mysteries, you may make God's children both in body and soul those who are anointed with you for the forgiveness of all sins: that their bodies may be sanctified for the reception of all

eumdem Dominum nostrum Jesum Christum, qui venturus est judicare vivos et mortuos et saeculum per ignem.
R. Amen.

[The mitre is removed.]

V. Dominus vobiscum.
R. Et cum spiritu tuo.
Oremus.
Deus, incrementorum omnium et profectuum spiritualium remunerator, qui virtute Sancti Spiritus imbecillarum mentium rudimenta confirmas, te oramus, Domine, ut emittere digneris tuam + benedictionem super hoc oleum, et venturis ad beatae regenerationis lavacrum tribuas, per unctionem hujus creaturae, purgationem mentis et corporis; ut si quae illis adversantium spirituum inhaesare maculae, ad tactum sanctificati olei hujus abscedant; nullus spiritualibus nequitiis locus, nulla refugis virtutibus sit facultas, nulla insidiantibus malis latendi licentia relinquatur. Sed venientibus ad fidem servis tuis, et Sancti Spiritus tui operatione mundantis, sit unctionis hujus praeparatio utilis ad salutem, quam etiam caelestis regenerationis nativitate in sacramento sunt baptismatis adepturi. Per dominum nostrum Jesum Christum Filium tuum, qui venturus est judicare vivos et mortuous, et saeculum per ignem.
R. Amen.

spiritual grace. Through the same Jesus Christ our Lord, who shall come to judge the living and the dead and the world by fire.
R. Amen.

V. The Lord be with you.
R. And with your spirit.
Let us pray.
O God, you reward all spiritual growth and progress and by the power of the Holy Spirit strengthen the first efforts of feeble wills; be pleased, Lord, we pray you, to send down your + blessing upon this oil, and grant that all who come to the water of baptism may, through being anointed with this your creature, be cleansed in mind and body; that if any pollution of their spiritual enemies has adhered to them, it may depart at the touch of this hallowed oil; let there be no place for the wickedness of evil spirits, no occasion for the apostate angels, no power of concealment left to the snares of sin; but to your servants who come to the faith and are cleansed by the operation of the Holy Spirit, let the preparation of this unction be of help to them for salvation which they are to obtain when born by heavenly generation in the sacrament of baptism. Through our Lord Jesus Christ, your Son, who shall come to judge the living and the dead, and the world by fire.
R. Amen.

[The bishop and priests salute
the oil three times before kissing
the vessel:]

Ave, sanctum oleum.   Hail, holy oil!

(B) *The anointing of the sick*

The Rituale Romanum *of 1614*

This translation of the order for administering the sacrament of
Extreme Unction given in the *Rituale Romanum* of 1614, and revised,
particularly in the 1925 *editio typica*, was authorized by the American
bishops in April 1964 and by the Vatican in May of the same year as
part of the introduction, before the general revision of liturgical texts
after Vatican II, of the vernacular for certain rites. The instructions
and other prayers are summarized and the text of the anointing is
given in full. The rubrics, printed here in italics, are those given in the
rite. The historical development of this rite may be summarized as
follows (i) The three introductory prayers remind us that the visit to
the sick was the first element of the rite from AD 800 onwards. (ii)
The confession is a vestige of the infiltration of the rite of death-bed
penance into the rite of anointing. (iii) The prayer 'In the name of the
Father' reflects eighth/ninth-century ideas of the devil as the cause of
illness. (iv) The form of anointing is one of three types. This one
comes from Cluny by way of the Franciscans. (v) The prayers after
anointing look back to life and not forward to death and are prayers of
recovery.

When the priest enters the place where the sick person is he says:

V. Peace to this house.
R. And to all who dwell herein.

The oilstock is placed on the table, on which is a cross and two lighted
candles. The priest puts on a surplice and a purple stole and then
sprinkles the sick person, the room and those present with holy water.
He says the *Asperges me*:

Sprinkle me, O Lord, with hyssop, and I shall be purified; wash
me, and I shall be whiter than snow.

Three prayers may follow which involve the blessing of the dwelling
and the summoning of angels to dwell therein. There is then provision
for particular sacramental confession and/or the general confession
and absolution, and then, in the American order, a reading (Matt.
8.5–10, 13) and a short litany.

*Next, the priest extends his right hand over the head of the sick person
and says:* [This imposition of hands was restored in the 1925 edition of
the ritual.]

185

In the name of the Father + and of the Son + and of the Holy + Spirit. May any power that the devil has over you be utterly destroyed, as I place my hands on you and call upon the help of the glorious and holy Mother of God, the Virgin Mary, and of her illustrious spouse, Joseph, and of all the holy Angels, Archangels, patriarchs, prophets, apostles, martyrs, confessors, virgins, and all the saints. Amen.

[The invocation of Mary and Joseph, which does not appear in the 1614 edition, was introduced by Leo XIII. The original prayer, following the theme of the previous prayers, invoked the angels and archangels first.]

Then, having dipped his thumb in the holy oil, the priest anoints the sick person on the parts of the body indicated below, making the sign of the Cross and saying the words of the form in the following way:

THE EYES

May the Lord forgive you by this holy + anointing and his most loving mercy whatever sins you have committed by the use of your sight. Amen.

After each anointing, the priest wipes the anointed spot with a fresh cotton ball. These cotton balls are later to be burned.

THE EARS

May the Lord forgive you by this holy + anointing and his most loving mercy whatever sins you have committed by the use of your hearing. Amen.

THE NOSTRILS

May the Lord forgive you by this holy + anointing and his most loving mercy whatever sins you have committed by the use of your sense of smell. Amen.

THE MOUTH, WITH THE LIPS CLOSED

May the Lord forgive you by this holy + anointing and his most loving mercy whatever sins you have committed by the use of your sense of taste and the power of speech. Amen.

THE HANDS
A priest's hands are anointed on the back, not on the palm.

May the Lord forgive you by this holy + anointing and his most loving mercy whatever sins you have committed by the use of your sense of touch. Amen.

186

THE FEET

For any reasonable cause, this feet anointing may be omitted.

May the Lord forgive you by this holy + anointing and his most loving mercy whatever sins you have committed by the use of your power to walk. Amen.

[The *Rituale* of 1614 included the following:

Ad lumbos sive renes.

Per istam sanctam Unctionem, + et suam piissimam misericordiam, indulgeat tibi Dominus quidquid per lumborum delectationem deliquisti. Amen.

Tit. V, c.1, n. 15 and the rubric given in the rite itself already required the omission of this anointing for women and for men who were too infirm to be moved. The *Propaganda Fide* admitted further limitations because of cultural norms in the East and the omission was made general by the Holy Office in 1889. The Code of Canon Law of 1916, canon 947, section 2, states *unctio renum semper omittatur* and the text was omitted from editions of the *Rituale* thereafter.]

In cases of necessity, a single anointing, to be made on the forehead if that is possible, suffices. These words are used:

Per istam sanctam Unctionem indulgeat tibi Dominus quidquid deliquisti. Amen.

May the Lord forgive you by this holy + anointing whatever sins you have committed. Amen.

Having cleansed his hands, the priest said a short litany followed by three prayers:

Domine Deus, qui per Apostolum tuum . . .
Respice, quaesumus Domine . . .
Domine sancte, Pater omnipotens

(C) Other anointings

Baptism
There are two anointings in the *Rituale*. The first, with the oil of catechumens, follows the renunciation of Satan. The sign of the cross is made on the chest and between the shoulders; the priest says:

Ego te linio + Oleo salutis in Christo Jesu Domino nostro, ut habeas vitam aeternam.

After the baptismal washing the child was anointed, again in the sign of the cross, *in summitate capitis*, on the crown of the head, with chrism; the priest saying:

> *Deus omnipotens, Pater nostri Jesu Christi, qui te regeneravit ex aqua et Spiritu Sancto, quique dedit tibi remissionem omnium peccatorum, ipse te liniat + Chrismate salutis in eodem Christo Jesu Domino nostro in vitam aeternam.*

Confirmation

The most common way of conferring confirmation given by the rubricists is this: the candidate kneeling before him, the bishop dipped his right thumb into the chrism, placed his right hand on the candidate's head, and makes the sign of the cross on his forehead, saying:

> *N., signo te signo Cru + cis*

Then he raised his right hand and made the sign of the cross three times over the candidate's head, saying:

> *Et confirmo te Chrismate salutis: In nomine Pa + tris, et Fi + lii, et Spiritus + sancti.*

Ordination of priests

Before Vatican II, the oil of catechumens was used for the anointing at ordination. The bishop dipped his thumb in the oil and anointed the open hand of the newly ordained priest, tracing the form of a cross, and then anointed the palm all over. While anointing, the bishop said:

Consecrare et sanctificare digneris Domine, manus istas per istam unctionem, et nostram bene + dictionem. R. Amen.

Be pleased, Lord, to consecrate and sanctify these hands by this anointing, and our ble + ssing. R. Amen.

Ut quaecumque benedixerint benedicantur; et quaecumque consecraverint, consecrentur et sanctificentur, in nomine Domini nostri Jesu Christi. R. Amen.

That whatsoever they bless may be blessed, and whatsoever they consecrate may be consecrated and sanctified in the name of our Lord Jesus Christ. R. Amen.

Consecration of bishops

Chrism was used for the consecration of bishops. The candidate was first anointed on the crown of the head in the form of a cross and then the rest of the crown was anointed. While performing the anointing, the consecrating bishop said:

> Ungatur et consecretur caput tuum caelesti benedictione, in ordine pontificali.

Blessing of the font

The blessing of the font, at the Paschal Vigil and on the eve of Pentecost (until 1955) and at other times according to necessity, required the oil of catechumens and chrism. The rite, largely drawn from the Gelasian Sacramentary, was very complex; only the part involving the oils, which is later than the Gelasian and probably came into the Roman rite about AD 1000, concerns us here.

Some of the oil of catechumens was poured into the font cross-wise, the celebrant saying:

Sanctificetur, et foecundetur fons iste oleo salutis renascentibus ex eo, in vitam aeternam. R. Amen.	May this font be sanctified and made fruitful by the oil of salvation for such as are born anew therein unto life everlasting. R. Amen.

Then some chrism was poured in the same way, saying:

Infusio Chrismatis Domini nostri Jesu Christi, et Spiritus Sancti Paracliti, fiat in nomine sanctae Trinitatis. R. Amen.	May this infusion of the chrism of our Lord Jesus Christ, and of the Holy Spirit the Comforter be made in the name of the Holy Trinity. R. Amen.

Then some oil of the catechumens and some chrism were poured together, cross-wise, saying:

Commixtio chrismatis sanctificationis, et olei unctionis, et aquae baptismatis, pariter fiat in nomine Pa+tris, et Fi+lii, et Spiritus + Sancti. R. Amen.	May this mixture of the chrism of sanctification, with the oil of unction, and of the water of baptism, be made in the name of the Father +, and of the Son +, and of the Holy + Spirit. R. Amen.

The oil was then mixed with the water and spread throughout the font, and baptisms followed immediately.

Blessing of bells

Anointing was part of the pontifical blessing of a bell which, apart from Spain, would not have been usual before the eighth century. The dedicatory prayers first appear in the Carolingian period and are found in full in *Ordo L*, also known, in part, as the *Ordo Romanus Vulgatus*, which formed some of the original material of the Romano-Germanic pontifical of the tenth century. After the bell was washed and dried, the Master of Ceremonies marked it, in chalk, with seven crosses equidistant from each other on the outside lip, four on the inside lip, and one in the middle of the outer surface. In silence, the bishop, wearing the mitre, anointed the place on the outer surface in the form of a cross with the oil of the sick. The chalk mark was first wiped off. The bishop then removed his mitre, prayed *Deus, qui per beatum Moysen*, made the sign of the cross over the bell, received his mitre and then wiped the oil off. The bell was then anointed at the seven points on the outer lip, with oil of the sick. Each time there was a double unction, followed by three signs of the cross, and the words were said. The four inner anointings were done with chrism. At the conclusion, the mitre removed, the bishop said the prayer *Omnipotens sempiterne Deus*. The rite concluded with the censing of the bell and, a later addition, the chanting of the Gospel (Luke 10.38–42).

Finally, some practical details should be noted. When anointing, a gremial or apron was spread over the bishop's knees, to protect his vestments. Following anointing, bishops used cotton wool and slices of lemon and breadcrumbs to cleanse their fingers (and priests, just bread) before washing their hands. The breadcrumbs and the water used for washing were consigned to the sacrarium. The oil used for anointing people was wiped off using cotton wool; this was to be burned and the ashes consigned to the sacrarium.

The reformed Roman rites[2]

The blessing of oil

Blessing of the oil of the sick

There are three forms for blessing of the oil of the sick. The first is that used by the bishop at the Chrism Mass or by a priest during the rite of anointing:

God of all consolation,
you chose and sent your Son to heal the world.
Graciously listen to our prayer of faith:
send the power of your Holy Spirit, the Consoler,
into this precious oil, this soothing ointment,
this rich gift, this fruit of the earth.

Bless this oil + and sanctify it for our use.

Make this oil a remedy for all who are anointed with it;
heal them in body, in soul, and in spirit,
and deliver them from every affliction.

We ask this through our Lord Jesus Christ, your Son,
who lives and reigns with you and the Holy Spirit,
one God, for ever and ever.

The second is a responsive form with a trinitarian structure and is to be used by a priest during the rite. With a different concluding prayer, it is used as a prayer of thanksgiving over oil that has already been blessed:

Praise to you, God, the almighty Father.
You sent your Son to live among us
and bring us salvation.

R. Blessed be God who heals us in Christ.

Praise to you, God, the only-begotten Son.
You humbled yourself to share in our humanity
and you heal our infirmities.

R. Blessed be God who heals us in Christ.

Praise to you, God, the Holy Spirit, the Consoler.
Your unfailing power gives us strength
in our bodily weakness.

R. Blessed be God who heals us in Christ.

Almighty God,
come to our aid and sanctify this oil
which has been set apart for healing your people.
May the prayer of faith and the anointing with oil
free them from every affliction.
We ask this through Christ our Lord.

The third form comes in the provision for exceptional circumstances, in this case a continuous rite of penance, confirmation (if necessary), anointing and viaticum. The introduction to this rite acknowledges the confusion that can be caused by laying on of hands twice and anointing twice, so the laying on of hands associated with anointing the sick is omitted. The blessing of oil is very short:

Bless, + Lord, your gift of oil
and our brother/sister *N*.
that it may bring him/her relief.

Blessing of the oil of catechumens
Lord God,
protector of all who believe in you,
bless + this oil
and give wisdom and strength
to all who are anointed with it
in preparation for their baptism.
Bring them to a deeper understanding of the gospel,

help them to accept the challenge of Christian living,
and lead them to the joy of new birth
in the family of your church.
We ask this through Christ our Lord.

Consecration of the chrism
Let us pray
that God our almighty Father
will bless this oil
so that all who are anointed with it
may be inwardly transformed
and come to share in eternal salvation.

Then the bishop may breathe over the opening of the vessel of chrism. [The
Ceremonial of Bishops says, 'As circumstances suggest, he may then
breathe over the vessel of chrism.' It does not indicate what
circumstances will govern his actions.]

Consecratory Prayer (A)
God our maker,
source of all growth in holiness,
accept the joyful thanks and praise
we offer in the name of your Church.

In the beginning, at your command,
the earth produced fruit-bearing trees.
From the fruit of the olive tree
you have provided us with oil for holy chrism.
The prophet David sang of the life and joy
that the oil would bring us in the sacraments of your love.

After the avenging flood,
the dove returning to Noah with an olive branch
announced your gift of peace.
This was a sign of a greater gift to come.
Now the waters of baptism wash away the sins of men,
and by anointing with olive oil
you make us radiant with your joy.

At your command,
Aaron was washed with water,
and your servant Moses, his brother,
anointed him priest.
This too foreshadowed greater things to come.

After your Son, Jesus Christ our Lord,
asked John for baptism in the waters of Jordan,

you sent the Spirit upon him
in the form of a dove
and by the witness of your own voice
you declared him to be your only, well-beloved son.
In this you clearly fulfilled the prophecy of David,
that Christ would be anointed with the oil of gladness
beyond his fellow men.

*All the concelebrants extend their right hands towards the chrism, without
saying anything, until the end of the prayer.*

And so, Father, we ask you to bless + this oil you have created.
Fill it with the power of your Holy Spirit
through Christ your Son.
It is from him that chrism takes its name
and with chrism you have anointed
for yourself priests and kings,
prophets and martyrs.

Make this chrism a sign of life and salvation
for those who are to be born again in the waters of baptism.
Wash away the evil they have inherited from sinful Adam,
and when they are anointed with this holy oil
make them temples of your glory,
radiant with the goodness of life
that has its source in you.

Through this sign of chrism
grant them royal, priestly, and prophetic honour,
and clothe them with incorruption.
Let this be indeed the chrism of salvation
for those who will be born again of water and the Holy Spirit.
May they come to share eternal life
in the glory of your kingdom.

We ask this through Christ our Lord.

Consecratory Prayer (B)
Father,
we thank you for the gifts
you have given us in your love:
we thank you for [the] life itself and for the sacraments
that strengthen it and give it fuller meaning.

In the Old Covenant you gave your people
a glimpse of the power of this holy oil
and when the fulness of time had come
you brought that mystery to perfection

in the life of our Lord Jesus Christ, your Son.
By his suffering, dying, and rising to life
he saved the human race.
He sent your Spirit to fill the Church
with every gift needed to complete your saving work.

From that time forward,
through the sign of holy chrism,
you dispense your life and love to men.
By anointing them with the Spirit,
you strengthen all who have been reborn in baptism.
Through that anointing
you transform them into the likeness of Christ your Son
and give them a share
in his royal, priestly, and prophetic work.

All the concelebrants extend their right hands towards the chrism, without saying anything, until the end of the prayer.

And so, Father, by the power of your love,
make this mixture of oil and perfume
a sign and source + of your blessing.
Pour out the gifts of your Holy Spirit
on our brothers and sisters who will be anointed with it.
Let the splendour of holiness shine on the world
from every place and thing
signed with this oil.

Above all, Father, we pray
that through this sign of your anointing
you will grant increase to your Church
until it reaches the eternal glory
where you, Father, will be all in all,
together with Christ your Son,
in the unity of the Holy Spirit,
for ever and ever.

(B) *The anointing of the sick*

The liturgy of anointing forms a part of a larger whole. It may be used within Mass, outside Mass, and in a hospital or institution, which is, of course, its shortest form. Its full form is:

- Litany (a responsive intercession)
- Laying on of hands
- Prayer over the oil (thanksgiving or blessing)
- Anointing

- Prayer after anointing
- The Lord's Prayer (outside Mass)

The priest lays on hands on the head of the sick person in silence, then says the thanksgiving over the oil, or blesses it if necessary. The priest then anoints the sick person with the blessed oil, first on the forehead, saying:

> Through this holy anointing
> may the Lord in his love and mercy help you
> with the grace of the Holy Spirit.
> R. Amen.

Then he anoints the hands, saying:

> May the Lord who frees you from sin
> save you and raise you up.
> R. Amen.

The Latin text, as given in the Constitution of Paul VI, is: *Per istam sanctam unctionem et suam piissimam misericordiam, adiuvet te Dominus gratia Spiritus Sancti, ut a peccatis liberatum te salvet atque propitius allevet*. These words constitute the sacramental form and they are not repeated, though according to local culture and traditions the priest may anoint additional parts of the body. There are several alternative prayers after anointing. The first general prayer asks God to grant comfort 'through this holy anointing'. That for the terminally ill refers to anointing for healing of body and spirit and that for those 'in advanced age' says that the person asks in the anointing 'for healing in body and soul'. In the prayer after anointing a child, the oil is called 'the oil of healing and peace'.

(C) Other anointings

The texts for the anointings at baptism, confirmation, ordination and for the dedication of an altar and a church are given in Chapter 9. Anointing no longer forms part of the blessing of bells. Nor is there mention of breadcrumbs and lemon slices, but only of 'the requisites for the washing of hands after anointing'.

Contemporary Anglican rites[3]

There is a considerable diversity in the provision for anointing in Anglican liturgies, as can be seen from Table 1. There has been a gradual recovery of the practice. This has been easier with regard to healing because of the explicit testimony of James. Although many

Anglicans favour baptismal anointing, it would be difficult to maintain that it is necessary given that there is no clear biblical warrant and no continuous tradition of use in the Anglican Church. Though actively encouraged in some provinces and tolerated in others, all anointings remain optional.

Table 1   Official provision for anointing

Province	Sick	Pre-baptismal	Post-baptismal	Confirmation	Ordination
America	√	×	√	×	×
Australia	×	×	×	×	×
Canada	√	×	√	×	×
England	√	√ or	√	√	×
Ireland	×	×	×	×	×
New Zealand	√	×	√	×	×
South Africa	√	×	×	√	√
Wales	√	×	√ or	√	×

(A) The blessing and consecration of oils

In the American *Book of Common Prayer* (1979) the consecration of chrism is integral to the rite of baptism. Following the thanksgiving over the water, the bishop places a hand on the vessel of oil and says the prayer 'Eternal Father, whose blessed Son . . .' given below. When administering confirmation, the bishop may also consecrate chrism for subsequent use at baptism. He may use just the prayer given in the rite of baptism or the prayer with an introduction as given in the *Book of Occasional Services*. This form is used after the post-communion prayer, when olive oil, to which oil of balsam or other fragrant oil has been added, is presented to him and placed either on a small table or on the altar:

> *Facing the people, the bishop addresses them in these or similar words:*

> Dear Friends in Christ: In the beginning, the Spirit of God hovered over the creation; and, throughout history, God, by the gift of the Holy Spirit, has empowered his people to serve him. As a sign of that gift, the priests and kings of Israel were anointed with oil; and our Lord Jesus Christ was himself anointed with the Holy Spirit at his Baptism as the Christ, God's own Messiah. At Baptism, Christians are likewise anointed by that same Spirit to empower them for God's service. Let us now set apart this oil to be the sign of that anointing.

Let us pray. [*Silence*]

The Bishop then places a hand on the vessel of oil and prays

Eternal Father, whose blessed Son was anointed by the Holy Spirit to be the Savior and servant of all, we pray you to consecrate this oil, that those who are sealed with it may share in the royal priesthood of Jesus Christ; who lives and reigns with you and the Holy Spirit, for ever and ever.

The prayer 'Eternal Father' was composed especially for the book, but it did have an earlier form in the 1973 authorized services. Comparison shows that the understanding of what anointing means and its relation to Jesus' own ministry became clearer with experimental use:

Eternal Father, whose Son Jesus Christ was anointed by the Holy Spirit to be the servant of all, we pray you to consecrate this oil; that those who are sealed with it may share in the ministry of our great High Priest and King; who lives and reigns with you and the Holy Spirit, one God, for ever and ever.

The *Book of Common Prayer* also gives the following blessing of oil for the sick, said by a priest:

O Lord, holy Father, giver of health and salvation: Send your Holy Spirit to sanctify this oil; that, as your holy apostles anointed many that were sick and healed them, so may those who in faith and repentance receive this holy unction be made whole; through Jesus Christ our Lord, who lives and reigns with you and the Holy Spirit, one God, for ever and ever. Amen.

Of those provinces that make full provision for the blessing of oils, the American Church is alone in making the blessing parochial and omitting reference to Maundy Thursday. The Canadian *Book of Alternative Services* includes the blessing of oil in its episcopal services. Two oils are blessed, for the sick and for baptism (chrism). The oil, according to the rubrics, is normally olive oil 'or, according to circumstances, other plant oil'. It is noted that oil of balsam or other fragrant oil is added to chrism. The Canadian book has a full set of rules concerning oil, several of which concern the ordering of the service. It specifically points out that it does not specify the day on which blessing takes place. It recognizes that gatherings of clergy and laity may be possible in *urban* dioceses on Maundy Thursday, but that they are impossible when large distances are involved. It recommends an occasion, such as a synod, when many clergy and laity are gathered 'so that the blessing of oil will be seen as an action of the whole diocesan Church'. Three of the practical regulations are worthy of note: that the blessed oil is to be kept reverently and in a safe place; that the oil is to be renewed each time the bishop blesses oil and that old oil is to be either poured to earth or poured into some absorbent material and burnt; that the oil for anointing is to be used only by clergy and appropriately authorized laypersons.

The Province of Southern Africa provides a form in its prayer book for the blessing of oils. Two oils are blessed at the Chrism Eucharist on Maundy Thursday: the oil of the sick and the holy chrism. The blessings are reserved to the bishop and take place before the Peace. They follow the shape and frequently the language of the reformed Roman rite.

The oil of the sick

Lord God, our loving Father, you bring healing to the sick through your Son, Jesus Christ. Hear us as we pray in faith, and send your Holy Spirit, our helper and friend, upon this oil. We ask you to bless those who will be anointed with it, and heal them in body, mind and spirit. Merciful Father, bless this oil for the ministry of healing, in the name of our Lord Jesus Christ. Amen.

The blessing of chrism is concelebrated. The priests extend their right hands towards the chrism, in silence, from 'And So, Father' until the end.

The oil for the holy chrism

Father, we thank you for the gifts you have given us in your love. We thank you for life itself and for the sacraments that strengthen it and give it fuller meaning.

Under the old covenant you inspired your servants to use oil to set men apart as kings and priests; in the fulness of time you anointed your perfect Son, Jesus Christ, as our eternal Priest and King.

By his suffering, dying and rising to life he saved the human race. He sent your Spirit to fill the Church with every gift needed to complete your saving work.

From that time forward, by anointing them with the Spirit, you strengthen all who are baptized. You transform them into the likeness of Christ your Son, and give them a share in his prophetic, priestly and kingly work.

And so, Father, by the power of your love, bless to our use this mixture of oil and perfume as a sign and means of your heavenly grace. Pour out the gifts of your Holy Spirit on those who are anointed with it. Let the splendour of your holiness shine on the world from every place and thing signed with this oil.

Above all, Father, we pray that through this sign of your
anointing you will grant increase to your Church until it attains
to the eternal glory where you, Father, will be all in all, together
with Christ your Son, in the unity of the Holy Spirit, for ever
and ever. Amen.

The New Zealand Prayer Book only makes suggested provision for
the blessing of oil, called 'setting apart', for anointing after baptism. It
may be used by either a bishop or a priest, though it is noted that it is
appropriate that it should be done by the bishop on Maundy
Thursday:

God of all creation, at baptism your Son was anointed by the
Holy Spirit; in Christ's name we set apart this oil. Grant that
those who are signed at their baptism with the cross of their
Saviour in this holy oil, may be sealed by your Spirit as yours for
ever, and share in the royal priesthood of your Church, for you
live and reign one God for ever. Amen.

Although the *Alternative Service Book* provides a collect and readings
for a Eucharist for the blesing of oils, no prayers for blessing were
agreed by the General Synod. This prayer, dependent upon that in the
American Prayer Book, is provided in *Ministry at the Time of Death*
(1991) for use by a priest when oil consecrated by the bishop is not
available:

Lord, holy Father, giver of health and salvation, as your
apostles anointed those who were sick and healed them, so
continue the ministry of healing in your Church. Sanctify this
oil, that those who are anointed with it may be freed from
suffering and distress, find inward peace, and know the joy of
your salvation, through your Son, our Saviour Jesus Christ.
Amen.

The English liturgist Michael Perham notes that there is an 'oil is oil'
school of thought in the Church of England which, affirming that the
same processes are at work in initiation and in healing, believes their
unity should be maintained by blessing only one oil. The General
Synod was asked, contrary to the tendency elsewhere in Anglicanism,
to allow for the blessing of three oils: of the sick, 'for the signing with
the cross before baptism', and chrism for post-baptismal anointing
and for use at confirmation. Though not agreed to by the Synod, this
threefold blessing is widely practised in the Church of England.

(B) The anointing of the sick

The new rites of the major Anglican Provinces are considered here in
chronological order – that is, those of America (1979), England (1983

and 1991), Wales (1984), Canada (1985), South Africa (1989), and New Zealand (1989). The Australian Prayer Book (1978) and the *Alternative Prayer Book 1984* of the Church of Ireland do not have a form of anointing.

The Book of Common Prayer (1979) of the American Episcopal Church includes both the laying on of hands and anointing in the order for ministration to the sick. The laying on of hands is the normative form and anointing is an optional supplement. First, a blessing of oil is provided, said by the priest. There is no provision for the blessing of oil at another time and the intention is that the priest should bless the oil at the time of anointing. (The text has already been given above.) After the laying on of hands, the priest may anoint by dipping a thumb in the holy oil and making the sign of the cross on the person's forehead, saying:

> N., I anoint you with oil in the Name of the Father, and of the Son, and of the Holy Spirit. Amen.

The priest may then add this prayer which is essentially abridged from the 1549 statement, portions of which were derived from the Sarum use:

> As you are outwardly anointed with this holy oil, so may our heavenly Father grant you the inward anointing of the Holy Spirit. Of his great mercy may he forgive you your sins, release you from suffering, and restore you to wholeness and strength. May he deliver you from all evil, preserve you in all goodness, and bring you to everlasting life; through Jesus Christ our Lord. Amen.

The rubrics allow a deacon or lay person, in case of necessity, to perform the anointing, using oil blessed by a bishop or priest.

In 1983 the Church of England produced a set of texts separate from the *Alternative Service Book* entitled *Ministry to the Sick*. This was followed in 1991 by a further booklet, *Ministry at the Time of Death*. The former provision expects the laying on of hands with prayer and anointing to take place at the Holy Communion or at Morning or Evening Prayer. It allows for modification to be made by the president, but it expects the presence of a congregation. The latter booklet draws on the former, but is more appropriately arranged for home, hospital or hospice. It provides, as its title suggests, the last rites of the Church.

The 1983 order assumes that the laying on of hands will always take place and may be followed by anointing. These words may be used or, if anointing is to follow, the laying on of hands may be done in silence:

> In the name of our Lord Jesus Christ who laid his hands on the

sick that they might be healed I lay my hands upon you, N. May almighty God, Father, Son, and Holy Spirit, make you whole in body, mind, and spirit, give you light and peace, and keep you in life eternal. Amen.

The anointing is given by making the sign of the cross on the sick person. The rubric does not state where. Canon B37 says on the forehead and note 11 to the rite provides that other parts of the body may be anointed in addition. These or similar words are used:

N., I anoint you with oil in the name of our Lord Jesus Christ. May our heavenly Father make you whole in body and mind, and grant you the inward anointing of his Holy Spirit, the Spirit of strength and joy and peace. Amen.

The 1991 order allows that the minister may be a bishop or priest, or a deacon authorized by the bishop. As noted above, a form for blessing oil is provided. The anointing is given by making the sign of the cross in oil on the person's forehead. The hands may also be anointed. The following words are said:

N., I anoint you with oil in the name of the Lord Jesus Christ. May the Lord in his love and mercy uphold you by the grace and power of the Holy Spirit. Amen.

After the anointing, the minister may add this prayer based on the American rite:

As you are outwardly anointed with this holy oil,
so may our heavenly Father grant you
the inward anointing of the Holy Spirit.
Of his great mercy may he forgive you your sins
and release you from suffering.
May he deliver you from all evil,
preserve you in all goodness,
and bring you to everlasting life;
through Jesus Christ our Lord. Amen.

The Welsh *Book of Common Prayer* (1984) contains an extensive section that bears the slightly misleading title 'The Ministry of Healing'. It contains five sections: communion of the sick; a form of confession and absolution with the laying on of hands and anointing (as one section); the ministry of deliverance; acts of devotion; and the commendation of the dying. The preamble to the anointing, if it is not done within the Eucharist, is a reading, profession of faith and confession and absolution. The rite prescribes that the oil be pure olive oil and, if it has not been blessed by the bishop, the priest says this prayer:

Almighty God, who hast taught us by thine apostle James to anoint the sick in the name of the Lord that they may be healed: Bless this oil that *he* who is now anointed may be delivered from all troubles of body, mind and spirit: through Jesus Christ our Lord. Amen.

The priest then lays his hands on the sick person's head and says:

As with this holy oil you are outwardly anointed, so may our heavenly Father grant that you be inwardly anointed with the Holy Spirit. Amen.

Then the priest is to anoint the person on the forehead with the sign of the cross saying:

N., in the Name of our Lord Jesus Christ, I anoint you with this holy oil that you may receive the healing of all your infirmities of body, mind and spirit. May the merciful Father give you comfort and sure confidence in him and keep you in perpetual peace and safety, through the same Jesus Christ our Lord. Amen.

The Book of Alternative Services of the Anglican Church of Canada (1985) teaches that the laying on of hands and anointing 'provide the moment when the prayer of the Church for the healing power of God is made specific and particular in relation to this sick person. It is also a sign of forgiveness and consequently of reconciliation in and with the Christian community.' The rubrics stress that the oil will have been blessed by the bishop. A form is provided for this. The oil may be used only by clergy and by those laypersons who have received authorization by the diocesan bishop. The minister anoints the person's forehead with oil, making the sign of the cross and saying:

N., through this holy anointing may the Lord in his love and power uphold you by the grace and power of the Holy Spirit. Amen.

This is followed by the prayer 'As you are outwardly anointed . . .' found in the American rite.

An Anglican Prayer Book of the Province of Southern Africa contains a full order for anointing with a preparation, including a general confession, brief ministry of the word, statement of faith in God and in his power to help, laying on of hands, anointing, thanksgiving and blessing, the parts being used according to necessity. The rubrics state that the priest is the proper minister of the rite, but that deacons may be authorized and lay ministers licensed to administer it. The oil is the oil of the sick blessed by the bishop. In case of grave necessity, the priest may bless 'natural vegetable oil' in these words:

Almighty God, giver of health and salvation, sanctify this oil for the healing of your people; through Jesus Christ our Lord. Amen.

The laying on of hands is the essential pre-condition for anointing in this rite and so the whole text is given:

The Minister may invite others present to join him as he lays hands on the sick person. He may pray in silence, or say

In the name of God most high, Father, Son and Holy Spirit, may release be given you from your pain according to his will; may new life quicken your mind and body; and may perfect health abound in you.

If the Priest considers it appropriate, he may use the following form

N., may Christ, the Light of the world, drive away from you all darkness and all assaults of evil. In the name of God, Father, Son, and Holy Spirit, I lay my hands upon you: may he fill you with his healing, his light and his peace.

The minister then anoints the sick person, saying

N., I anoint you with oil in the name of our Lord Jesus Christ. May our heavenly Father make you whole in body and mind, and grant you the inward anointing of his Holy Spirit, the Spirit of strength and joy and peace. Amen.

    The Almighty Lord, who is a strong tower to all who put their trust in him, be now and evermore your defence, and make you believe and trust that the only name under heaven given for health and salvation is the name of our Lord Jesus Christ. Amen.

The preliminary rubrics in *A New Zealand Prayer Book* (1989) describe anointing as 'a vivid, sacramental expression of God's love in time of sickness' and stresses that it is helpful at the onset of illness as well as in times of crisis. Its purpose is to convey healing in all sickness, not just when a Christian is dying. It is stated three times in the order that the oil for the anointing of the sick is only to be used by a priest! This is the text for the act of anointing:

The priest dips a thumb in holy oil and makes the sign of the cross on the person's forehead, saying

N., I anoint you with this holy oil.
Receive Christ's forgiveness and healing.
The power of the Saviour who suffered for you
flow through your mind and body,
lifting you to peace and inward strength.
Amen.

If the person wishes, other parts of the body may also be anointed. When the anointing is completed, the priest continues

God our healer,
keep us aware of your presence,
support us with your power,
comfort us with your protection,
give us strength
and establish your peace.

(C) Other anointings

The new American rite of baptism of 1973, which was carried through, with little modification, to the 1979 Prayer Book, was the first Anglican rite that made provision for anointing with chrism. As noted above, it is consecrated by the bishop at the baptism. If a priest anoints at baptism, rather than a bishop, he must use episcopally consecrated chrism. The action of baptizing is followed either by a prayer of thanks and anointing or by anointing and then the prayer of thanks:

Heavenly Father, we thank you that by water and the Holy Spirit you have bestowed upon these your servants the forgiveness of sin, and have raised them to the new life of grace. Sustain them, O Lord, in your Holy Spirit. Give them an inquiring and discerning heart, the courage to will and to persevere, a spirit to know and to love you, and the gift of joy and wonder in all your works. Amen.

Then the bishop or priest places a hand on the person's head, marking on the forehead the sign of the cross (using chrism if desired) and saying to each one:

N., you are sealed by the Holy Spirit in baptism and marked as Christ's own for ever. Amen.

In the Church of Canada, the signing comes first, with the words 'I sign you with the cross and mark you as Christ's own for ever.' Then the prayer 'Heavenly Father, we thank you . . .', as in the American book, is said. The Church of the Province of New Zealand simply provides that the sign of the cross after baptism may be made 'with oil set apart for this purpose either by the bishop or by a priest'. The accompanying words are 'We sign you with the cross, the sign of Christ'.

In the Church of England there are a number of options for anointing in the initiation rites of the *Alternative Service Book*:

(a) when administering baptism, and confirmation, the bishop may anoint as he makes the sign of the cross before or after baptism with 'oil blessed for this purpose' and after laying his hands on the candidate's head.

(b) a priest may also anoint with 'oil blessed for this purpose' before or after baptism when making the sign of the cross.

(c) the bishop may anoint at confirmation 'with oil which he has previously blessed for this purpose'.

(d) anointing may be omitted altogether.

This confusion stems in part from the way anointing came to be permitted and in part from the arrangement of baptism in which the signing with the cross, and accompanying anointing, is not considered to be an essential element. A commission in 1958 stated that it did not consider that anointing would gain much support. The Ely report on initiation commended it as a rite that could enhance baptism, but the Liturgical Commission did not include it in the draft Series 3/ASB rite. In November 1978 the Revision Committee provided for the optional use of chrism and it moved the consignation from after baptism to the decision before the washing, while keeping the post-baptismal option. Ronald Jasper reported that this was a move urged by Charles Whitaker 'for it clearly indicated that consignation was not to be regarded as part of the sacrament'. In Series 2, the Liturgical Commission had attempted to clarify matters by making the signing a post-baptismal ceremony, but ASB associates it with the decision, and its connection with delivery from the powers of darkness, in the pre-baptism position, is suggestive of the link of anointing with exorcism in the Roman rite. When used post-baptismally that connection is, of course, not made. If anointing is to be done before baptism it cannot be done with chrism. If it is to be done at all it must be with an oil 'blessed for this purpose' which is akin to the oil of catechumens. A post-baptismal anointing cannot in the tradition or usual practice of the Church, Roman Catholic or Anglican, be done with any oil other than chrism. It must be said that the words 'I sign you with the cross . . .' do not embody the traditional understanding of the joyful post-baptismal anointing. The signing with the cross in the baptismal liturgy of the American Episcopal Church does, by contrast, sound a note of joy and fulfilment. It is also clear that the ASB baptism rite will not allow anointing before *and* after baptism, as, apart from anything else, it only provides one set of words. Wherever it is done and whatever reason the minister may have for doing it, ASB does not count it as necessary and is not prepared to give it a particular meaning. The same might be said for confirmation. Anointing is allowed, but not encouraged. The matter of the rite is the laying on of the bishop's hand. The form, as determined by the Church of England, is the words 'Confirm, O Lord . . .'

An alternative order for the baptism of infants and for baptism with confirmation was authorized for experimental use by the Governing Body of the Church in Wales in September 1990. It provides for the signing with the cross, without any form of anointing, when the candidates are presented. Unless baptism is followed by confirmation, the minister anoints the newly baptized on the crown of the head with the oil of chrism. The prayer follows closely the text of the Roman rite:

> God the Father of our Lord Jesus Christ
> has set you free from sin,
> given you new birth by water and the Holy Spirit
> and welcomed you into his church.
> He now anoints you with the oil of salvation.
> In the name of Christ,
> the anointed Priest, Prophet and King,
> may you live always as a member of his Body,
> sharing everlasting life.

The same prayer is used by the bishop if he anoints at confirmation immediately following baptism.

The Southern African Church provides for a post-baptismal anointing by the bishop in confirmation and not at the celebration of baptism. He may sign them on the forehead using chrism and say:

> N., I sign you with the sign of the cross and I lay my hand upon you. Lord, confirm and strengthen with your Holy Spirit this your child and empower *him* for your service.

It is the only one of the provinces we are considering that makes provision for anointing at the ordination of priests. It follows the ordination prayer and the vesting and precedes the giving of the Bible, chalice and paten. As with the blessing of oils, the prayer follows the Roman formula:

> *The bishop may anoint his palms with chrism, saying*:

> As the Father anointed his Son with the power of the Spirit, so may Jesus Christ preserve you to sanctify his people and to offer sacrifices of praise and thanksgiving.

The absence of official provision at provincial level does not necessarily mean absence of practice in dioceses or parishes. For example, until the authorization of the alternative rite of baptism, there was no occasion on which the Welsh Church officially permitted anointing, other than of the sick, yet three oils were regularly blessed in Llandaff Cathedral on Maundy Thursday. Such blessing would certainly suggest use of the oils.

(D) Other rites

The American *Book of Occasional Services* (2nd edn, 1988) contains a blessing of an aumbry for the oils:

> Antiphon.
> The Israelites and Levites shall bring grain, new wine, and oil to the rooms where the vessels of the sanctuary are kept.
> V. You have anointed my head with oil:
> R. My cup is running over.
> Let us pray.
> O Lord God of hosts, who commanded priests of the Old Covenant to set apart oil for the anointing of kings and priests, and by your Apostle James commanded the presbyters of your Church to anoint the sick: We here offer to you this aumbry for the safe-keeping of the oils set apart for the anointing of baptism and for the ministry of healing; through him who was anointed as the Christ, and who lives and reigns for ever and ever. Amen.

(E) Conclusion

It is less than twenty years since anointing, whether of the sick or in initiation, was generally reintroduced in Anglicanism. It has inevitably been a period of experiment and of reception. A broad pattern has emerged in liturgical imagery and in practice – that is, of blessing only two oils, that of the sick and chrism, of giving a single post-baptismal anointing in initiation, and of using the anointing of the sick more sparingly than the laying on of hands in the healing ministry. The diversity of prayers connected with the anointing of the sick is related to a wider uncertainty about the meaning of the Christian ministry of healing. Future development would helpfully include provision of introduc-tions, such as those in the Canadian book, to rites involving anointing, the encouragement of provinces that have no provision to permit anointing, and the use of a single post-baptismal anointing. Further work is needed on the way in which healing liturgies express reasonable expectations of health and salvation and on the traditional link between Maundy Thursday and the blessing of oils.

The Lutheran churches in America and Canada[4]

In the revised liturgical texts, these churches followed the lead of the American Episcopal Church, though the Inter-Lutheran Commission on Worship adapted developments and texts according to its own tradition.

(A) *The blessing of oil*

The Lutheran book entitled *Occasional Services* provides a form for
dedication of worship furnishings. It consists of unchanging introductory and concluding sections and a changeable section appropriate
to what is being dedicated – for example, cross, candles, paraments,
window, etc. The prayer, which is said by the presiding minister, an
ordained pastor, is used during the liturgy of Holy Communion
between the presentation of the gifts and the offertory prayer. Oil is
dedicated in the following way:

> Blessed are you, O Lord our God, king of the universe. You
> have enriched our lives with every good and perfect gift; you
> have commanded us to show your splendour to our children and
> to praise you with lives of love, justice, and joy.

> Accept this oil which we offer in thanksgiving; may those who
> look to you for health and salvation be filled with the power of
> your Holy Spirit and become radiant with the goodness of life
> which has its source in you.

> Bring us all at length to your perfect kingdom, where you live
> and reign with the Son and the Holy Spirit, now and forever.

Another prayer is provided in the order for the laying on of hands and
anointing the sick. The rubric prescribes that the oil used for
anointing should be olive oil 'to which an aromatic ingredient such as
synthetic oil of cinnamon or oil of bergamot may be added'. When it
has been prepared, this prayer is said by an ordained pastor:

> Lord God, you bring healing to the sick through your Son, Jesus
> Christ our Lord. May your blessings come upon all who are
> anointed with this oil, that they may be freed from pain and
> illness and be made whole. Amen.

(B) *The anointing of the sick*

A note to the services involving anointing points to the biblical
association between anointing and the activity of the Holy Spirit,
especially in relation to the healing of sickness or infirmity. 'In recent
decades,' the note continues, 'many have rediscovered the value of the
laying on of hands and anointing with oil, both in the visitation of the
sick and in public services of healing.'

The Service of the Word for Healing, a public and corporate
service, provides for the laying on of hands with suitable words or the
laying on of hands in silence followed by anointing of the person's
forehead with the sign of the cross using these words, which, in

common with the Episcopalian blessing of the oil of the sick, derives from an old Roman form:

> O God, the giver of health and salvation: As the apostles of our Lord Jesus Christ, at his command, anointed many that were sick and healed them, send now your Holy Spirit, that *[name]*, anointed with this oil, may in repentance and faith be made whole; through the same Jesus Christ our Lord.

In the private administration, the pastor simply says:

> *[name]*, I anoint you with oil in the name of the Father, and of the Son, and of the Holy Spirit.

(C) Anointing at initiation

After baptism the minister marks the sign of the cross on the forehead of each of the baptized. This may be done in oil 'prepared for this purpose', presumably using the form given in the dedication of church furnishings. Whether oil is used or not, the words said are the same:

> *[name]*, child of God, you have been sealed by the Holy Spirit and marked with the cross of Christ forever.

No other anointings are provided for in the Lutheran liturgy.

Notes

1. The *Pontificale Romanum* was used in an edition published by Dessain, Mechlin 1895 and in the *editio typica* of 1962 (Vatican City). The text of the blessings, with the English translation used here, appears in the *Saint Andrew Daily Missal* (Bruges 1962). Reference was also made to the historical sources of the blessings: H. A. Wilson, *The Gelasian Sacramentary* (Oxford 1984); A. Chavasse, *Le Sacramentaire Gélasien* (Paris 1957); J. Deshusses, *Le Sacramentaire Grégorien* 3rd edn (Fribourg 1992). M. Andrieu, *Le Pontifical Romain au Moyen-Age*, 1 (Vatican 1938).

    The ritual was used in three editions, each following from that of Paul V (1614): as revised by Benedict XIV, 3rd edn (Ratisbon 1882); the *editio typica* of Leo XIII in 1884 revised by Pius X in 1913 and again under Pius XI in 1925 to bring it into line with the new Code of Canon Law (Ratisbon 1926); and in the form with an authorized English translation *Collection Rituum – The 1964 English Ritual* published in 1964 (College-ville). Reference was also made to the *Excerpta E Rituali Romano* (London 1959), which was prepared shortly after Pope John XXIII allowed some use of the vernacular in the rites. This was itself derived from the old *Ordo Administrandi Sacramenta*, the English ritual. The rites were elucidated by reference to W. Dunne, *The Ritual Explained*

(London 1928) and J. Wuest, T. Mullaney and W. Barry, *Matters Liturgical* (New York 1959).

The ceremonial details for episcopal rites were drawn from P. Ahearne and M. Lane, *Pontifical Ceremonies* (London 1942).

2.   The following liturgical texts were used: *Missale Romanum, editio typica altera* (Vatican City 1975); *Pontificale Romanum: De Ordinatione Diaconi, Presbyteri et Episcopi, editio typica* (Vatican City 1968); *Ceremonial of Bishops* (Collegeville 1989); *Dedication of a Church and an Altar* (Washington DC 1989); *The Ordination of Priests* (London n.d.); *Pastoral Care of the Sick* (London 1982); *The Rites of the Catholic Church*, 2 vols (Collegeville 1990); *The Sacramentary* (New York 1985).

3.   Anglican liturgical books:
Canada The Book of Alternative Services of the Anglican Church of Canada (Toronto 1985).
England The Alternative Service Book 1980 (Cambridge and London 1980). *Ministry to the Sick* (London 1983). *Ministry at the Time of Death* (London 1991).
New Zealand A New Zealand Prayer Book/He Karakia Mihinare o Aotearoa (London and Auckland 1989).
Southern Africa An Anglican Prayer Book 1989 (London 1989).
United States The Book of Common Prayer . . . According to the Use of The Episcopal Church (New York 1979). *The Book of Occasional Services*, 2nd edn (New York 1988).
Wales Y Llyfr Gweddi Gyffredin i'w arfer yn Yr Eglwys yng Nghymru/ The Book of Common Prayer for use in The Church in Wales, 2 (Penarth 1984). *Bedydd Cyhoeddus Babanod, Bedydd gyda Chonffyrmasiwn/Public Baptism of Infants and Baptism with Confirmation* (Penarth 1991).

4.   Texts are contained in *Occasional Services: A Companion to the Lutheran Book of Worship* (Minneapolis 1982).

15

Blessings of Oil and Anointings: The Byzantine Rite

W. Jardine Grisbrooke

The Byzantine rite makes use of the three traditional oils – chrism, the oil of catechumens, and the oil of the sick. Chrism is blessed by the bishop on Maundy Thursday (in practice only by patriarchs and primates, and only from time to time when a new supply is needed). The oil of catechumens and the oil of the sick are blessed by a priest on the occasions when they are to be used.

(A) Blessing of chrism

1.   Byzantine chrism is a very complex confection. The basis is olive oil, to which are added numerous aromatic substances (the number varying from thirty-eight to fifty-seven according to different usages). Most of these are boiled together, and then left to cool, clarify and almost solidify, while some are added at the cooling stage. The complexity and costliness of these operations accounts for the practical restriction of the blessing of chrism to a small number of great churches, and also for the fact that it does not take place annually, but only in those years when a new supply is needed.
2.   The preparation of the chrism takes place from Monday to Wednesday of Holy Week, each stage being marked by a brief liturgical ceremony. During the boiling, which continues day and night, the chrism is watched over by priests and deacons (deacons only, according to some usages) and others charged with the confection of it, and during this continuous vigil the Gospels are read.

211

3.   The blessing of the chrism takes place at the liturgy on Maundy Thursday. The chrism is brought in with the eucharistic gifts at the great entrance; it is blessed after the eucharistic prayer. There are three principal parts to the rite: (i) a triple signing with the sign of the cross, (ii) the actual prayer of blessing, (iii) a 'prayer of inclination'. The texts of the two prayers are as follows:

O Lord of mercy and Father of lights, the giver of every good and perfect gift, grant to us, unworthy though we be, the grace to fulfil the ministry of this great and lifegiving mystery, as you gave it to Moses your faithful steward, and to Samuel your servant, and to your holy apostles, and send your Holy Spirit upon this chrism:

Make it a royal anointing, a spiritual anointing, a safeguard of life, a hallowing of souls and bodies, an oil of gladness, which was prefigured in the Law, and which shone forth in the New Covenant:

For by it were anointed priests and high priests, prophets and kings,[1] and your holy apostles,[2] and all who have been reborn through the washing of new birth, by them, and by the bishops and priests who have followed them, even to this day.

So,[3] Lord God Almighty, by the coming of your holy and adorable Spirit, make it a garment of immortality, a perfecting seal which imprints your divine Name, and that of your only-begotten Son, and that of your Holy Spirit, on those who have received your divine washing:

That they may be known before your face, that they may be of your household and of your city, your servants and handmaids; that they may be delivered from all evil and redeemed from all sin;

That they may be recognized by the angels and archangels and all the powers of heaven, as having put on the garment of your immaculate glory, and may strike fear into all evil and impure demonic powers;

That they may be a people set apart, a royal priesthood, a holy nation, signed through this immaculate mystery, so that you, O God and Father, may dwell in them through the Holy Spirit.

For you, our God, are holy, and you dwell in the holy places among those who are holy,[4] and to you do we give glory, to the Father, and to the Son, and to the Holy Spirit, now, and always, and for ever and ever. Amen.

212

To you, O God and King of all, do we bow the neck of our heart, giving thanks because you have judged us worthy to become the ministers of these your divine mysteries: we proclaim the mercy, which you have poured out upon us with such abundance: and we pray that we may receive your hallowing, like the chrism which is poured upon our heads, since the chrism which is poured out is the Name of your only-begotten Son, Christ our God, through whom the whole world, visible and invisible, is sweetly scented:

For you are everywhere to be adored and glorified, and to you do we give glory and worship, to the Father, and to the Son, and to the Holy Spirit, now, and always, and for ever and ever. Amen.

(B) Anointing with chrism

1.   The principal and primary use of chrism, as is reflected in the prayer for its blessing, is in the sacrament of chrismation (confirmation), which immediately follows baptism, for infants as well as for adults. After the neophyte has been baptized and clothed, the priest says this prayer over him:

Blessed are you, O Lord God Almighty, the fount of all that is good, and the sun of righteousness, who through the appearing of your only-begotten Son and our God have made the light of salvation to shine upon those who were in darkness, and have granted to us, unworthy though we be, blessed cleansing through holy baptism and divine hallowing through lifegiving anointing; who also have now been pleased to regenerate your newly-enlightened servant through water and the Spirit, and have given him forgiveness of his sins, both voluntary and involuntary.

Do you yourself, O Master, the King of all, the compassionate, give to him also the seal of the gift of your holy and all-powerful and adorable Spirit, and make him a partaker of the holy Body and the precious Blood of your Christ. Guard him by your hallowing, and confirm him in the Orthodox faith; deliver him from the evil one and all his works, and through a saving fear of you keep his soul in purity and righteousness, that he may be well-pleasing to you in his every work and word, and so become a son and inheritor of your heavenly kingdom.

For you are our God, the God who has mercy and saves, and to you do we ascribe glory, to the Father, and to the Son, and to the Holy Spirit, now, and always, and for ever and ever. Amen.

After the prayer the priest anoints the newly baptized with the chrism, making the sign of the cross on the forehead, eyes, nostrils, mouth, ears, breast, hands and feet, saying:

The seal of the gift of the Holy Spirit. Amen.

2. Chrism is also used at the consecration of a church, with both the altar and the interior walls being anointed.

3. Chrism was also formerly used at the coronations of the Byzantine and Russian emperors.

(C) *Blessing of the oil of catechumens*

1. The blessing of the oil of catechumens takes place not, as one might expect, in the order for the making of a catechumen (the first part of the baptismal service), but in the order for baptism proper, after the blessing of the baptismal water and before the baptism itself.

2. The priest breathes three times on the vessel of oil, and signs it with a triple sign of the cross, and then says this prayer:

Master, Lord God of our fathers, who sent to those in the ark of Noah a dove with a twig of olive in its mouth as a symbol of reconciliation and of deliverance from the flood, and thereby prefigured the mystery of grace; who supplied the fruit of the olive for the fulfilment of your holy mysteries, and through it filled those under the Law with the Holy Spirit, and make perfect those under grace: Do you yourself also bless this oil with the power, the working, and the coming of your Holy Spirit, that it may become an anointing of incorruption, an armour of righteousness, a renewal of soul and of body, a defence against all the works of the devil, and a deliverance from all evils, for those who in faith are anointed with it or partake of it: to your glory, and that of your only-begotten Son, and that of your all-holy, good and lifegiving Spirit, now, and always, and for ever and ever. Amen.

(D) *Anointing with the oil of catechumens*

1. Singing 'Alleluia' three times with the people, the priest pours some oil into the baptismal water, making the sign of the cross with it three times. He then sings 'Blessed be God, who enlightens and hallows every man who comes into the world, now, and always, and for ever and ever. Amen.'

2. He then takes some of the oil, and makes the sign of the cross on the forehead, breast and back of him who is about to be baptized (and in practice also on his ears, his hands and his feet), saying:

[At the forehead] The servant of God, N., is anointed with the oil of gladness, in the Name of the Father, and of the Son, and of the Holy Spirit. Amen.
[At the breast and back] For the healing of soul and body.
[At the ears] For the hearing of faith.
[At the feet] That he may walk in the way of your precepts.
[At the hands] Your hands have made me and fashioned me.

(Some editions have the anointing of the feet before that of the hands, and some have that of the hands before the feet. The earliest surviving text has the priest anointing forehead, breast and back with the main formula, and then the deacon anointing the whole body without any formula.)
Baptism follows at once.

(E) *The office for the anointing of the sick*

The Byzantine office for the anointing of the sick (or, to give it its proper title, the order of the sacrament of the holy oil), which includes the blessing of the oil, is extremely lengthy (it is, of course, greatly abbreviated in an emergency), and the end product of a long and complicated historical development. Ideally, it should be celebrated in church, if the condition of the sick person or persons allows, and by seven priests. In outline, the order of service is as follows:

1. The office of consolation (Gk: *paraklesis*, Slav.: *moleben*), comprising various prayers, psalms and anthems.
2. The blessing of the oil, comprising:
   (i) a litany;
   (ii) the actual prayer of blessing of the oil;
   (iii) anthems (*troparia*), mostly in honour of saints notable for their powers of healing.
3. The anointings, seven in number, each comprising:
   (i) gradual, Epistle, alleluia and Gospel;
   (ii) a prayer for the sick person or persons;
   (iii) the anointing.
Each anointing is performed by one of the seven priests.
4. The concluding rite, comprising:
   (i) the imposition of the book of the Gospels on the head of the sick person or persons, with a prayer;
   (ii) anthems (*troparia*) in honour of the 'unmercenary' saints and the Mother of God. ('Unmercenary' is a technical term, denoting saints who gave their services – in particular, medical ones – freely to the poor.)
   (iii) dismissal.

215

The prayers ask for both bodily and spiritual healing, and for the forgiveness of sins, and are clearly directed towards both recovery of health and, if appropriate, preparation for death.

Comparison with related services in other rites (notably the Coptic) and the evidence of ancient Byzantine documents suggests that the requirement of seven priests, and the sevenfold series of readings, prayers and anointings, indicate that the present service is in fact a conflation of seven services which were originally held on seven different days; similarly, the order of the office of consolation with which the service opens reflects the fact that at one time it was celebrated in the context of matins, just as at another time (and this is reflected in the arrangement of readings and their accompanying chants) it was celebrated in the context of the eucharistic liturgy. (An account of the involved historical development of the service will be found in E. Mélia, 'The Sacrament of the Anointing of the Sick: Its Historical Development and Current Practice' in *Temple of the Holy Spirit* (New York 1983) pp. 127–160.

(F) *The blessing of the oil of the sick*

The text of the prayer, which is said by all the concelebrant priests together, is as follows:

> O Lord, who in your mercy and compassion heal the disorders of our souls and of our bodies: do you yourself, O Master, hallow this oil, that it may become a healing remedy for those anointed with it, and may set them free from all suffering, from all defilement of flesh and of spirit, and from all that is evil: that so also your all-holy Name, of the Father, and of the Son, and of the Holy Spirit, may thereby be glorified, now, and always, and for ever and ever. Amen.

(G) *The anointing with the oil of the sick*

The text of the prayer, which is said in turn by each of the concelebrant priests, is as follows:

> Holy Father, physician of souls and bodies, who sent your only-begotten Son our Lord Jesus Christ, to heal all manner of sickness, and to deliver from death, heal also this your servant (N) from all the illness with which he is beset, whether of body or of soul, and give him life through the grace of your Christ; at the prayers of our most holy Lady the Mother of God and ever-virgin Mary; through the power of the precious and lifegiving Cross; through the protection of the honourable bodiless powers

216

of heaven; [at the prayers[5]] of the honourable and glorious prophet and forerunner John the Baptist; of the holy and glorious Apostles, renowned throughout the world; of the holy, glorious and victorious Martyrs; of the holy and God-bearing Fathers; of the holy and unmercenary Healers Cosmas and Damian; of Cyrus and John; of Panteleimon and Hermolaus; of Sampson and Diomede, of Photius[6] and Anicetas; of Thalelaius and Tryphon; of the holy and righteous forebears of God Joachim and Anna; and of all the Saints. For you are the fount of healing, O Christ[7] our God, and to you we ascribe glory, to the Father, and to the Son, and to the Holy Spirit, now, and always, and for ever and ever. Amen.

(H) Extension of anointing with the oil of the sick

The administration of the oil of the sick is not confined to those gravely ill, and Orthodox theologians have in the past castigated the West for so confining it. But an Orthodox practice that sometimes causes *admiratio*, even scandalized *admiratio*, in the West, is its administration to those who are not apparently physically ill at all. This is commonly done among the Greeks in Holy Week as a preparation for Easter communion. The Greek practice is to celebrate the rite in its entirety, apart from the fact that the anointing is conferred once only, after the imposition of the book of the Gospels. In pre-revolutionary Russia this was done in the cathedral of the Assumption in Moscow, and in the principal church of the great monastery of the Holy Trinity in Sergievo (and anciently also in the church of the Holy Wisdom in Novgorod); but certain changes were introduced into the service that indicated that this was not considered to be the actual sacrament. Similarly, those of the Byzantine rite in communion with Rome who keep up this practice make changes in the service – for example, the Melkites omit the prayer 'O Holy Father . . .' which is considered to be the 'form' of the sacrament. In justification of the practice it is argued, not unreasonably, that we are all physically or spiritually sick, and all in need of healing. It has been suggested (cf. Mélia, 'Le sacrament de l'Onction des malades dans son développement historique et quelques considérations sur la pratique actuelle') that this practice may be the relic of an ancient rite for the reconciliation of penitents which included an anointing.

Notes

1. The words 'and kings' are omitted in the current Greek text, and were already so omitted by the seventeenth century – cf. Goar, *Euchologion*, rev. edn 1730, p. 507, note 19.
2. The words 'and your holy apostles' are not in the Greek text, but are clearly implied in a way difficult and clumsy to reproduce in a modern vernacular; I have therefore followed the Chevetogne edn, *La Prière des Églises de Rite Byzantin*, in inserting them explicitly.
3. Literally, 'Yes'.
4. 'you dwell . . . holy': literally, 'repose among the holies'.
5. Not in the text, but must be understood.
6. Greek texts currently in use read 'Mokius', but Goar, *Euchologion*, does not mention this reading, and Photius (an early martyr, not the famous patriarch of Constantinople), who was a relation of Anicetas and died with him, is paired with him in the calendar.
7. In all texts, but surely an interpolation, in the light of the opening and closing of the prayer.

Index